AF805099

THE POLITICS OF
FAIR TRADE

THE POLITICS OF **FAIR TRADE**

A SURVEY

FIRST EDITION

UWE Bristol
26 JUL 2011
BNE
Library Services
46999

Editor: Meera Warrier

Routledge
Taylor & Francis Group
LONDON AND NEW YORK

First Edition 2011
Routledge
Albert House, 1–4 Singer Street, London EC2A 4BQ, United Kingdom

Simultaneously published in the USA and Canada
by Routledge
711 Third Avenue, New York, NY 10017

Routledge is an imprint of the Taylor & Francis Group, an informa business

© 2011 Routledge

All rights reserved. No part of this publication may be photocopied, recorded, or otherwise reproduced, stored in a retrieval system or transmitted in any form or by any electronic or mechanical means without the prior permission of the copyright owner.

Trademark notice: Product or corporate names may be trademarks or registered trademarks, and are used only for identification and explanation without intent to infringe.

The publishers make no representation, express or implied, with regard to the accuracy of the information contained in this book and cannot accept any legal responsibility for any errors or omissions that may take place.

Library of Congress Cataloging Publication Data
The politics of fair trade : a survey / editor, Meera Warrier. – 1st ed.
p. cm.
Includes bibliographical references and index.
1. International trade. 2. Competition, Unfair. 3. International trade–Case studies. 4. Competition, Unfair–Case studies. I. Warrier, Meera.
HF1379.P654 2011
382'.3–dc22
2011011773

ISBN 978-1-857-43512-2 (hbk)
ISBN 978-0-203-83110-6 (ebk)

Typeset in Times New Roman
by Taylor & Francis Books

Editor Europa New Projects: Cathy Hartley

Printed and bound in Great Britain by
CPI Antony Rowe, Chippenham, Wiltshire

Contents

List of tables

The editor and contributors

Meera Warrier is Research Development Co-ordinator at the University of Leicester. She has several years' experience in research management and communicating research to non-academic audiences such as journalists, the charity sector and policy makers. Her current research interests include globalization and the politics of development, and the globalization and internationalization of higher education.

Graeme Auld is an Assistant Professor at Carleton University in the School of Public Policy and Administration. He holds a PhD from Yale University (2009) in Environmental Governance, an M.S. from Auburn University (2001) and a B.S. in Forestry from the University of British Columbia (1999). His primary research focus examines the emergence, evolution and impacts of non-state and hybrid forms of global governance, with particular attention to social and environmental certification in the agriculture, forest and fisheries sectors. Secondary interests include the efficacy and consequences of information disclosure and transparency policies and policy for climate change. He is co-author (with Ben Cashore and Deanna Newsom) of *Governing through Markets: Forest Certification and the Emergence of Nonstate Authority* (Yale University Press, 2004) and has published in the *Annual Review of Environment and Resources, Journal of Forest Policy and Economics, Global Environmental Politics, Journal of Strategic Management Education, Business and Politics, Journal of Environmental Management,* and the *Review of European Community and International Environmental Law.*

Amanda Berlan is a Social Anthropologist based at the Brookes World Poverty Institute and Sustainable Consumption Institute of the University of Manchester. She has been working on social issues in cocoa production since 2000 and has carried out fieldwork with cocoa producers in West Africa, India and the Caribbean. Her main research interests include fair trade, sustainability, incomes and productivity, child rights and education.

Catherine S. Dolan is a Fellow of Green Templeton College and a University Lecturer in the Marketing, Culture and Society Programme at the University of Oxford. She is an anthropologist specializing in the cultural and political economy of development, and has published extensively on agro-food commodity chains, sustainable agriculture, and alternative trade networks. She has served as a senior consultant to the World Bank, DFID, USAID, and UNIFEM on issues of gender, trade, and poverty, and has led several research projects on pro-poor growth, livelihood diversification, and corporate social responsibility for international aid agencies. She is currently engaged in a research programme on markets, gender equity and poverty reduction, examining the potential for partnerships between non-profit entities and global corporations to deliver development benefits through new forms of entrepreneurship.

Daniel Jaffee, PhD. is Assistant Professor of Sociology at Washington State University, USA. His research examines the effects of economic globalization and neoliberal policies on social and environmental conditions for rural communities in the global South, particularly Latin America. He focuses on fair trade as an alternative model of international economic exchange, examining the benefits and limitations of participation in fair trade and organic markets for peasant commodity producers. He has conducted extensive field work in rural Mexico, both on coffee production and on the indigenous community forestry movement. He is the author of *Brewing Justice: Fair Trade Coffee, Sustainability and Survival*, published by University of California Press in 2007, which won the C. Wright Mills Book Award from the Society for the Study of Social Problems. His additional interests include social movements around sustainable agriculture and resource use in both North and South; the effect of global trade rules on environmental protection and regulation; and issues of access to and commodification of common resources, particularly water.

Sam Knowles is Planning Director of salt, a PR agency specializing in developing communications programmes for clients inspired to 'do well by doing good'. This practice at salt is called Marketing with a Mission, and Sam has been involved in developing partnership and social mission programmes for Lipton (with the Rainforest Alliance), Domestos (with the World Toilet Organization), and RBS/NatWest. Sam holds a doctorate in Experimental Psychopharmacology, and also applies the principles of behavioural psychology to developing communications programmes designed to motivate behaviour change.

Peter Luetchford is lecturer in Anthropology at the University of Sussex and is the author of *Fair Trade and A Global Commodity: Coffee in Costa Rica*. He has carried out ethnographic fieldwork in Costa Rica and Spain. His work focuses on ethical and political ideas on the economy.

Patrick C. Wilson is Associate Professor of Anthropology at the University of Lethbridge, Canada. He has conducted extensive fieldwork in Amazonian Ecuador and more recently in Andean Ecuador and Spain on themes related to indigenous social movements, development and non-governmental organizations, and race, ethnicity and indigeneity. His recent publications include *Editing Eden: A Reconsideration of Identity, Politics, and Place in Amazonia* (University of Nebraska Press, co-edited with Frank Hutchins) and *Federaciones indígenas, ONG y el Estado: el desarrollo y la politización de la cultura en la amazonía ecuatoriana* (Indigenous Federations, NGOs and the State: Development and the Politicization of Culture in Amazonian Ecuador, Ediciones Abya-Yala).

Jens-Uwe Wunderlich is lecturer of International Relations at the School of Languages and Social Studies, Aston University. His research and teaching focus on Comparative Regionalism and on International Relations theory, European Integration and Globalization. Recent publications include *Regionalism, Globalisation and International Order: Europe and Southeast Asia* (Ashgate), *A Dictionary of Globalization* (Routledge, together with M. Warrier) and *The EU and Global Governance: A Handbook* (Routledge, together with D.J. Bailey).

Abbreviations

ACP	African, Caribbean and Pacific
AoA	Agreement on Agriculture
ATO(s)	Alternative Trading Organization(s)
CAP	Common Agricultural Policy
CCC	Clean Clothes Campaign
CSR	corporate social responsibility
EFTA	European Fair Trade Association
ETI	Ethical Trading Initiative
EU	European Union
FACE	Farmers' Advisory Cell
FDI	foreign direct investment
FLO	Fairtrade Labelling Organizations International
FTF	Fair Trade Federation
FTO(s)	Fair Trade Organization(s)
FWF	Fair Wear Foundation
g	gram(s)
GAP	Good Agricultural Practices
GATT	General Agreement on Tariffs and Trade
ha	hectare(s)
ICAs	international commodity agreements
IFAT	International Fair Trade Association/International Federation for Alternative Trade
IFOAM	International Federation of Organic Agriculture Movements
IGO(s)	international governmental organization(s)
IMF	International Monetary Fund
INGO(s)	international non-governmental organization(s)
IPC	Integrated Programme for Commodities
ISO	International Standards Organization
lb	pound(s)
LI	Labelling Initiative(s)
m.	million
MFA	Multifibre Arrangement
MFN	most favoured nation
MNCs	multinational companies/corporations
NAFTA	North American Free Trade Agreement
NGO(s)	non-governmental organization(s)

NIs	National Initiatives
NICs	newly industrializing/industrialized countries
OECD	Organisation for Economic Co-operation and Development
RA	Rainforest Alliance
SKU	stock-keeping unit
SFTMS	Sustainable Fair Trade Management System
TNCs	transnational corporations
TRIPS	Trade-Related Intellectual Property Rights
UK	United Kingdom
UN	United Nations
UNCTAD	United Nations Conference on Trade and Development
US(A)	United States (of America)
WFTO	World Fair Trade Organization
WTO	World Trade Organization

Essays

Introduction

Meera Warrier

From humble beginnings as an alternative trading movement slowly picking up momentum from about the 1970s, 'fair trade' has come a long way. Fair trade campaigners argued that the market confines poor countries to export goods whose prices are historically low and vulnerable to fluctuations. Furthermore, the internationalization of production has led to the exploitation of workers in the developing world, leading to a lowering of labour standards and wages. Following fair trade campaigns, increasing numbers of people in richer countries began demanding goods produced in socially and environmentally friendly conditions. And fair trade has been expanding, becoming almost a brand in itself, with all major retailers and supermarkets in richer countries stocking ethically produced commodities, and with buyers willing to pay a higher price for these products.

In 2009 there were 827 organizations in 60 countries spanning three continents producing Fairtrade goods. The expanding reach of fair trade with respect to producers has been equalled and exceeded by its reach with customers. In what has been one of the most difficult economic years in recent times, consumers spent an estimated €3,400m. on Fairtrade products in 2009, a good 15% increase over the previous year. Fairtrade gained new customers in Eastern Europe and many countries in the Global South. And existing Fairtrade markets showed strong growth, with a 12% growth in the UK and 7% in the USA. Australia and New Zealand too showed a big leap, with consumers significantly increasing their Fairtrade shopping (by 58%).

Sales in Fairtrade herbs and spices multiplied as Fairtrade Labelling Organizations International opened its scope to include all varieties of herbs and spices. Coffee, the pioneer Fairtrade product, grew steadily at 12%. The products to see the greatest increases were cocoa (35%) and sugar (57%), brought about in no small part by the 100% commitments by global chocolate and confectionery brands including Cadbury Dairy Milk, Nestlé's Kit Kat, Green & Black's, and Ben & Jerry's.

Growth, however, has brought its own challenges, including fair trade's relationship with the mainstream market. But first, some clarification on terminology is called for. The most common signifier of fair trade for consumers has become the Fairtrade Mark, the distinct blue, green, white and black mark with FAIRTRADE spelt out below it. This mark, adopted by Fairtrade Labelling Organizations International in 2002, assures retailers and consumers that the producers of that commodity in the developing world are getting a better deal. It suggests that certain minimum standards have been met with respect to social, economic and environmental requirements. Built into it are also progress requirements that encourage continuous improvement of farmers' organizations or the situation of estate workers (see Graeme Auld's chapter for more on fair trade standards and certification).

However, 'fair trade' is much broader than 'Fairtrade', the brand, and spans a wide range of commodities and activities. It includes agencies like Oxfam, Traidcraft and Twin Trading with close links to producer groups and their own retail outlets; labelling organizations like Max Havelaar in the Netherlands and the Fairtrade Foundation in the UK; co-operatives like the USA's Equal Exchange; ethical businesses like the Body Shop and Green and Black's chocolate company; NGO-sponsored products like Cafédirect; plus a range of umbrella organizations. Fair trade is the global movement responsible for unique and progressive companies like Divine Chocolate Ltd and AgroFair.

The Fairtrade mark, as stated above, is a symbol of the product certification system that offers consumers (mainly food) products made under 'fair trade' conditions. The Fairtrade mark is peculiar to the multitude of labelling initiatives under the umbrella Fairtrade Labelling Organizations International (FLO), which was created through the merger of the labelling initiatives Max Havelaar, Transfair and Fairtrade (of the Fairtrade Foundation in Britain). FLO can claim to be the largest fair trade initiative in existence. It has grown from a small non-governmental organization to a global enterprise, with 21 international bodies which set the standards for certification. Estates are checked and certificates awarded by FLO-CERT. The list of products certified Fairtrade is growing steadily. Amongst products currently receiving certification are coffee, tea, rice, fresh fruit, juices, cocoa, sugar, honey, sports balls, and flowers. Products currently in development include avocado and other fresh fruits and vegetables, cereals including quinoa, spices, dried fruits and nuts, and more wines.

This volume provides an overview of the current global fair trade scenario, with in-depth analyses of fair trade's successes, its compromises, and glimpses of the road ahead. The first half of the book provides a critical examination of both the principles behind fair trade as well as its operationalization. Each chapter presents a particular facet of the fair trade story, and can be read alone or in conjunction with the others. The section concludes with a case study each on handicrafts, cocoa and coffee. Each of these three case studies is unique in some way. The nascent beginnings of the fair trade movement were through the sale of handicrafts from the developing world in special outlets like the worldshops. Coffee was the first product to be certified and is a commodity that is still showing steady growth in the fair trade market. Unlike other fair trade products, cocoa reaches the Northern consumer not as it is, but as processed chocolate, and the processing is mostly done in the North.

The latter half of the book provides a cross-referenced glossary of over 150 key terms associated with fair trade, as well as some recent statistics on fair trade.

When there are ethical issues at stake, as in 'fair' trade, there will no doubt be contentions as to what constitutes 'fairness'—fair to what or whom. As such, none of the chapters are neutral—they bring their authors' reasoned arguments, based on evidence, as to the perceived 'fairness' in current arrangements, the opportunities to explore and possible pitfalls.

FAIR TRADE: THE DILEMMAS AND THE OPPORTUNITIES

In April 2010 a press release from the Fairtrade Foundation announced that the organization had been awarded the Queen's Award for Enterprise in the Sustainable Development category. The Queen's Award notification cited the Fairtrade Foundation as 'making a tangible difference to the livelihood and quality of life of local communities within some of the world's poorest regions and is an outstanding demonstration of the benefit which sustainable consumerism has on communities across the globe' (see www.fairtrade.org.uk/press_office/press_releases_and_statements/april_2010/fairtrade_foundation_wins_queens_award_for_enterprise.aspx).

Then, in August 2010, the Fairtrade Foundation became one of two British recipients of the Ruban d'Honneur Award for Corporate Sustainability in the European Business Awards. The European Business Awards, sponsored by HSBC, is an independent awards programme designed to recognize and promote excellence, best practice and innovation in the European business community, in line with the broad aims of the European Union and business representative groups across the member states (see www.fairtrade.org.uk/press_office/press_releases_and_statements/august/fairtrade_foundation_scoops_major_business_award.aspx).

These two awards may not constitute the Oscars in business awards, but are nevertheless indicative of the accolades fair trade has earned in recent times. The intentions and actions of an organization like the Fairtrade Foundation are to be lauded. Indeed, the spirit of solidarity and the antipathy to the corporatization of production and the loss of connection between producer and consumer that lay at the heart of the earliest efforts at setting up an alternative trading system stand as beacons of hope for the possibility of change. Yet, niggling doubts remain—is it corporate sustainability that fair trade is aiming for?

It was Michael Barratt-Brown (1993), one of the earliest writers on fair trade, who described fair trade as being both 'in and against' the market. The worry today is whether fair trade is more 'in' the market than against it. What are the compromises this entails? Can fair trade be against the market while being in it without losing something of itself?

There is no doubt that in many ways fair trade is very much working within the capitalist paradigm. Consider, for instance, fair trade's marketing of its products. The advertising strategies that evoke an individually named small producer, in his or her verdant farm, picking tea or coffee, and directly addressing the consumer to tell him or her of the benefits the fair trade premium has brought to producers' lives, is a supreme example of the movement having commandeered the tools of corporate business to good effect. The string of advertisements put out by Cafédirect, a pioneer in the fair trade arena, is just one illustration of this. Indeed, there are those who would argue that through a typically capitalist sleight-of-hand, fair trade has been subjugated to the ethos of consumption. The onus is now on the consumer to be socially responsible through consumption. It is through consuming [fair trade goods], the subtext reads, that the world can be made a better place. Catherine Dolan discusses this further in her chapter.

In taking the certification route too, fair trade might be said to have placed itself quite squarely within the logic of capitalism. The originally conceived shortening of the supply chain is effected today through a more depoliticized technical solution—certification. Products to be certified have to adhere to a set of minimum standards. There is no denying the usefulness of standards, but a certification system does take away from the more personal, solidary relationship between producer and consumer that was envisaged in the early days of the alternative trade movement.

But that may be a price that fair trade needs to pay to grow the market. Certification has facilitated the entry of more mainstream players. And whilst the presence of bigger players with much greater resources has meant a further push for fair trade product sales, it raises the question of whether the original concerns of fair trade may not be diluted; whether fair trade might not have sold its soul to big corporations. The small, marginalized producers, whom fair trade sought to represent and provide a sustainable livelihood to, are likely to struggle to compete with larger players, who can undercut prices and use non-fair trade lines to cross-subsidize the sale of fair trade products. It also blurs important differences for the consumer who sees the same logo, whether it is Tesco's own fair trade coffee, or coffee sold by a small company exclusively selling fair trade produce.

Is anything left of fair trade then that is 'against' the market? Pre-financing, the minimum price and the premium, it can be argued. Fairtrade guarantees a minimum price to farmers, which is set at a level that ensures that producer organizations receive a value covering the cost of sustainable production. However, this is not a living price, and a lot of the value of the minimum price for coffee, for instance, has been eroded over time by inflation. And it has not been easy for producers—even very small incremental changes to the minimum price have been difficult to secure, as witnessed, for instance, in the case of Arabica. Under consistent pressure from producer groups, the minimum price for this coffee went up marginally from US $1.21 per pound to $1.25 and the social premium rose from $0.05 to $0.10 per pound (the last increase had been in 1989!). The premium is another incentive for producers. Whilst it has proved to be useful for inputs and equipment in farmers' co-operatives, criticisms have been levelled on the ground that they are not high enough, or that the benefits do not spread to a large enough group of growers, or, as in the case of plantations, for instance, that the total premium does not make it back to the growers.

The definition of fair trade suggests that it is:

> a trading partnership, based on dialogue, transparency and respect, that seeks greater equity in international trade. It contributes to sustainable development by offering better trading conditions to, and securing the rights of, marginalized producers and workers – especially in the South. (http://www.fairtrade.org.uk/what_is_fairtrade/fairtrade_foundation.aspx)

This definition provides a model of trade that achieves certain social objectives such as better trading conditions and the securing of rights, while at the same time seeking to challenge the orthodoxy, and raising consumer consciousness in the North to this end. It has promoted better working conditions, with fair trade buyers guaranteeing minimum price, advancing loans to help producers avoid getting into debt, ensuring that trade is as direct as possible bypassing intermediaries, and thereby ensuring that producers get a higher share of the final price. It is also designed to create the development of higher value-added packaging facilities in less developed countries, and a niche for traditionally made products in the global market. However, fair trade can only encourage good practice; it is powerless to do anything actively to discourage bad practice. Buying into fair trade certification is a purely voluntary gesture, and does not mean a corporation has to be bound by the certification guidelines for all their product lines or business processes, thus allowing big corporations to jump on the fair trade bandwagon to improve their brand positioning by converting just a few product lines to fair trade, whilst not changing their overall business practices. And in the absence of efforts to secure responsible market management, there is a limit to what fair trade can achieve.

AIM AND STRUCTURE OF THE VOLUME

This volume provides an incisive introduction to fair trade, placing it in the context of neoliberal globalization and free trade, and understanding the paradoxes and contradictions fair trade poses by being both part of the market and yet against it. It looks at its governance structures, the way it is experienced by both producers and consumers, and asks where the opportunities are for fair trade in developmental terms.

The central goal of the fair trade movement has been to create more direct, socially just and environmentally responsible trade relations, where the link between producer and consumer is shortened, and a greater part of the value of the product goes back to the producer. To understand the full import of the metaphorical distance to be shortened we need only consider that the 'producers' are all in developing, Southern countries, and the consumers are in the more developed, Northern countries.

What has made for these rather extended and unequal relations? Jens-Uwe Wunderlich's chapter places fair trade in the context of the neoliberal organization of trade, and the global institutions managing it. It looks at the rhetoric around 'free' trade, and asks whether 'free' trade can be 'fair' trade or whether the two are anathema to each other. He takes us back to the liberal, mercantilist and critical traditions to provide us with the analytical toolkit to analyse the arguments for and against free trade, whilst at the same time training the spotlight on the gap between the theory and practice of free trade. Whilst developed countries have been pushing developing countries to liberalize their trade and open up their borders to exports from the North, they themselves have kept their doors firmly shut in the face of the largely primary commodity exports from the South. Furthermore, the agricultural sector in a number of these countries is hugely subsidized, and the large food surpluses generated are dumped in poorer country markets, robbing Southern producers of their livelihoods, both from domestic markets and exports. If the North practised what it preached, and opened up its borders to primary commodity exports from the developing world, that alone could achieve more than the aid currently provided to these countries. An Oxfam report, *Make Trade Fair*, estimates that African countries would generate about US $70,000m. if their share of exports were increased by just a single percentage point. And this would be approximately five times what the continent currently receives in aid.

But despite protests, campaigns and lobbying by both Southern countries and those in solidarity with them in the North, little has been achieved. Indeed, the product of the Uruguay Round, the World Trade Organization (WTO), is seen by critics as having only laid the ground for large multinational corporations to claim more rentier income. The WTO's Agreement on Agriculture, for instance, has yet to show any real teeth in effecting far-reaching policy changes. And the use of the term 'fair' in the trade discourse in these circles has quite a different meaning and import than that used by advocates of a fairer trade regime. Fairness has been used in the context of 'levelling the playing field', with demands for harmonizing labour and environmental standards, so that developing countries would not have an 'unfair advantage' such as lower labour costs or less stringent environmental regulations that will render Northern countries less competitive.

The success of fair trade products, whilst still only a tiny proportion of total sales, has whetted the appetite of large multinational corporations to build an image of 'fairness' or of environmental, social and/or economic sustainability into their brands. The labelling and certification industry in socially, ethically and environmentally responsible practices has burgeoned since 1988, when the first fair trade label, Max Havelaar, was launched as an initiative of the Dutch development agency, Solidaridad, selling 'Fairtrade' coffee from Mexico in Dutch supermarkets. Just nine years later, FLO was established in Bonn, Germany, to unite various national labelling initiatives under one umbrella to establish worldwide standards and certification.

Third party certification was just what corporations needed to give them that edge of credibility in the public's eye, argues Sam Knowles in his chapter, 'The Commodification of Ethics'. There are several different forms of certification now available, and corporations can 'fairwash' their image in one fell swoop through strategic advertising, even if they are certifying only a small proportion of their product lines. And whilst it is not profits that motivate them, certifying bodies nevertheless need a steady and growing demand to stay in business. Competition amongst them is every bit as fierce as that between their corporate counterparts, contends Knowles. Their internal organizations also often mirror mainstream corporations with client services and accounting teams.

In 'Branding morality: The case of Fairtrade', Catherine Dolan trains the spotlight on the fair trade brand, which is not just the commodities sold but which embraces the entire context of consumption—the ideas, attitudes, values and experiences. She looks at the different ways this consumption is manipulated and managed, so that the advertisement is used as a cultural intermediary to both educate the public about the Third World, whilst also competing for their hearts and minds. The images used act as symbolic carriers of race, gender and class identities. And in commodifying the lives of producers, their landscapes and production processes, the brand is effectively divesting the exchange of sociality, in complete contradiction to the original intention of the movement, which was to put people and sociality back into the equation.

We see fair trade most often from the consumption end. What about the lived experiences of the producers themselves (rather than the rarefied versions on advertisements)? How do they understand 'fair trade'? Peter Luetchford, in 'Falling foul of fair: The politics of supply chains' casts his gaze on a group of coffee producers in Costa Rica. He finds that the fair trade discourse elides various categories of producers under the term 'small farmers'. There is a whole range of 'smallness', from those who own less than a hectare to those who own several hundred hectares. And this still does not take into account the family members, migrants and others who are part of the coffee farming process, but who do not even appear on the fair trade radar screen. The typecasting of small producers as a monolithic category thus obscures the power relations between different parties at the production end of the fair trade supply chain. Furthermore, fair trade here is still experienced as trade, as a market relationship with all that it entails. NGOs and co-operative managers are the de facto middlemen here, brokering the relationship and (re)presenting producers in certain ways to secure the higher prices offered by fair trade. They have to walk the tightrope of being seen as able to produce specialty coffee, while positioning themselves as being disadvantaged enough to need help.

Can and will advocacy-led certification transform corporate practices, asks Graeme Auld in 'Certification as governance: Current impacts and future prospects'. The chapter looks at the origins and spread of certification systems, the structures and functions of certification and certification as a tool of governance. The certification of fair trade, Auld argues, has professionalized it and given it a certain credibility, but in the process it has depersonalized the exchange for producer organizations, alienated the very people fair trade seeks to empower.

There is also a question mark as to whether it reaches those who need it most, for participation in the certification system requires a certain level of capacity to meet and comply with standards. Furthermore, the competition amongst certifiers could see either a race to the bottom or a ratcheting up of standards. Fair trade, he argues, has still a lot going for it due to the credibility it has established through the commitment shown by the early Alternative Trading Organizations. However, its continued success and progress will depend on its ability to show why and how it is different.

Daniel Jaffee asks whether fair trade is fulfilling its promises, and looks at the developmental role fair trade plays or has the potential to play in 'Fair trade and development: A changing paradigm'. He revisits the early inspiration behind fair trade to find it has not been one vision, but five different strands underpinning the idea of fair trade, each of which he explores in some detail. These include: (i) livelihood improvements for farmers living in severe rural poverty in the South; (ii) empowering small producers and waged labourers; (iii) as a tool for redistributing wealth; (iv) as a tool for internalizing the social and environmental costs of conventional trade and business practices; and (v) as a device for leveraging greater corporate responsibility. Fair trade has seen considerable growth in recent times, but what would constitute success for fair trade—would it be its ability to adhere to its values and principles, or is its growth indicative of success? And here is the kernel of the dilemma currently facing fair trade. Jaffee sees possibilities for a more radical reform of trade today as neoliberal dogma begins to lose face. He concludes by providing glimpses of the possible road(s) ahead.

In the case study section, Patrick Wilson examines the role of handicrafts in the early days of the growth of Alternative Trading Organizations, and explores the reasons for its subsequent decline, and the challenges currently confronting handicrafts. Amanda Berlan delineates the growth of fair trade cocoa, and the impact this has had on producers. She uses Kuapa Kokoo, a highly successful fair trade model, to study fair trade arrangements in cocoa. And finally, Peter Luetchford writes about coffee, and discusses the key characteristics which make it sit at the centre of the fair trade imaginary, including the political economy of coffee production, the social relations and politics behind production, distribution and consumption, and the distinctiveness of coffee in terms of the cultural practices and meanings attached to it.

BIBLIOGRAPHY

Barratt-Brown, M., *Fair Trade: Reform and Realities in the International Trading System*, London, Zed, 1993.

De Neve, G., Luetchford, P., Pratt, J. and Wood, D. (eds), 'Hidden Hands in the Market: Ethnographies of Fair Trade, Ethical Consumption, and Corporate Social Responsibility', *Research in Economic Anthropology* (28), 2008.

Fridell, G., *Fair Trade Coffee: The Prospects and Pitfalls of Market-Driven Social Justice*, Toronto, University of Toronto Press, 2007.
Jaffee, D., *Brewing Justice: Fair Trade Coffee, Sustainability, and Survival*, Berkeley, CA, University of California Press, 2007.
Nicholls, A. and Opal, C., *Fair Trade: Market-Driven Ethical Consumption*, London, Sage, 2005.

Free trade, fair trade and globalization

JENS-UWE WUNDERLICH

Trade constitutes an essential building block for all economies, and development policy often underscores the importance of expanding trade. Despite trade continuing to expand for the world as a whole, it has become a deeply divisive issue and an anchor point for the grievances of the global justice movement. An Oxfam report, drawing in findings from more than 80 developing countries, suggests that the huge increase in wealth generated by trade under globalization has not been matched by parallel progress in poverty reduction, or even in broader progress towards human development. Scant attention has been paid to whether and to what extent the trade regime has overall coherence or consistency with the development goals of poorer countries, despite lip service to the development agenda. Increasing socio-economic tensions in both developed and developing countries is prompting a recontestation of the multilateral trade regime.

The bases for the current imbalances in the trade regime may, to a great extent, be attributed to the imbalances in trade agreements themselves, which, in turn, have prejudiced trade outcomes. As such, the benefits of increased trade are often skewed heavily in favour of developed countries that already enjoy a lead in both the firm-level capacity to compete in world markets as well as the national capacity to implement trade-related reforms and comply with WTO discipline (Mendoza and Bahadur 2002).

The debate on trade often appears as a debate between 'free' and 'fair' trade, with arguments suggesting that 'fair' is anathema to 'free'. This is often based on the assumption that the trade regime, as it exists today, is 'free'. Despite the rhetoric to that effect, however, and the calls for liberalization and opening up of borders on the part of the gatekeepers of the current trade system like the WTO, trade is by no means 'free', as protectionism in its various guises is still rampant in both the developed and developing worlds. If trade were to become 'free' in its purest sense, would it accomplish the benefits developing countries desire? What is meant by 'fair' anyway? Arguably, 'fair' can be a very context-specific term, and can mean different things even in the context of trade. And where do 'fair trade' certified goods fit into the equation? Does it ensure a 'fair' deal that is also sustainable?

These are some of the questions this chapter purports to raise. It is more important to pose these questions; arguably we are still a long way from finding the right answers or, indeed, finding more pragmatic, workable solutions to what could become a trading stalemate between developed and developing countries. The chapter will begin with an attempt to place in context current trade theories and debates by examing on the three classical theoretical traditions of international political economy which inform all today's discussions—liberalism, mercantilism and critical approaches (following Gilpin's (1987) classification). One big question links all the various strands of this multifaceted and complex debate: Is a free trade system largely beneficial for all participants? Or are there winners and losers?

FREE TRADE: THE THEORETICAL ARGUMENTS

The theoretical debate on the relative merits and problems of trade regimes is well established in the political economy literature. It is imperative to recapitulate the main arguments in the context of this volume since they provide the philosophical foundations for many contemporary discussions about trade politics and the costs and benefits of free trade.

Traditionally, international political economy distinguished between three schools of thought—liberalism, mercantilism and critical approaches. None of them can be conceived as a coherent theory in the traditional sense. Rather, they are broad intellectual traditions bringing together scholars who share a particular normative and ideological outlook. Furthermore, there is substantial room for disagreement not only between the three classical schools, but even within each perspective.

The essence of a free trade regime is the absence (or at least the limitation) of all barriers to trade. The strongest advocates of free trade come from within the liberal tradition, and can be traced back to Adam Smith and his famous 1776 book *The Wealth of Nations* (Smith 1983). Smith, a prominent figure of the Scottish Enlightenment, argued that a competitive market, regulated only by the pressures of demand and supply, would ultimately generate the most efficient allocation of resources. Market forces generate their own regulatory pressures, the so-called 'invisible hand', forcing producers to offer products and services that consumers really want and forcing them to sell those products at the lowest possible price. Smith expounded the positive role of the market for society where individuals' rational profit-seeking behaviour leads to a collectively beneficial outcome by increasing overall prosperity and wealth.

In the early 1800s, building on Smith's insights, David Ricardo put forward the theory of comparative advantage, according to which countries can benefit from specialization and trade because all countries are relatively more efficient in the production of a particular good or service compared to other countries. This theory underwent further refinement in the 1920s when Eli Hekscher and Bertil Ohlin contended that trade patterns emerge according to a country's relative endowments of production factors. Over time, liberal trade theory has been further burnished with the human capital argument, the inclusion of intra-industry and intra-firm trade, product-life cycle theory and the notion of a shifting comparative advantage. It is worth noting that these refinements do not fundamentally challenge the essence of liberal trade theory which remains Ricardo's concept of comparative advantage, suggesting that the economy of each country will prosper and economic growth and living standards will improve if a free trade system is adopted.

The contemporary neoliberal orthodoxy promoted by global financial institutions and the developed states in the Global North draws on these traditions. They argue that the liberalization of trade flows also enhances competition within domestic markets. Domestic monopolies, for example, will lose their dominating position when faced with foreign competitors. Increased competition tends to lower prices, increase consumer choice and domestic development. Furthermore, trade flows are seen to generate patterns of complex interdependence, helping to foster international cooperation and peace.

Mercantilist thinking offers a strong counter argument to the liberal tradition. Mercantilism can be traced back to the emergence of the Westphalian-state system in Europe in the 15th and 16th centuries. Early mercantilists believed that a country's wealth was best measured by the amount of gold bullion stored in the treasury (O'Brien and Williams 2004: 142). Trade was regarded as a zero-sum game where one country's gain equated to another's loss. The export of products and services was to be actively encouraged to yield an inflow of bullion as payment, and imports had to be restricted. By extension, domestic markets had to be actively protected, and measures put in place to achieve a trade surplus.

Early mercantilist critics of liberalism argued that a free trade system is only beneficial for countries at equal levels of economic development. Developing economies needed to industrialize in the insulation offered by a curtain of tariffs and other barriers to trade, before opening up to free trade. This provided the foundation for the contemporary infant-industry argument. (Temporary) protectionist barriers are designed to enable industrial development and should be removed as soon as the protected industry has reached a certain level of maturity and self-sufficiency. The danger with protectionism, however, is that all too often it moves from a temporary to a permanent feature and quickly becomes entrenched in the system with powerful interest groups lobbying for its continuation (consider, for instance, the European Union's Common Agricultural Policy—CAP).

Contemporary mercantilism also finds expression in the 'developmental state' argument, a view very popular among opponents of free trade in the developing world. This school holds that the state rather than the market should sit in the driving seat. Governments should use industrial policies, trade protection and other forms of state intervention to actively guide and shape the industrial and technological structure of the economy. The success of the newly industrialized countries (NICs) in East Asia—Hong Kong, Singapore, South Korea and Taiwan—is seen as supporting this position. The success of the NICs, as also Japan, is put down to careful macroeconomic planning by powerful institutions of the state.

Critical approaches see free trade flows as a threat to adequate wage levels and incomes, health and safety standards, environmental protection, human rights, gender equality and child welfare. These concerns are often captured in the phrase: 'race-to-the-bottom'. This is a game theoretical concept, with a logic similar to the 'prisoner's dilemma', describing a situation where individual rational behaviour leads to a collectively suboptimal outcome. 'Race-to-the-bottom' suggests that government regulations such as corporation tax, welfare standards, health and safety laws and environmental protection, will be lowered in a competitive free trade environment where companies are free to relocate to countries with more 'business friendly' attitudes (i.e. less regulation and public obligation). To secure industrialization, therefore, and to be 'competitive', tax and wages levels are adjusted downwards, and environmental strictures relaxed.

To demonstrate the embedded inequalities in the system they point to the imbalance in the mobility of production factors which, to a large extent, is a direct result of the structure of the international political economy and the form globalization has taken. While trade liberalization and the removal of capital controls have been high on the political agenda, immigration controls have increased and labour migration made more difficult (EU citizens' migration within the EU being an exception). Thus, developed economies have been able to call the shots, thus emphasising trade liberalization and capital mobility from their more privileged vantage points.

Critical approaches point out that relations of power run through all economic exchanges and theoretical arguments. They argue that free trade theorists not only turn a blind eye to the historical construction of inequality, but in doing so also freeze a particular status quo, making it impossible for poorer countries to develop, while economic wealth continues to accrue to wealthier nations, perpetuating relations obtaining in the imperialist past—the colonizers are now the Global North, and the colonized constitute the Global South. However, a contextualization and study of the historical origins of the current trading system indicates that it is neither static nor 'natural'. As such it can be changed and this drive for changing the status quo is an important thread uniting critical approaches. Under this broad rubric are included a vast variety of Marxist-informed approaches, critical theory, dependency theory, world systems theory, feminism and green political thought.

The three broad schools of thought outlined above—liberalism, mercantilism and critical approaches—provide us with the vocabulary and the theoretical toolkit to understand current discourses and practices in the trade arena. Let us now look at the major institutions that have fundamentally shaped the development of the contemporary trade order, and the role of 'free' trade here.

TRADE ORDER AND TRADE LIBERALIZATION

The contemporary trade order has its roots in the immediate post-World War environment and the Bretton Woods system. The post-war international economic order was shaped by American power, and naturally reflected American preferences. It firmly embedded liberalism, legalism and multilateralism in the emerging trade order, and laid the foundations for the rapid neoliberal wave of globalization. The Bretton Woods system created many of the multilateral institutions that still dominate the international economy, such as the International Monetary Fund (IMF) and the International Bank for Reconstruction and Development (IBRD), now known as the World Bank. The proposal for an International Trade Organization (ITO) was less successful, and the General Agreement on Tariffs and Trade (GATT) was instituted in its place as an interim arrangement in 1947, which acted as a standby until the foundation of the WTO in 1995.

The GATT was designed to facilitate trade liberalization among signatory countries by securing a reduction in tariffs and preventing the introduction of new barriers to trade. It was based on four principles: the most favoured nation clause, reciprocity, market access and fair competition. The work of the GATT was conducted through eight negotiating rounds, each leading to a refinement of the existing rules. The process of pursuing trade liberalization was negotiated among countries through reciprocal market access and non-discrimination, and involved the harmonization of trading rules and the reduction of barriers to trade (tariffs and quotas).

The last round of GATT, the Uruguay round (1986–94), resulted in the creation of the WTO which, unlike the GATT, is a fully-fledged international organization with a legal personality. It has a much wider remit than the GATT, presiding also over a General Agreement on Trade in Services (GATS) and Trade Related Aspects of Intellectual Property Rights (TRIPS) and a mechanism for dispute settlement. The WTO (www.wto.org) fundamentally transformed the international trade system. First, it engineered a shift away from trade liberalization based on tariff reduction to a focus on domestic economic policies, institutional practices and regulations. Second, it enhanced the scope of trade liberalization by including new sectors (services, intellectual property rights, agriculture). There has also been a shift in emphasis away from cumbersome negotiations on tariff concessions on single products and product groups to discussions over policies that shape the very nature of competition. And, third, the WTO has initiated a drive towards policy harmonization. As such it is seen as effectively reinforcing the neoliberal economic orthodoxy.

The GATT proved to be rather successful in the setting up of an international liberal trade system. International trade increased significantly as a result of trade liberalization until the economic upheavals of the 1970s ended the post-war boom and slowed trade liberalization. Faced with recession and rising unemployment, governments were less willing to expose their economies to international competition. The recession of the 1970s also brought into focus several of the key weaknesses of the GATT. Countries were putting in place new protectionist measures based on non-tariff barriers such as quotas, subsidies, and preferential state procurement or 'voluntary' export restraints, all of which were outside GATT's remit. Furthermore, it was clear that the developed world was in the driving seat, determining the direction and design of the trading system.

The agricultural sector, for example, was excluded until the Uruguay round of negotiations (1986–94). Primary commodities, the major category of export from developing countries, did not get a successful hearing in other international fora either. It was at the first United Nations Conference on Trade and Development (UNCTAD) in 1964 that industrialized countries acknowledged the need for a coherent programme on primary commodities to address poorer countries' developmental needs. The result was the Integrated Programme for Commodities (IPC), launched under UNCTAD auspices 12 years later. The IPC sought to create market structures which achieved remunerative and stable prices, while taking into account the interests of consuming countries. A Common Fund was established to maintain buffer stocks that would be increased (through purchasing operations) when prices were low, and reduced (through sales) when prices went up. The resulting international commodity agreements (ICAs) covered a range of commodities including sugar, rubber, coffee and cocoa. But it did not live long. By the end of the 1980s the price-stabilizing functions for all of them, except rubber, had either collapsed or been abandoned (Jaffee 2007).

Amongst the reasons attributed for the collapse of ICAs are: first, the hostility of Northern governments to market interventions they saw as inherently inflationary; second, the attempt to defend reference prices that were far removed from underlying realities; and third, there were new low-cost suppliers of commodities like coffee and cocoa in East Asia who were well placed to benefit from the higher prices generated by African and Latin American governments, whilst not being interested in restricting their own output to keep prices up.

As world prices have declined, some producing countries, especially with respect to coffee, have gone back to supply management principles, trying to hold back stock, for instance, until prices rose again. However, these plans rarely translated into action due to developing countries' desperate need for foreign exchange. Most also lack the storage capacity to withhold stocks, or the financing capacity to buy produce from farmers without exporting it immediately.

The record on commodity-market interventions leaves little room for optimism. Northern governments have favoured the interests of powerful food companies in getting cheap raw materials rather than the interests of developing countries in getting remunerative prices. The argument that market-management agreements are inherently doomed also does not bear up to the fact that Northern governments have intervened in other types of markets (like the currency market) when they considered their own interests to be at stake.

FREE VERSUS FAIR TRADE?

There is clearly a justification for policies to create a level playing field for all players. For instance, there is a need to enable developing countries to compete in world markets. But northern countries place numerous barriers before primary exports from developing countries. Furthermore, there are entrenched disincentives to developing countries processing primary products, as higher tariff rates are often applied for higher value-additions. For example, developing country exports of chocolate to the developed countries often face tariff barriers that are up to eight times higher than those that apply to unprocessed cocoa (UNCTAD 2000). Measures such as these lock in developing countries' comparative advantage in low value-added products, seriously impeding development efforts, and sustaining the inequalities in trade.

A possible starting point in the effort to rebalance the trade regime would be to phase out agricultural subsidies and strengthen special and differential treatment. Reforming the imbalanced decision making and bargaining power exercised in the WTO would therefore be key to bringing about a more level playing field. At the Uruguay round, the Agreement on Agriculture (AoA) brought national agricultural policies under multilateral rules and disciplines, with the long-term objective of establishing a fair and market-oriented agricultural trading system through substantial progressive reductions in agricultural support and protection. It included specific binding commitments by WTO members to improve market access and to reduce production- and trade-distorting domestic support and export subsidies. A basic motivation for the AoA was the need to reduce surplus production generated through rising levels of subsidies and protection in developed countries during the 1980s and early 1990s (see www.fao.org/trade/docs/ur.htm). By agreeing to cap and reduce these subsidy levels and import barriers, the developed countries hoped to bring an end to the 'subsidy wars' that were draining their national budgets and driving down world commodity prices. The vast majority of developing countries, on the other hand, entered the Uruguay round with underdeveloped agricultural sectors and insufficient resources to raise productivity and output in line with their food needs and production potential. Additionally, their farmers were being forced to compete with the agricultural outputs of the world's richest countries, both in export markets and in their home markets. The AoA was expected to generate slightly higher and more stable world prices for agricultural products and to improve the trade prospects of non-subsidizing exporters, including many developing countries. However, relatively small policy changes have occurred, and their impacts have been correspondingly small.

Furthermore, nations and national interests are only a small part of the story. A significant share of global capital, technology, trade flows and market access are controlled today by large multinational corporations (MNCs) (Held *et al.* 1999; Appadurai 1990). These MNCs account for about two-thirds of all global exports of goods and services. The power concentrated within these large corporations and the transnational nature of their operations enables them to influence political, economic and social realities around the world. They are able to manipulate national policy-making and international agenda setting, as well as bypass unions, labour laws and environmental standards. They are accused of being at the heart of the 'race-to-the-bottom', keen to achieve the lowest costs regardless of their human and environmental consequences.

There are also problems inherent in the theoretical logic of free trade. The drive towards more free trade was premised on Ricardo's theory of comparative advantage, which is driven by inherent differences in capacity, and hence in the cost, of producing different products and services across countries. In the age of globalization and an ever intensifying global division of labour, advocates of protectionism might point to the domestic consequences of a shifting comparative advantage—the relocation of industries to cheaper locations and, subsequently, unemployment. Protectionism can thus be found amongst some of the most vocal backers of liberalization, like the EU or the USA, in high-tech sectors such as computer manufacturing and electronics, in traditional manufacturing sectors like the automobile industry or even in primary sector industries like agriculture. It can also be found in industries that are deemed to be important for national security.

Pursuing more trade without developing comparative advantage could erode the gains from trade over time, particularly for developing countries. Trade among non-equals (i.e. producers in developed versus developing countries) can potentially lead to the decimation of nascent industries in some developing countries. Similarly, simply expanding the realm of free trade has, in many cases, resulted in an actual increase in poverty and environmental degradation, and has had an adverse impact on women and food security across the developing world, undermining efforts to achieve sustainable human development (Mendoza and Bahadur 2002).

While the static mutual gains from trade (and, by extension, Ricardo's theory) remain unchallenged, the gains over time need to be evaluated as well, which begets the question as to how far and how long a comparative advantage can be sustained. Building dynamic comparative advantage often requires some degree of protection in order to develop competitiveness in certain sectors, thus going against the process (at least temporarily) of levelling the playing field (Mendoza and Bahadur 2002).

An additional yet equally important concern is the adjustment cost related to trade liberalization. Free trade dictates that the forces of competition bring about an efficient market outcome, but among unequal competitors, the relative costs of adjustment differ significantly (Mendoza and Bahadur 2002). Adjustment is typically more protracted and costly in the developing world for the obvious reason that there are fewer resources to help facilitate such adjustment. Another facet of these adjustment costs deals with the implementation of trade-related regulations and reforms (i.e. import licensing procedures, customs valuation, sanitary and phytosanitary standards, trade-related legal reforms). Many compliance measures emanate from the developed world that already have these in place. But for countries with meagre resources it would be an additional and onerous burden. Stiglitz and Charlton (2006), for instance, argue that developing countries have to incur several additional costs if they are to realise the full benefits of new market opportunities. In many cases they lack the necessary exporting infrastructure (e.g. efficient ports, adequate roads, reliable electricity and communications) or lack the necessary technology and knowledge to meet product standards prevailing in high value markets (sanitary measures, technical barriers, certification, etc.). It was an acknowledgement of these differences in capacities that led to the setting up of the aid for trade agenda.

Thus, the current system is inherently discriminatory. Not only do many developed countries break the rules of the liberal trading system to protect their own, but the structural power relationships and political agreements do not lead to the full incorporation of the underdeveloped world into the global trading system. To make trade 'fair', Stiglitz and Charlton (2006), for instance, suggest a combination of state policy, better adherence to liberal rules and a more participatory, redistributive global trading system.

WHEN IS TRADE 'FAIR'?

Neoliberal globalization with its emphasis on trade liberalization is seen as both negative and limited, largely benefiting the developed world and already powerful TNCs, and leading to 'corporate globalization' or 'globalization-from-above' (Steger 2003). It is argued that this proliferation of global capitalism is a form of neo-colonialism, undermining the political, social and economic fabric of many societies, making them vulnerable to the volatility of markets, systematically destroying the environment, endangering the rights of minorities and, ultimately, rendering ineffective democratic principles (Held and McGrew 2002).

Fundamental to a fairer trade regime would be a level playing field between trade partners, with everyone coming to it with similar capacities and adhering to the same principles, norms and rules. The fair trade initiative is seen as an international movement bringing together Northern activists and impoverished producers from the Global South in the search for global economic justice promoting equitable labour, production, trade, environmental and welfare standards (Raynolds 2000). The Fair Trade Labelling Organizations International (FLO) definition sees fair trade as 'a trading partnership, based on dialogue, transparency and respect, that seeks greater equity in international trade. It contributes to sustainable development by offering better trading conditions to, and securing the rights of, marginalised producers and workers – especially in the South' (EFTA 2006).

The FLO definition is a very particular take on the notion of fairness. In trade parlance, 'fairness' has historically been understood in the context of competition. For instance, there have been demands for harmonization of labour and environmental standards on the grounds that southern countries might otherwise have an 'unfair' advantage in cost. Under this definition 'unfair trade practices' would include the broad field of non-tariff barriers like subsidies or social, labour, health and environmental standards which lead to distortions in global trade relations and cause 'unfair' advantages. Thus, lower labour costs or weaker environmental regulations in developing countries are cited by developed countries as unfair advantages, as they lower the cost of production, undercutting competitiveness of developed country producers. There is an implied norm of fairness here, which suggests that no matter what the economic, historical or other justifications for the existence of such differential standards, they constitute a lack of symmetry for competing firms in an industry in different nations and hence are unacceptable (Bhagwati and Hudec 1996). Such interpretations of fairness have led some economists to ask whether labour, environmental or human rights conditions are appropriate to a body like the WTO, or whether such 'social' conditions represent the most recent incarnation of protectionism in the North against imports from developing countries. It is difficult to distinguish where legitimate non-trade concerns end and trade protection begins.

Proponents of fair trade propagate a very different economic development model compared to neoliberalism. Rather than free market forces, the price mechanism and comparative advantage, it emphasises 'fairness' in the economic relations between the Global North and South. Its stated aims are: to regard trade as a mutual beneficial partnership based on dialogue, transparency and respect; to support organizational capacity-building for democratic groups that are required to represent small-scale producers (co-operatives) and workers (trade unions); to offer guaranteed prices that are higher than market rates; to provide a social premium to finance community projects such as schools, clinics and environmentally sustainable production.

Implicit in the fair trade movement is the recognition that conventional free trade rhetoric deliberately de-emphasizes the power asymmetry in most trade relations as well as its negative social and environmental impacts. As a solution it promotes a bottom-up version of globalization directly linking consumers in the Global North with otherwise marginalized and disenfranchised producers and workers in the Global South via the market (the mechanisms by which this connection is articulated is explored in other chapters in this book).

Since the 1990s trade in fair trade certified products has grown dramatically. Typical commodities include tea, coffee, cocoa, sugar, bananas, honey, fresh and dried fruits, fruit juices, vegetables, rice, wine, nuts, oilseeds, cut flowers, ornamental plants and cotton, and plans for the certification of other products are under way (Murray and Raynolds 2007). Public support and recognition of fair trade certification has grown in Europe and North America as fair trade has increasingly become a recognized brand with certified products available from most large-scale retailers. In the Global South, the initiative has attracted many local producers in search of higher and reliable commodity prices, as well as the promise of benefits to the wider community (ibid.).

The enthusiasm for fair trade's success thus far is, however, tempered by an increasing concern that this might be the end of the road for a movement that still works within the current market paradigm. The mainstreaming of fair trade is particularly raising fears that its central messages, and indeed, its principles, are being diluted, as large multinationals join the bandwagon to get a few product lines certified, and bask in the halo this provides for their business practices in entirety. Indeed, as Daniel Jaffee argues, 'If fair trade is to move beyond creating islands of relatively greater well-being in a rising sea of inequality, it will do well to link its work to that of broader movements for global justice, with their ambitious vision of creating alternative economic institutions, radically changing existing ones, and redefining the purpose of trade itself' (Jaffee 2007: 10).

BIBLIOGRAPHY

Appadurai, A., 'Disjuncture and Difference in the Global Culture Economy' in *Theory, Culture, and Society,* 7: 295–310, 1990.

Archer, C. and Fritsch, S., 'Global Fair Trade: Humanizing Globalization and Reintroducing the Normative to International Political Economy' in *Review of International Political Economy*, 17(1): 103–28, 2010.

Bhagwati, J. and Hudec, Robert E. (eds), *Fair Trade and Harmonization: Prerequisites for Free Trade? Volume 1: Economic Analysis*, Cambridge, MA, and London, MIT Press, 1996.

EFTA (European Fair Trade Association), 'EFTA: Joining Fair Trade Forces'. The Netherlands, EFTA, available at www.european-fair-trade-association.org/efta/Doc/What.pdf, 2006.

Gilpin, R., *Global Political Economy: Understanding the International Economic Order*, Princeton, NJ, and Oxford, Princeton University Press, 1987.

Held, D. and McGrew, A. (eds), *Governing Globalisation*, Cambridge, Cambridge University Press, 2002.

Held, D., McGrew, A., Goldblatt, D., Perraton, J., *Global Transformations: Politics, Economics and Culture*, Cambridge, Polity Press, 1999.

Huang, H., *Politics in Pacific Asi*a, London, Macmillan, 2009.

Jaffee, D., *Brewing Justice: Fair Trade Coffee, Sustainability and Survival*, Berkeley, CA, University of California Press, 2007.

Mendoza, Ronald U. and Bahadur, Chandrika, 'Towards Free and Fair Trade: A Global Public Good Perspective', unedited draft, 25 June 2002, available at www.undp.org/globalpublicgoods/globalization/pdfs/Free-and-Fair-Trade-25June-02.pdf (accessed on 6 August 2010).

Murray, D. L. and Raynolds, L. T., 'Globalization and its Antinomies: Negotiating a Fair Trade Movement' in Raynolds, Murray and Wilkinson (eds) *Fair Trade: The Challenges of Transforming Globalization*, London and New York, Routledge, 3–14, 2007.

O'Brien and Williams, *Global Political Economy–Evolution and Dynamics*, Basingstoke, Palgrave, 2004.

Raynolds, L., 'Re-embedding Global Agriculture: The International Organic and Fair Trade Movements' in *Agriculture and Human Values,* 17: 297–309, 2000.

Raynolds, L. T., Murray, D. and Wilkinson, D., *Fair Trade: The Challenges of Transforming Globalization*, London and New York, Routledge, 2007.

Ricardo, D., *From 'On the Principles of Political Economy and Taxation'*, 2002.

Smith, A., *The Wealth of Nations,* New York, Penguin, 1983.
Steger, M. B., *Globalization: A Very Short Introduction*, Oxford, Oxford University Press, 2003.
Stiglitz, J. and Charlton, A, 'Aid for Trade: A Report for the Commonwealth Secretariat', March 2006, available at http://works.bepress.com/cgi/viewcontent.cgi?article=1008&context=joseph_stiglitz (accessed on 4 August 2010).
——. *Fair Trade for All: How Trade can Promote Development*, revised edition. Oxford, Oxford University Press, 2007.
United Nations Conference on Trade and Development (UNCTAD), 'Opening Doors for LDC Exports', Geneva, UNCTAD (www.unctad.org/conference/e-press_kit/ldc_exports.pdf), 2000.
White, G., *Developmental States in East Asia*, London, Macmillan, 1988.

The commodification of ethics

Sam Knowles

The coalition of non-governmental agencies, led by Oxfam and their certified commercial partners in the Fairtrade movement, hold an annual Fairtrade Fortnight (www.fairtrade.org.uk/get_involved/fairtrade_fortnight/fairtrade_fortnight_2009/default.aspx) in the UK in the first quarter of the calendar year. For two weeks, producers, NGOs and retailers focus media and consumer attention on the issue of sustainable sourcing from the majority world. This is the annual opportunity for brands and NGOs to inform consumers about the progress they are making towards sustainable consumption and production.

In early March 2009 Britain's biggest chocolate manufacturer, Cadbury, stole the headlines of Fairtrade Fortnight by announcing that it was doubling the quantity of cocoa it sources from smallholders in the majority world (www.guardian.co.uk/environment/2009/mar/04/cadbury-fair-trade-dairy-milk, www.ft.com/cms/s/0/cbd96894–0848–11de-8a33–0000779fd2ac.html, www.telegraph.co.uk/finance/newsbysector/retailandconsumer/4933531/CadburyDairy-Milk-to-be-fairtrade.html). It committed to pay an extra US $150 per ton for Fairtrade cocoa, ensuring farmers were paid a minimum of $1,600 per ton. Cadbury's initiative was projected to grow British Fairtrade chocolate sales from £45m. to £225m., increasing chocolate carrying the Fairtrade imprimatur to 15% of all chocolate sold in the UK, and increasing Fairtrade's £700m. UK sales by 20%. In its press statements at the time of the announcement, Cadbury emphasized that its action aimed to change the choice of Fairtrade chocolate from 'a niche preference to a mainstream ethical benchmark' (Wiggins 2009). Harriet Lamb, the chief executive of the Fairtrade Foundation, was reported in the *Financial Times* as saying that the move 'really does set the pace for the mainstream [chocolate] industry' (ibid.).

Cadbury's move was bold and attention-grabbing. The company—which had suffered a series of dents to its reputation over recent years, including a salmonella outbreak which closed its factories and stopped production for weeks in 2006 (http://news.bbc.co.uk/1/hi/5112470.stm)—had rewritten the rules of ethical trading in chocolate overnight. Turning its flagship stock-keeping unit (SKU), Cadbury's Dairy Milk, from uncertified to certified was bold indeed, and while it may be impossible for the company to achieve the switch to Fairtrade immediately, the company's message to the outside world was clear. It values the working and employment conditions of those who provide ingredients for its biggest-selling SKU so highly that it is prepared to invest in the independent, third-party certification process run by Fairtrade, and absorb the estimated £1.5m. annual cost for certification itself (http://cadburydairymilk.typepad.com/fairtrade/, http://www.cadbury.com/media/press/Pages/cdmfairtrade.aspx). The deployment of the independent third party was designed to serve as a signifier of due diligence, the shorthand in today's market for: 'If you're the sort of person who does not trust big corporations, that is fine; we are independently vetted and verified by this credible third party.'

There is nothing to suggest that the takeover of Cadbury by Kraft will affect the company's decision to make Dairy Milk Fairtrade, a certification deal that was already well advanced when the takeover was announced. The brand would be vulnerable to attack and direct consumer action if it were to reverse this policy decision. The new parent company also has a long track record in working with the Rainforest Alliance to certify its Kenco coffee brand.

Cadbury's move shows a confidence and an understanding of consumer motivation; motives shared by the world's biggest tea company, Unilever, which in 2007 announced its intention to certify as sustainable by the Rainforest Alliance the 12% of the world's tea crop it buys annually for its Lipton and PG Tips brands (www.rainforest-alliance.org/news.cfm?id=unilever). This applies to tea sold in Europe by 2010, 2015 in the rest of the world. Likewise, in recent years, Kraft has been slowly increasing the proportion of the coffee beans in its popular Kenco SKUs that are certified by the Rainforest Alliance. At the time Lipton announced the Rainforest Alliance certification programme in June 2007, marketing blogger *the brand gym* commented in a post tagged 'Lipton to make the only "green" tea':

> What is smart, and brave, about this move is trying to give the whole brand stronger ethical credentials by being values-led: integrating the ethical principles into the way of doing business. This feels much more powerful than the more commonly used, quicker fix of launching an 'ethical version'.
>
> (http://wheresthesausage.typepad.com/my_weblog/2007/06/lipton_to_make_.html)

THE EVOLUTION OF BRANDS AND THEIR MEANING

In the early part of the 20th century, when brands started to emerge in a form that today's consumers would recognize, they differentiated themselves with verbal and visual identities. At that time, brands were designed to fulfil functional needs. Soap cleaned hands and eliminated germs to keep users healthy, while the first processed foods added missing nutrients to the working man's diet. As affluence spread across the West after the Second World War—and particularly in North America and Western Europe—brands were increasingly promoted for the emotional needs they could fulfil, elevated in both their ability to command attention and in Maslow's hierarchy of needs (Maslow 1943). Hairspray was able to enhance feelings of femininity and self-confidence, while chocolate bars could enable and symbolize sexual liberation.

In the early part of the 21st century, many brands have chosen to go beyond fulfilling purely functional and emotional needs. To succeed today, a growing number of consumer products sold in the minority, developed world—and particularly food and drink products made out of raw ingredients sourced from majority, developing economies—claim that they are able to fulfil social needs (see Catherine Dolan's chapter in this volume for a deeper elaboration on this point). The very act of consumption brings with it social benefits to those who tend the raw materials; it is a way for concerned global citizens to extend the ethics of care to the distant poor through their everyday purchasing behaviour.

In a world where all flavours of corporate behaviour are instantly narrow-cast by citizen journalists and non-governmental organizations (NGOs), some brands are choosing to base their marketing strategy on the sustainable credentials of their supply chain. As public understanding of sustainability becomes increasingly sophisticated, consumers are not just demanding 'greener' products which have less impact on the environment; to earn and deserve their loyalty, many consumers demand that their shopping basket brands are properly sustainable in terms of social and economic as well as environmental impact.

In the battle to secure advantage over branded rivals and private label products, many brands have realized that they also need to do good—to build in social capital into their brand story—in order to do well. After all, it is the responsibility of all boards of directors of publicly-listed companies to maximize returns for shareholders. Brand custodians are primarily in the business of making money, growing brands and market share, and not saving the world. So—the argument goes—in this new environment, if they are able to build meaningful sustainability into the very act of consumption, they are likely to fulfil their primary objective faster and more successfully than their rivals.

But consumers have also learned to be cynical about the overzealous claims some marketers make for their products in the name of differentiation and share of attention. To reassure consumers, many brands therefore now choose to outsource the job of guaranteeing the sustainable credentials of their raw materials and supply chain to independent, third party bodies which certify different stages of the growing, production, packaging, distribution and reuse cycle. These certification bodies and schemes—including Fairtrade, the Rainforest Alliance and the Soil Association—use different models and criteria to satisfy themselves, legislators, the retail trade and the buying public, that the products they approve meet internationally-agreed standards. This shift reflects the shift in power from advertising to public relations. If advertising is what you say about yourself, public relations is what others say about you. If as a corporation you are able to secure—through transparent, carefully-audited associations—the imprimatur of an independent, third-party NGO, a mistrusting public is much more likely to give you, your products and the sustainable claims you make for those products the benefit of the doubt.

Although the organizations which administer the certification schemes do not operate in the same way or for the same reasons as the companies whose business practices they are commissioned to scrutinize and certify, the competition between these organizations can be every bit as fierce as the competition between branded rivals. Their continued success depends on growth, and for these organizations, growth means more producers commissioning them (and not their rivals) to assess and certify their supply chains. The revenue they generate is not returned to shareholders, but rather invested in stakeholders—the farmers who are audited, the communities in which they and their dependents live, and the infrastructure.

One route to growth for the NGOs that certify sustainable production is to become increasingly well-known and sought-out by consumers as a signifier of sustainable business. Wider recognition is, therefore, both an end in itself and integral to increased success. So while these organizations' behaviour and business models are designed to be very much more like an NGO than a consumer goods company, their partnership with consumer goods companies and rivalry with other certifying bodies makes them behave more like their commercial partners than they might think.

CERTIFYING AND ACCREDITING ORGANIZATIONS

Brand owners of products with a global distribution—companies with the scale of operation to be able both to afford the costs of certification and, therefore, to make a significant impact on the lives of hundreds of thousands of farmers through their buying behaviour—are a relatively small group of multinational corporations. This group includes Kraft, Nestlé, Unilever, Cadbury Schweppes, Heinz and Campbell's—a collection of multi-billion dollar corporations headquartered in the USA, the UK or mainland Europe.

The NGOs that have developed and diversified their services to ensure a more equitable relationship between consumer countries in the minority world and supplier countries in the majority world, between multinational corporations and farmers, are even thinner on the ground than the corporations they are now busy certifying. This is partly because the certification route is little more than 25 years old, partly because the costs involved in creating a proper certification network are prohibitive and classically chicken-and-egg, and partly because the market for their services is still in its infancy. For while the number of fairly traded brands arriving in Western supermarkets is growing every week, compared with the total number of products available and the total turnover of the global food industry, they still represent less than 1% of total global consumption.

The two biggest competing brands in the market for certification are Fairtrade and the Rainforest Alliance (RA); Utz Certified is a third (see glossary for further details). While the RA has, since its foundation, existed as a certifying body, the many different partners in Fairtrade—particularly Oxfam—have different objectives and both campaigning and crisis response arms that give them at least the perception of more independence from the industries whose raw materials they are also now certifying. This means that, while the RA seeks to deliver social, economic and environmental benefits to farms and farmers as a direct result of creating a more equitable relationship between growers and manufacturers, this is only part of Oxfam's role and motivation. This principal point of difference has led to tensions between the two camps, with the RA at times being accused of being in industry's pocket. It has also meant, historically, a relatively lower profile for the RA. The RA argues that this is because it spends all the money it receives from certification on certification and it does not have a mandate to campaign actively for change.

Oxfam, the Fairtrade Foundation and the RA are, like many national and global NGOs, now coming to be structured in a way that mirrors the commercial partners with whom they work, with client services and account teams. In effect, this means that they work with their commercial partners in a way that is not unlike the way their commercial partners work with their retail partners. The principal difference can be found in the motivations of those who seek to work in the commercial versus the NGO sector. Just as brands are evolving to have social meaning, as described above, the energetic and demanding Generation Y which populates many key roles in certifying NGOs are asking that their job provides social meaning as well as a means to earning a living (functional benefits) and status (emotional). Moreover, as an increasing number of companies are taking the sustainability of their supply chain seriously, the structure and availability of roles in branded goods companies is also changing, to mirror the relationships and partnerships that they need to maintain with NGOs. As a result, there is also increasingly frequent movement between in-house corporate social responsibility and sustainability roles in corporations, and the client or account management roles in NGOs.

DIFFERENT BRANDS, DIFFERENT BRAND OWNERS, DIFFERENT APPROACHES

The initiatives to turn category-leading brands over to sustainably sourced raw ingredients is not the only approach taken by consumer goods brands to building social capital into their product stories. That said, many commentators believe that it is only by turning mainstream, mass consumer brands over to production regimens that are independently certified can any real change be brought to the long-term economic, environmental and social status of growers in emerging, producing economies. For it is only mainstream brands, which have regular dialogue with their consumers through advertising and other marketing channels and in particular public relations, that are willing and have the economies of scale to absorb the cost of certification within their operating and production costs.

By contrast, some brands have chosen to introduce small, niche, upmarket SKUs which are sustainably sourced. Critics have branded the development of products of this sort—such as Nestlé's Partners' Blend coffee—as a cynical attempt to make consumers think that they have fundamentally changed their business model when no real change has been effected (www.just-food.com/store/product.aspx?id=52125). Instead of following the Cadbury, Unilever and Kraft model, they argue, niche sustainable products are generally agreed to be little more than tokenistic gestures.

However, that three of the world's biggest food and drinks companies are now prepared to turn the entire supply chain of raw ingredients to sustainable sources for their most important SKUs speaks volumes about both consumer demand and consumer desire to have an ethical dimension built into their day-to-day consumption behaviour. On the one hand, manufacturers are being pulled into a new ethics of production by consumers. On the other hand, they are being pushed into it by retailers, who are increasingly demanding a more sustainable approach to production from their suppliers. This, in turn, is driven by consumer demand. But more than push and pull, some corporations now appear to understand the value of building social value into their brand DNA and communicating this aggressively.

Many of the roots of social concern might also be seen with the great Victorian philanthropists such as Cadbury and Lever. In some cases, such as Unilever's vast tea plantation at Kericho in Kenya, working practices certified as best practice by independent NGOs which accredit production have been in development and refinement for the best part of a century (www.lipton.co.uk/gb_en/Lipton_history – 0,68.aspx).

The battle between the different certification bodies—between Fairtrade, the Rainforest Alliance and Utz Certified; between the Soil Association and competing organic certification schemes—is just as cutthroat as the battle between Nestlé and Kraft, between Wal-Mart and Tesco, and between Lipton and Tetley. They exist to make money—out of certification—just as their commercial peers seek to worst their branded competitors. While certification bodies may seek to win over farmers and governments, they also look to generate revenue to further their aims and objectives.

GOING IT ALONE

Some brands, particularly those with a more family culture and background, often companies that are neither publicly quoted nor owned and operated by multi-national corporations, have chosen to capitalize on their individual way of doing business to tell their own sustainability stories. They do not feel the need to engage independent third parties to validate or certify the way they do business, but rather take an idiosyncratic approach to tell their tale of corporate social responsibility.

Table 2.1 Categories/brands certified by Fairtrade and the Rainforest Alliance

Category	*Fairtrade*	*Rainforest Alliance*
Chocolate	Pioneered by Divine, Traidcraft and Oxfam Most brands have Fairtrade SKUs, including Green & Blacks, M&S, Sainsbury's, Waitrose, Thorntons	Cocoa Cultures, Kraft, Whole Foods Market
Coffee	Cafedirect, M&S, Nescafé, Rombouts Starbucks, Waitrose	Costa, easyjet, Holiday Inn (US), Kenco, McDonalds, Whole Foods Market
Fruit	Co-op, Riverford Organics, Waitrose, Whole Foods Market	Chiquita Bananas, innocent (smoothies – bananas), Whole Foods Market
Ice cream	Ben & Jerry's (three flavours) M&S, Sainsbury, Tesco Cotswold Ice Cream Company	Ben & Jerry's (coffee ice cream)
Tea	Clipper, Equal Exchange, M&S, Purely Organic, Teadirect	Lipton, McDonald's, PG Tips

Source: Fairtrade (http://www.fairtrade.org.uk/products/retail_products/default.aspx)
Rainforest Alliance (http://www.rainforest-alliance.org/agriculture.cfm?id=main)
* The figures against these products represent the cocoa part of all products containing cocoa and the honey part of all products containing honey.
** Following review, some of the 2007 figures have been amended but the total remains the same.

Take Tilda, for example. From modest beginnings as an importer of rice and pulses in the early 1970s, privately-owned Tilda has changed the way the developed world and the Middle East thinks about and eats rice. Passionately championing the finest cultivar of the world's most prized, rare breed of rice, Basmati, Tilda has almost single-handedly shifted public perception that rice is simply a commodity carbohydrate and taken value and volume leadership of rice in dozens of countries including its home base, the UK (Tilda 2008).

The company's route to success has been its obsessive focus on Basmati. For instance, it runs the world's only DNA testing facility for rice, ricesearch. Every batch of Basmati that Tilda buys at the open, government-controlled auction is tested for genetic purity. This is a hugely important benchmark, as some batches of rice purporting to be Basmati are frequently adulterated with inferior quality, hybrid Basmati strains or, worse, non-Basmati, long-grain strains (details on www.tilda.com, Genuine Story, Purity and DNA tested).

To achieve a consistent supply of finest-quality, unadulterated Basmati, Tilda has made a considerable investment in building relationships with the tens of thousands of individual, independent, small-holding farmers in the only area in northern India where genuine Basmati can be grown—the foothills of the Himalayas. Getting to know so many individuals by name through its contact and advice programme, known as the Farmers' Advisory Cell (FACE), has been vital to its corporate success. FACE provides authenticated Taraori seed at cost with no compulsion for farmers to sell their final crop back to Tilda, and by sharing best practice from its field-scale Basmati farm, FOSTER, Tilda practises what it calls a 'fair play' system. The company also runs a number of cultural, health, social and education programmes at a community level—the kinds of corporate behaviours that certificating bodies routinely look for and tick off on the journey to certifying brands as triple bottom-line.

The difference with Tilda—and other independent, family-culture companies independently active in this way, such as family tea and coffee merchants Taylors of Harrogate—is that sustainable sourcing is the way they have always done business. The only change from when they started to trade and today is scale. They do not appear to believe that they need the independent, third-party imprimatur of certification to validate their way of working. This is a confident, if understated, approach in a world in which corporate behaviour is more open and accessible than it ever has been. For although Taylors does buy a lot of its coffee from Fairtrade certified co-operatives, the company has been buying coffee ethically since long before the Fairtrade mark was developed, and this behaviour has always been an important and very public part of the company's philosophy and behaviour. Some commentators—particularly in the blogosphere—also welcome companies bold enough to go it alone as, they argue, consumers are suffering from 'label fatigue' in the face of yet another logo denoting sustainability.

RETAILER PRESSURE

The world's biggest and most high-profile retailers have become key players in the commodification of ethics as they embrace a mixture of local and global sustainability strategies at the heart of their day-to-day business and communications strategies. Despite, or perhaps because of, a less than positive public and media profile, in the USA this has been pioneered by Wal-Mart (see, for instance, the cinema-released, 2005 documentary, *Wal-Mart: The High Cost of Low Price*). In the UK, Marks and Spencer (M&S) has been the public and media champion of sustainability with its much-publicized Plan A ('... because there is no Plan B') initiative (http://plana.marksandspencer.com). M&S' much bigger rival, Tesco, has also been extremely active in this area, although consumers and the media have not reported or heard about Tesco's Community Plan nearly as often or as favourably as M&S's Plan A, in part the result of Tesco's more negative reputation as the nation's biggest retailer (see, for instance, the community of organizations and individuals actively working against Tesco's perceived stranglehold on the UK retail market, http://www.tescopoly.org). In the UK, Waitrose and Sainsbury's have also gained traction, column inches and significant consumer support for what they are doing to minimize the impact their business has environmentally, while maximizing the impact they have economically (better prices for suppliers, better value for consumers) and socially (better conditions and returns for producers in the majority world).

What the bigger retailers have in common—and what they have learned from smaller players such as Whole Foods Market, whose corporate philosophy is based on being a good corporate citizen (http://www.wholefoodsmarket.com/values/corevalues.php)—is a desire to differentiate themselves from their competitors on their sustainable credentials. Since retailers sit between producers and manufacturers on the one side and consumers on the other, they are uniquely sensitive to concerns and issues on both sides. It is this unique position that has seen retailers take a leadership role in both the debate about what sustainability in consumption means, in changing producer and manufacturer behaviour (reduced packaging, local sourcing) and deploying these developments to motivate consumer behaviour (carbon/food miles labelling, charging for plastic bags, creating bags for life, encouraging the switch to concentrated products).

The example of Whole Foods Market is instructive for what consumers are increasingly expecting of their retailers and retailers are increasingly requiring producers and manufacturers to deliver as a condition of the retailers continuing to stock and promote their products. The company, whose origins go back to the late 1970s in Austin, Texas, now operates almost 300 stores in the USA, Canada and the UK (www.wholefoodsmarket.com/stores/all/index.php). The company boasts that it sells the highest quality natural and organic products available and actively campaigns to reduce, and where possible eliminate, plastic from packaging and bags. It is involved in local community projects related to local suppliers and the local environment, and advocates the humane treatment of animals in the food production chain. In this context it was an early member of the Marine Stewardship Council, a global NGO promoting sustainable fishing practices.

Although an early pioneer in building sustainability into both its philosophy and operating practice, Whole Foods' approach to sustainability was equally ahead of its time by virtue of being holistic. From the start, the company took a triple bottom-line approach, ensuring that the products it sold and the packaging that held them had a neutral effect on the environment, a positive effect on the economic life of the producers, and a positive impact on the social conditions of the producers and their communities.

To the lay, consumer audience, sustainability often means little more than 'not harmful to the environment'. But triple bottom-line programmes today typically seek to ensure that: (a) workers in the majority world are paid well above average or minimum wage, so they benefit from the production cycle economically; (b) production, waste and recycling policies ensure that the land used to produce the raw ingredients is not exploited, is well looked after with the prospects of future generations factored in; and (c) that workers, their families and dependents receive a good level of social welfare, including health and safety, healthcare provision and education. These principles have been neatly captured in the Brundtland definition of sustainability: 'Sustainable development is development that meets the needs of the present without compromising the ability of future generations to meet their own' (United Nations 1987).

Retailers have been shouting loudly about their ethical policies in the opening years of the 21st century, talking about how this benefits all stages of their supply chain and in particular their consumers. They have adopted, and indeed anticipated, consumer demand for products that commodify ethics. As the middlemen between the producer and the consumer, they have been able to leverage consumer concern and demand to compel producers to put their houses in order as a condition of continued access to the market. Of course the retailers have had to introduce their own sustainable standards into their business practices, but they have also secured the benefit in consumers' eyes of stocking increasingly sustainable inventories while doing little more than introducing more stringent criteria on their suppliers. They have been able in part to secure competitive advantage with consumers by virtue of the reflected glory of their suppliers.

An example from the USA makes this point. In the early 2000s retail giant Wal-Mart was looking for ways to increase the number of SKUs in its laundry category without increasing the shelf space given over to the category in the stores. Wal-Mart knew that manufacturers had experimented with super-concentrated laundry liquids in the 1990s, but, in a time before mass consumer understanding of environmental concerns, the products had not done well.

With the surge in environmental consciousness in the early 2000s as the lever, Wal-Mart, approached the leading laundry liquid manufacturers and challenged them to produce a new generation of super-concentrated liquids. Less water in the product would mean smaller bottles (less plastic), fewer lorries on the road, and less water transported unnecessarily. It would also mean more shelf-space for Wal-Mart to stock a wider variety of SKUs. Several manufacturers responded quickly to Wal-Mart's challenge, with All Small & Mighty the first to market (www.sustainableisgood.com/blog/2007/09/concentrated-la.html). The All brand was able to present itself as being environmentally aware and active, but so too was Wal-Mart. The retailer may have been the catalyst to the manufacturer's innovation, but it was also able to take credit for that innovation without needing to invest itself.

A FLOURISHING MEDIA—AND NEW MEDIA

Media, and particularly new media, holding self-proclaimed ethical brands to account have flourished in recent years. This is true from both a business-to-consumer-facing perspective (see, for instance, *Ethical Consumer* magazine and online resource www.ethicalconsumer.org) and a business-to-business standpoint (see *Ethical Corporation* www.ethicalcorp.com). Modern ethical publications, whether business- or consumer-focused, are today available to all at the click of a mouse. Perhaps most importantly from the perspective of the modern consumer activist is the blogosphere. Where now everyone is a potential contributor to, as well as a consumer of, online journalism, the line between editor and reader has become blurred to such an extent that yesterday's conversation in the pub is tomorrow's opinion-leading point of view.

THE IMPACT OF THE GLOBAL RECESSION

In late 2008 and early 2009 many countries in the G20 group of industrialized and developing nations entered recession. The global financial crisis, sparked by a combination of financial mismanagement and risk-taking, reckless deregulation of the banking sector, and unfettered consumer lending, is anticipated to leave few corners of the world economy untouched for many months if not years to come.

As discussed, many major consumer brands have made significant investment in securing their raw ingredients from sustainable sources. Some of these brands, for the short to medium term, have absorbed the on-costs of sustainable sourcing and not increased retail prices. Others have chosen to pass the costs of certifying their supply chain as sustainable with premium pricing.

The extent to which consumers will abandon more expensive, premium products and brands and trade down to cheaper, more commodified products is yet to be fully established. Initial indications are that, although many consumers' ability to spend the same amount on food and drink as they could before the recession began is unchanged—most consumers have not lost their jobs, after all, and plummeting interest rates have reduced the cost of tracker mortgage repayments significantly—spending on both small and particularly big ticket items has reduced, while saving has increased (http://news.bbc.co.uk/1/hi/business/7967597.stm). Retailers have reported that private label, generic commodities are doing better than previously, at the expense of their branded rivals, and this includes branded products which have been certified as sustainable (Benady 2008).

Experience from previous, admittedly less severe recessions in 1991–93 and 2000–01, suggests that those brands which sustain, or better increase, marketing spend during a recession tend to do significantly better once economic growth returns. So it is reasonable to assume that mass consumer products that did not increase their price when they were certified as sustainable, and continue actively to differentiate themselves on their sustainable credentials during the recession, should do disproportionately well come the projected bluer economic skies of 2011 and 2012.

Indeed, compassion fatigue is not a necessary corollary of national and personal economic hardship. Many charities are thriving during the recession on the grounds that 'those who need it most need our help more than ever during hard times'. This argument was deployed at every turn by film director Richard Curtis, the creator and figurehead of Comic Relief's Red Nose Day in the UK in 2009. As a result, donations to the telethon for UK and African projects rose from a previous record of £40m. in 2007 to £57m. in 2009 (http://news.bbc.co.uk/1/hi/entertainment/7939425.stm), an outcome which is at the very least counter-intuitive. This outcome may be good news for sustainable consumer brands during the current recession.

THE FUTURE OF COMMODIFIED ETHICS

At the time of Cadbury's announcement of its commitment to Fairtrade in March 2009, the company's chief executive said: 'If there are only small players in Fairtrade, it's sort of self-defeating ... If big businesses get behind it, you can have a much bigger impact on agricultural societies' (Wiggins 2009).

The history of engaging affluent, minority world consumers with the ethical dilemmas and contradictions inherent in consuming products grown and produced in the majority world, largely by poor, agricultural labourers, was dominated at the outset by NGOs looking to do good by doing well. In the course of the past decade, and in response to both consumer and retailer demand, the custodians of many leading consumer brands have spotted the long-term commercial opportunity of evolving their brands to accommodate sustainability. For mainstream consumer brands to have a sustainable economic future in both the developed and emerging economies, marketers have followed the lead set by NGOs, and often partnered with them to certify their claims. Because of their expertise in both communication and persuasion, not to mention an established customer base and a marketing and distribution infrastructure, mainstream brands can achieve very much more than NGOs working alone to promote and support niche products.

Several brands are doing well, in terms of image, reputation and sales, by building consumer involvement in one or more aspects of sustainability into their brand promise and the very act of consumption. This analysis of the market and the issues driving the commodification of ethics suggests that successful brands in this sector share a number of distinct approaches, beliefs and behaviours: (a) they build a 'conscience' into the act of consumption. Buying their brand brings with it both a long-term commitment to sustainable sourcing and an immediate financial contribution to real people's lives in the majority world today; (b) they make it easy and undemanding for consumers to factor sustainability into their weekly shopping trips. In effect, they offer to subcontract an ethical approach to consumerism; (c) for this reason, they very frequently look to work with independent, third party organizations that can certify the ethical claims they make for their products. Consumers understand manufacturers' profit motives—they know very well that they are not in business just to do good or make themselves feel good. This is why it can be so valuable to commission an NGO to verify the claims the brands seek to make; (d) the big brands can absorb the costs of certification or partnership into their operating costs by tightly managing their supply chain. As such, they often do not increase the cost of their products once they acquire their new, sustainable status. This is especially true of mass consumption, commodity products which are notoriously sensitive to movements in price; (e) they turn their entire mainstream product supply chain over to sustainable sourcing and production. Actually delivering this—and particularly when it needs to be certified by a third party—can take many years, but in this case brands make a long-term commitment and often communicate updates. And as they acquire their new sustainable status, they invest time and money in communicating exactly what their consumers' consumption in the minority world is delivering for the growers, their families and communities in the majority world. They are selling a message and an attitude every bit as much as a product.

Perhaps most importantly from this exploration of the junction between market-leading brands and sustainability, there are several advantages when big, established, market-leading brands convert their lead SKUs to sustainable sources—as distinct from the pioneers of fairly-traded goods, which were small, niche products, sold at a price, quality and ethical premium compared with standard products. This approach normalizes the rhetoric and reality of sustainability in any given category, not least because if a big brand makes a commitment in this area, it is currently bound to leverage that commitment to branded advantage; one of the prime motivators for change is to hold on to a leadership position, to sustain a reputation for innovation. This also makes ethical considerations or sustainability the benchmark or entry-level standard for all other players in the market.

BIBLIOGRAPHY

Benady, D., 'Eat, Drink and be Merry', *Marketing Week*, 20 November 2008.

Maslow, A. H., 'A Theory of Human Motivation', *Psychological Review*, 50(4): 370–96, 1943.

Tilda, *The Tilda Basmati Report – 2008 Market Outlook*, Tilda, Rainham, 2008.

United Nations, *Our Common Future*, World Commission on Environment and Development, New York, 1987.

Wiggins, J., 'Cadbury Wraps Up Fairtrade Agreement', *Financial Times*, 4 March 2009. Available at www.ft.com/cms/s/0/cbd96894-0848-11de-8a33-0000779fd2ac.html.

Branding morality: The case of Fairtrade

CATHERINE S. DOLAN

INTRODUCTION

In an age of mass production and homogenous goods, the manufacture of difference through branding has become pivotal to corporate success. As the hallmark of contemporary capitalism (Holt 2006; Suchman 2007), brands enable companies to sustain customer loyalty, enhance shareholder value, and differentiate themselves in a postindustrial landscape sated with a seemingly infinite array of goods. Yet while brands dominate the marketplace, their power lies less in the utility and functionality of their products than in their intangible symbolic attributes. These intangible qualities are particularly salient in ethical brands such as Fairtrade where it is the moral rather than utilitarian connotations of the label that have inspired growing numbers of consumers to change their everyday purchasing practices.

Described as the 'archetypal brand' of the new economy (Paton 2006), Fairtrade is now the world's most recognizable ethical brand. Sales of Fairtrade products have experienced dramatic growth over the last decade, gaining increased market share across several categories and moving from the margins to the mainstream of commercial retailing. However, in contrast to other ethical brands, Fairtrade places market relations at the centre of consumer politics, aiming to restructure supply chain interactions by 're-embedding' economic exchange in social relations (Raynolds 2002; Polanyi 1957). This politics of reconnection forms the crux of Fairtrade's brand identity.

This chapter explores how the relational principles conveyed by Fairtrade—collaboration, partnership and long-term relationships—are produced and communicated through the brand. It focuses on the key arena in which brand identity is fashioned: the system of marketing that aims to differentiate Fairtrade products by conveying its alternative values of collaboration, trust and fairness. The marketing of Fairtrade-labelled goods, for instance, de-anonymizes the act of consumption through promotional campaigns that make visible the social effects of production and draw Northern consumers into moral relations with producers in the South (Watson 2007). Such campaigns provide a 'bridge to social justice', empowering consumers to participate in a moral act that strives to redraft economic (and social) ties between rich and poor and north and south. Yet while marketing seeks to reconnect producers and consumers through new aesthetic and discursive forms, the chapter suggests that such techniques may render these relations ever more idealized and remote. In fact while the Fairtrade brand has enjoyed tremendous success, the aesthetic and bureaucratic processes through which brand meanings are produced, conveyed and validated inhibit the moral contract that the movement seeks to create. Indeed, these processes may have the opposite effect, parlaying the subjectivities of producers into a source of economic value by commodifying their lives, landscapes and production practices. The chapter concludes that while the symbolic force of the brand may bestow credibility to Fairtrade, the process of brand-building may ultimately divest exchange of sociality, rendering the intended equality of North-South relations increasingly illusive and virtual.

BRANDING MORALITY

Over the last century brands have emerged as the leitmotif of consumer culture and have gained increased economic importance since the 1980s. Originally brands served as a trademark that signified quality and imbued anonymous mass-produced commodities with an identity by connecting them to an identifiable producer or personality (Klein 2005). Today the term no longer refers to a simple commodity but to an entire context of consumption—the ideas, attitudes, values and experiences that people attach to products (Hearn 2006; Klein 2005). Although marketing and advertising continue to permeate the marketplace, what now epitomizes consumer culture is the deepening penetration of brands, where icons like Apple, Sony, and Walmart signify entire environments of meaning, and where corporations sell affect, experience and lifestyles more than a thing (Banet-Weiser and Lapsansky 2008).

Brands are 'monetized symbols' (Gorz 2003: 60), a locus of both economic activity and socio-cultural meaning. These symbols and the meanings they convey do not simply reflect the creative capacity of marketers, who labour over logos and ad campaigns, but are constituted by consumers who invest brands with their personal and social identities (Foster 2008). The process of branding, for example, serves as a linking device between an alienated product and the realisation of social aspirations such that brands become an 'extension' of the self' (Belk 1988) or a 'badge of social belonging' (Zadek *et al.* 1998) that enable consumers to convey ideas about the kind of person they are and the sort of person they would like to be seen to be (Moore 1994; Baudrillard 1988; Banet-Weiser and Lapsansky 2008). As Arvidsson (2006: 82) writes, '[i]t is how you feel with the branded product, what kind of person it can make you become, that is what sets it apart' from the indistinguishable, generic products that clutter the marketplace.

Brands also act as a catalyst and a medium for social and political concerns, bridging the seemingly oppositional domains of citizenship and consumption (Soper 2007). In Britain concerns surrounding the morality of the market have often been part of consumer society, from the moral codes of respectability and virtuosity that inspired socially productive consumption in the

18th century to anti-slavery boycotts, co-operative movements, and Buy Empire campaigns in the 19th (Bushman 1992; Hilton 2003; Smith 2002; Trentmann 2007). During the 1990s, as media exposés and NGO campaigns highlighted the sweatshop conditions, ecological disasters and human rights abuses wrought by global multinationals, consumption became once again a key arena for political engagement. Public animosity toward unfettered markets and sybaritic corporations spawned myriad consumer resistance movements from 'buy nothing day' to culture jamming and ad-busting (Holt 2002; Penaloza and Price 1993; Rumbo 2002). Yet while a vigorous anti-branding movement flourished, not all resistance occurred outside the theatre of the market; rather the market itself was cast as the vehicle through which social and economic justice could be realized. Consumption itself became a locus of civic and political participation as citizens increasingly defined shopping as an arena in which they could 'cast their ballot – on a world scale, no less' (Beck and Gernsheim, 2001: 44).

The politicization of consumption entails a whole new level of self-responsibility as citizens are no longer obligated only to themselves but to humanity at large. As Sassatelli (2006:233) writes, '[b]lame, far from being externalized and placed on companies and authorities, is internalized and placed on the self as a consumer'. As a result, a plethora of market-based initiatives emerged to remoralize trade and right environmental and social wrongs through 'green', 'ethical', and 'sustainable', etc. forms of consumption. By 2004 65% of the UK public self-identified as 'green or ethical consumers' (Nicholls 2010) and by 2009 the UK ethical market had reached £43.2 billions up from £36.5 billion in 2007 (The Co-operative 2010). A growing proportion of the ethical marketplace is now captured by ethical brands such as Innocent Smoothies, Ecover, Divine Chocolate and Fairtrade.

Over the last decade Fairtrade has experienced impressive growth rates and increased levels of consumer loyalty. In the UK consumer awareness of the Fairtrade mark has grown from 20% of the population in 2002 to 82% in 2009, with consumers in Britain purchasing more Fairtrade-labelled products per capita than any other country (Fairtrade Foundation 2009). In 2008 retail sales of Fairtrade-labelled products topped £700m., with over 4,500 Fairtrade-certified products for sale in retail and catering outlets (Fairtrade Foundation 2009; Mintel 2009). Today, Fairtrade products capture substantial market share in some categories, comprising one-quarter of all bananas and one-fifth of roast and ground coffee sold in the UK (Mintel 2009).

THE GROWTH AND DIVERSIFICATION OF FAIRTRADE

Fairtrade promotes an ethical vision that seeks to marry tangible financial rewards with development outcomes such as empowerment, capacity building, and producer participation. While originally forged as a mechanism for humanitarian assistance, by the 1960s the Fairtrade movement, largely comprising faith-based, campaign, and community organizations, had shed its philanthropic associations and shifted its orientation toward a structural reform of capitalism. Recasting its mandate for development as 'justice instead of charity', these organizations aimed to alleviate poverty and injustice by instituting ethics into North-South trading relations through a system of direct and fair exchange (Schmelzer 2007; Scholte 2003). In the late 1980s these disparate Fair Trade Organizations and Alternative Trading Organizations (FTOs and ATOs) came together to form the International Fair Trade Association (IFAT), now the World Fair Trade Organization (WFTO), whose member organizations market goods that are produced, imported and/or distributed through 'alternative' market channels (Barrientos and Dolan 2006).

In the 1990s a second model, spearheaded by Fairtrade Labelling Organizations International (FLO), emerged to expand brand visibility and market access for Fairtrade goods (Bezençon and Blili 2006; Renard 2003). In contrast to the mission-driven ethos of ATOs, for whom Fairtrade is 'more than a market', FLO and its national affiliates are focused on building the business of Fairtrade, embracing corporate participation as a way to spread development benefits to a wider swathe of producers (Barrientos and Dolan 2006: 181; Raynolds 2009). Spawned by the establishment of the first Fairtrade label, Max Havelaar in 1988, FLO (through its National Initiatives) is today the worldwide standard-setting and certification organization for Fairtrade-labelled products. Following the adoption of the Fairtrade Certification Mark (CM) by FLO in 2002, labelled products quickly moved into the 'mainstream', penetrating the distribution and marketing channels of manufacturers and retailers (Bezençon and Blili 2006; Renard 2003).

Although IFAT and FLO are working towards a joint generic Fairtrade standard, the two systems tend to encompass different products, visions and branding strategies. For example, whereas the FLO mark certifies products (primarily agricultural commodities), the IFAT mark certifies organizations (primarily handicraft producers and importers) (Benzençon and Blili 2006). Yet even within the FLO system, the actors, institutions and trading relations vary as Fairtrade-labelled products enter the commercial mainstream through several market channels. This ranges from dedicated Fairtrade companies such as Cafédirect and Day Chocolate to branded manufacturers such as Procter & Gamble, Kraft, and Nestlé that now include Fairtrade products among their offerings. The Fairtrade lines carried by these companies, from Cafédirect to Kraft, are now sold in a growing number of large supermarket chains, with several UK retailers also converting their own-brand products to Fairtrade (Co-op, Sainsbury's, Marks and Spencer and Tesco).

This chapter is concerned with FLO-labelled products (i.e. those that carry the FAIRTRADE Mark), which have underwritten Fairtrade's spectacular market growth (Wilkinson 2007) and thrust Fairtrade into the centre of commercial retailing. The FAIRTRADE Mark (i.e. label, logo) is what 'singularizes' the brand, distinguishing its products from other brands in the marketplace by conveying both its moral claim and its credibility (Kopytoff

1986). This symbolic seal of fairness forms the basis of consumer trust, a determinant in the decision to purchase an ethical product. As Iain Bretman, the Deputy Director of the Fairtrade Foundation, noted upon receipt of a Superbrand award, '[T]he Fairtrade Mark … embodies the trust that shoppers place in the Foundation to operate a system of rules that deliver a better deal for disadvantaged farming families in the world's poorest countries' (Fairtrade Foundation 2005) and indeed, a recent study found that over 90% of people familiar with the Fairtrade brand trusted it. What consumers 'trust' is that Fairtrade delivers on its commitment to transform market relations by offering better trading conditions to marginalized producers in the South, that is, that it fulfils an ethic of universal rights and economic justice.

THE ETHIC OF FAIRTRADE

The Fairtrade mark guarantees that the movement's ethical principles are incorporated into the exchange process. The mark's moral claim, for example, is authenticated by a process of certification, which aims to translate brand values of economic justice and empowerment into a set of codified requirements (standards), thereby creating a system that consumers can trust. These standards typically consist of a hierarchy of principles, criteria and indicators, and provide the basis for internal and external processes such as monitoring and verification. The generic standards for small farmer organizations in Fairtrade, for example, contain requirements for social, economic and environmental development and stipulate that producers must receive a fair price and a social premium to invest in producer organizations and/or community improvements in healthcare, education, housing and local infrastructure (Barrientos and Dolan 2006; FLO 2007). While not legally binding, standards translate values of transparency, empowerment and equity into prescriptions for action, providing producers, traders, and buyers with a technical blueprint of their responsibilities.

The values encoded in standards are founded on moral universalism—what Smith (2000) describes as an 'ethics of impartiality'—a system of ethics that holds that 'if something's right for me, it's right for you; if it's wrong for you, it's wrong for me' (Chomsky cited by Schivone 2007). As the Fairtrade and organic coffee company, Café Campesino, describes it:

> Café Campesino envisions a world in which all trade is based on the tenets of the Golden Rule [providing] working women and men with equal opportunity, a fair price for the goods and services they produce, the ability to meet their basic needs, and a … dynamic future based on a respect for basic human rights, free enterprise and liberty.
>
> (http://www.cafecampesino.com/aboutus.asp)

In the context of Fairtrade, the Golden Rule reflects the spirit of relationality and sociality that underlies the exchange process of Fairtrade, and in particular its commitment to form long-term, direct supply chain relationships that embody trust and mutual respect (Raynolds 2002). For example, the mission statement of the fair trade movement's champion brand, Cafédirect, states that it aims 'to be the leading brand which strengthens the influence, income and security of producer partners in the South, by linking them directly to consumers in developed countries' (Cafédirect 2009; Davies *et al.* 2009). At the heart of this vision lies an ethics of care (Whatmore 1997) that aims to remoralize the economy by supplanting the calculation and abstraction of capitalism through exchange founded on mutual obligation, co-operation and interdependence. Importantly it is through the mediation of the brand that this politics of reconnection occurs. It is through the purchase of labelled Fairtrade products, for example, that consumers express their vision of global justice, conceiving the brand as aligned with their identity and ethical ideals.

This relational ethic constitutes Fairtrade's challenge to conventional economic relations and forms the crux of its brand identity. For example, what is most significant about Fairtrade transactions is not the status of the commodity per se, but the 'economy of moral cultivation' that the exchange engenders (Carrier 1991; Mahmood 2003). Consumers do not perceive the Fairtrade brand 'as a passive objective of marketing transactions' or as a form of charitable assistance, but as an animate, dynamic contributing partner in the relationship dyad (Fournier 1998). Yet how are these affective ties forged and through what mechanisms are the values of the brand conveyed, actualized and legitimated? As Barnett *et al.* note (2005, 29), ethical dispositions are 'worked up, governed, and regulated by' through a range of strategies, procedures and actors, which facilitate and shape the forms that ethical consumption assumes. In the following I examine a key arena in which Fairtrade's brand meanings are produced—the system of marketing and advertising that seeks to 'qualify' Fairtrade products by defetishizing the exploitative conditions of market exchange and constructing an emotional bridge between North and South (cf. Callon 1988). This process seeks to 'extend the consumers' sense of caring beyond the 'here' and 'now' (Goodman 2004, 903) by re-embedding exchange in a new moral economy of trade. However, as the following suggests, it can also produce the opposite effect, creating a disconnection between the values that the brand signifies and the means through which the values are communicated and deemed legitimate.

THE MARKETING OF FAIRTRADE: FROM PICTURES TO PURCHASES

The success of Fairtrade hinges on Northern consumers translating their perceived ethical responsibilities into a product purchase at the checkout till. However, moving from principle to practice requires knowledge of the social and environmental conditions confronted by Southern producers as only then can a sense of global moral responsibility be established (Sznaider 2001, 15). As described by Adam Smith:

> By the imagination we place ourselves in his situation, we conceive ourselves enduring all the same torments ... His agonies, when they are thus brought home to ourselves, when we have thus adopted and made them our own, begin at last to affect us, and we then tremble and shudder at the thought of what he feels.
>
> (Adam Smith 1759: 9)

In the absence of direct observation, this knowledge/information deficit is filled by the communications of media, NGOs and Fairtrade marketers, the 'ethical complex' that mediates between the world of producers and the ethical dispositions of consumers (Freidberg 2003; Watson 2007). Yet building brand equity is not only a matter of knowledge production—raising consumer awareness about the consequences of the products that they buy—but of moral solicitation. As Holt (2002) and Arvidsson (2006) note, marketers' efforts to boost brand value must tap into the ideas that people want to express through their consumption by fostering attachments around the brand through experiences, emotions, attitudes, and lifestyles, etc. In the world of moral marketing, this is not only achieved by constructing a vicarious experience of connection but by identifying the ingredients in that connection that will move an individual to act (i.e. buy) through 'culturally constructed stories and ideologies about commodity flows' (Appadurai 1986: 48). Marketing strategies, for example, deploy a range of aesthetic and discursive strategies to elicit sympathy for distant producers and translate ethical obligations into consumption practices (Barnett *et al.* 2005). They serve as cultural intermediaries who not only educate the public on the hardships of the Third World but compete for the 'hearts and minds' (and purchases) of consumers through advertising imagery and promotional techniques (Goodman 2004: 902). The politics of ethical consumption are thus carried out in the symbolic realm, where concerned citizens are exposed not to the 'classic hard sell of old-style marketers' but to images that induce sympathy, moral obligation and a shared sense of humanity (Cronin 2004: 351). In this regard Fairtrade marketers are less 'taste makers' than moral entrepreneurs, whose strategies of affect management turn mundane commodities such as coffee, tea and chocolate into cultural resources for consumers' ethical subjectivities (Dolan 2007; Goodman 2004; Holt 2002; Watson 2007; Wright 2004).

INTIMATE STRANGERS, DISTANT KIN

For Fairtrade to foster new (albeit imagined) relationships between cosmopolitan consumers and the 'have nots' of the global South, consumers must experience themselves as interacting not with a particular product but with the producer of that product (Watson 2007). As noted, this calls for marketing techniques that defetishize the conditions of market exchange such that an emotional bridge can be formed between North and South. This occurs through what Goodman (2004) describes as Fairtrade's 'political ecological imaginary, a regime of representation that shapes the moral economy of consumption by aestheticizing the livelihoods and landscapes of small farmers and depicting the power of Fairtrade to transform lives. This is most visible in the traffic of morally-tinged messages featured on press releases, in-store publications and corporate websites that seek to inspire concern for Third World poverty, competing for what Applbaum (1998: 334) terms a 'share of mind'. For example, in the US-based Fairtrade Resource Network's booklet, the Conscious Consumer, concerned citizens are invited to 'meet people in distant regions, learning how they work, live and raise their families' (Ericson 2002: 2). Such encounters abound in the virtual worlds of Fairtrade organizations and corporations where with a mouse click consumers are introduced to the baleful consequences of contemporary capitalism and afforded a voyeuristic tour of producers' lives transformed by the daily shopping of Northern consumers. A troll through the website of Tesco, the UK's largest supermarket, introduces us to Regina Joseph, a banana farmer and single parent of five children in Dominica for whom Fairtrade has provided a 'lifeline' for her and her family. Similarly, Cafédirect's website provides an opportunity to meet coffee growers like John, who says, 'I've been a grower since 1963 so I've seen many changes. The biggest change is that since Cafédirect's involvement we now get a fair price and can grow really great coffee for *you*' (http://brewing.cafedirect.co.uk/what-we-grow/#guillermo). By employing the pronoun 'you' to address me/us personally, these virtual encounters become intimate, instantaneously distinguishing the ongoing dialogue of Fairtrade from a one-off disinterested economic transaction (Lury 2004). Similarly, Marks and Spencer celebrated Fairtrade fortnight in 2008 through an emotive set of images that conveyed the social transformation afforded through ethical consumption. One poster claimed that 'Buying tea carrying the FAIRTRADE mark means that farmers like Alice are getting a better deal. The Fairtrade Premiums have enabled her local community in Kenya to extend their dispensary and set up a training centre for workers.' While such testimonials have been criticized for being 'morally bankrupt', affording Northern consumers an armchair experience of compassion at a distance, they also highlight the way producers now '*sell themselves*' in order to be chosen as a worthy partner in this social contract (Berlant 2004; Goodman 2009).

These strategies may provide an emotional (if not metaphorical) bridge for consumers, but they are also symbolic carriers of race, gender and class. Fairtrade advertisements, for instance, present ethnically and racially coded images, which while benignly multicultural nevertheless draw attention to the differences between the fortunate 'us' and downtrodden 'them', employing race as an empty signifier that can be infused with meanings of moral purpose and consumer citizenship (Banet-Weiser and Lapsansky 2008). As Gates (2006) drawing on Berlant (1996) suggests, these semiotics of 'the face' have permeated discourses of social justice in order to elicit personal identification with broader social concerns and spawn political action (e.g. 'the face of

AIDS', 'the face of welfare', 'the face of poverty', etc.). It is the commodification of this difference that ultimately refigures the meanings of exchange, converting the commodity and the relations that it enjoins from the abstract sphere of economic relations to what Carrier (1990) terms 'the symbolism of possession.' By implanting images of distant, less-privileged cultural worlds on website vignettes, for instance, marketers nurture a sense of global kinship, replacing the alienation of capitalism with an imagined experience of intimacy (Carrier 1990; Dolan 2007). This is illustrated in the symbol of the circle embodied in the logo of Cafédirect which according to the head of marketing reinforces 'the sense of family' between producers and consumers (McNally 2007). This 'sense' therefore is produced through the iconography of the brand, which exploits difference as a way to forge new moral connectivities between northern buyers and southern producers (Dolan 2007; Goodman 2004). Indeed, over the last year Cafédirect has built its brand strategy (the 'new look') around its partnerships with growers. As the organization states:

> We're proud of the direct relationships we have with our 39 grower partners, and they are proud of the excellent quality coffees, teas and cocoa that they grow for you. That's why our new packs feature our grower partners and their signatures – they've given each one their seal of approval.
>
> (Cafédirect, www.cafedirect.co.uk//our_products/newlook2)

Although these campaigns tend to render Fairtrade producers objects of mass consumption and a source of economic value in their own right (Goodman 2004; Lyon 2006; Wright 2004), it is not only the lives of producers that marketing appropriates as a catalyst for moral reflection but the landscapes of production. The commodification of nature has long been grist for the world of marketing, providing a cultural and spiritual loadstone for consumers alienated by urbanism and industrial capitalism (Wilk 2006). The marketing of Fairtrade recuperates this tradition, deploying images of tropical climes and pristine environments that draw a contrast between the simplicity of their untouched, natural worlds and the digital alienation of ours. Fairtrade brand communications have increasingly discarded grower testimonials in favour of a discourse of quality conveyed through 'natural' and 'unspoiled' images on product packaging; Cafédirect, for example, changed the name of their instant coffee to '5065'—the average elevation at which their coffee beans are grown (Davies *et al.* 2009). Through snapshots of verdant tea fields and mist-covered coffee farms consumers are immersed in a world where workers are contented and the earth is clean. The brand thus becomes the means by which consumers 'enter a virtual world' and form an intimate relationship with the 'location as well as the product' (Wright 2004: 674). As Wright intimates in her cogent analysis of a Cafédirect advertising campaign, these landscape aesthetics remove toil, labour and poverty from the marketing frame, converting agrarian environments into sites of purity and abundance.

The unadulterated, natural capital of these regions thus cleanses Fairtrade of its dour associations with poverty while reworking brand meanings to convey the high quality and superior taste that the 'rich soils, sunshine, rainfall and river water' of Machu Pichu and Mt Kilimanjaro endow (Wright 2004: 668). By creating a synergy between the landscape of producers and the quality of Fairtrade products, this brand positioning casts 'consuming, spending and enjoying' as congruent with, rather anathema to, the Fairtrade ethic (Bourdieu 2000: 311).

THE 'CELEBRIFICATION' OF FAIRTRADE

Brands must continually take the pulse of consumer society, staying abreast of the cultural, economic and media context in which its products circulate. The (re)positioning of consumerism as integral to Fairtrade's brand identity, for instance, reflects the growing tendency for Fairtrade to align itself with the lifestyles and tastes of middlebrow consumers by supplanting a motif of poverty with the symbols and icons of popular culture. Where Fairtrade once relied on the emotional appeal of 'Third World' producers and the ethical currency of ATOs to sell products, it now employs the techniques of Big Business, poaching the expertise of former marketers from GlaxoSmithKline, Mars and Nestlé (Davies *et al.* 2009) and pursuing strategies that aim to spectacularise as much as moralise. This can be seen in Cafédirect's recent promotional efforts to target public 'extravaganzas' such as the Glastonbury Rock Festival and the Edinburgh Fringe, highlighting the fact that Cafédirect is not 'just a niche brand but a mass-market competitor with a unique selling proposition' (Davies *et al.* 2009).

The process is also visible in the use of 'aid celebrities' to advertise Fairtrade products, with marketers appropriating the labour of celebrities to promote, if not augment, the brand (Arvidsson 2006). While celebrities have long been a ubiquitous feature in marketing, and served as ambassadors for charitable giving (McCracken 1989; Richey and Ponte 2008), their association with conspicuous consumption has traditionally weakened their appeal among ethical consumers. But today, celebrities are increasingly a proxy for brand integrity in the ethical marketplace. As part of a wider movement to market development through cultural spectacles such as Live 8 and the Make Poverty History Campaign, A-list 'responsibility celebrities' from Annie Lennox and Chris Martin, to Antonio Banderas and Colin Firth are now using their celebrity status to awaken the moral conscience of consumers (Biccum 2007). Colin Firth, for instance, underscoring the fact that 25m. coffee growers face poverty due to collapsing coffee prices, featured in a spread in which he endured cold coffee being poured over his head whilst Coldplay's Chris Martin confronted a deluge of rice to highlight how subsidies to US farmers impoverish rice producers in developing countries (Lee Potter 2005). In the same vein, Cafédirect commandeered the London Eye in 2005, with each pod serving as a venue for popular entertainers (Davies *et al.* 2009).

Notwithstanding these theatrics, the incidents highlight how the ethics of consumption are increasingly conflated with the stylistics of cool and the allure of Hollywood affluence. Indeed, with the front cover of the UK's *Daily Mirror* presenting Madonna in the image of an African woman (Davies *et al.* 2009), it is clear that 'buying Africa' [or poverty] increasingly sidesteps the injustices of international trade.

The role that trendsetting celebrities play as contemporary arbiters of morality and public opinion sits within a wider neoliberal framework in which 'expert' knowledge is circulated by certain political/cultural intermediaries who propagate and legitimize particular visions of consumption (e.g. food safety, hygiene, obesity, etc.). Yet this expertise is not only rational and calculative. Like the advertising campaigns previously described, the celebrity is an 'intimate stranger' (Schickel 1986; Rojek 2001). They are figures who traffic in social distance and affective proximity, serving as both envoys for poverty alleviation and touchstones for the enactment of consumers' desires and aspirations. As Goodman (2009) writes:

> …just as celebrities have bought into campaigns and can construct themselves and be seen as 'caring', 'good', 'political' and 'doing something', so too can we take on these characteristics – and, thus, create meanings for and about ourselves. …

Celebrity endorsers thus serve as instruments of meaning transfer, purveying an image 'of life not as it is, but life as it should be according to' an imagined ideal, imbuing the brand with a set of values, ideas and qualities that the consumer can draw from for their own identity construction (Cronin 2004: 363). Yet in contrast to the touristic imagery of distant peoples and places, celebrities are brands unto themselves and are thus pre-invested with a constellation of meanings. It is these meanings—what the celebrity stands for in the minds of consumers—that are transferred to Fairtrade and by consequence have reworked the image and conceptions of Fairtrade in the marketplace. Yet while the status of a celebrity is used to legitimate and proselytize the Fairtrade cause, this process of celebrification can also cloud the meanings that underlie the brand. The celebrity is after all 'industrially generated' and manufactured by consumer society (Yano 1997: 347), naturalizing a capitalist 'system of false promise' that offers a reward of affluence and stardom to a minority (Marshall 1997: 9).

The process of celebrification raises several questions on the synergies between brand values and the mechanisms through which those values are instilled. Does, for example, mining the terrain of popular culture and enlisting the 'celebretariat' (Goodman 2009) to advertise 'make trade fair dot com' in the newspaper sustain the values of Fairtrade? Are celebrities, as Richey and Ponte (2008) describe, the new 'totems of possibility' or simply another commodity fetish created in pursuit of an ethics of care? As Chris Martin, current front man for Fairtrade expressed:

> You can obviously question the power that musicians or actors have, because they don't really have any political power. What they do have is some effect on public opinion … It's all kind of farcical, really, but people like Bono understand they can get their causes across by allowing someone to have a photograph with the singer of U2. I know full well that you have to kind of whore yourself around. But we don't care about looking like idiots. [It] doesn't matter as long as you get the four words 'make trade fair dot-com' in the newspaper.
>
> (Turman 2004)

Of course, marketing is not the only arena in which the distance between Fairtrade's moral vision and its brand-building strategies are apparent. As other chapters in this volume highlight, the disconnection is also manifest in the abstracting processes of standard-setting and auditing, which like marketing ultimately convert the experiences and social lives of producers into a marketable commodity. Taken together these findings suggest that the 'ethics of care' (Whatmore 1997) extended through Fairtrade may unwittingly affirm if not create new forms of distance between 'moral' consumers and their purported beneficiaries.

CONCLUSION

Fairtrade initiatives are promoted as a way to rectify global inequalities through an ethics of care and responsibility that situates the consuming individual at the heart of social transformation and economic justice. Increasing numbers of consumers are positioning themselves as 'partners' in this market-based movement attempting to create more just and equitable North-South trading relations through their everyday consumption of the Fairtrade brand.

This chapter has explored the marketing process through which the brand values of Fairtrade are conveyed and rendered legitimate in the eyes of consumers, a process that has catapulted Fairtrade from a small niche market to a global retail phenomenon. Yet the remarkable growth of the brand has not been without its consequences. Critics have cast the increased corporate participation as green-washing, enabling companies to capitalize on the 'halo effect' of ethical branding while engendering formidable new barriers to entry (standards, quality requirements, certification, etc.) that cleanse fair trade of its oppositional and transformative elements (Dolan 2009).

However, this chapter has addressed a more fundamental issue at the heart of the brand, which is how producers—the object of ethical consumption and moral obligation—are defined in the exchange process. Although the brand rests on a maxim of 'Trade not Aid', it is no longer simply 'ethical' commodities that are exchanged but the lives, landscapes and production practices of producers. With their images and experiences abstracted from concrete life worlds and rendered as consumables in advertisements and product packaging, the connection between their lives and ours becomes increasingly remote. The brand may be a vehicle through which producers gain a measure of financial well-being and Northern consumers can both 'look good and do good' without changing their primary behaviour (Banet-Weiser and Lapsansky 2008). However, the circuits of inclusion the Fairtrade mark connotes remain largely symbolic. As Wilk (2006: 320) concluded, at the end of the day, 'brands can never fully substitute for the kinds of culturally meaningful objects and categories' that they strive to replace, including the experience of shared humanity and moral equivalence that today's ethical consumer seeks.

BIBLIOGRAPHY

Appadurai, A. 'Introduction: Commodities and the Politics of Value', in A. Appadurai (ed.), *The Social Life of Things: Commodities in Cultural Perspective*, Cambridge, Cambridge University Press, 1986.

Applbaum, K., 'The Sweetness of Salvation: Consumer Marketing and the Liberal-Bourgeois Theory of Needs', *Current Anthropology*, Vol. 39, No. 3, 1998.

Arvidsson, A., 'Brands: A Critical Perspective', *Journal of Consumer Culture*, Vol. 5, No. 2, 2006.

Banet-Weiser, S. and Lapsansky, C., 'Red is the New Black, Brand Culture, Consumer Citizenship and Political Possibility', *International Journal of Communication*, Vol. 2, 2008.

Barnett, C., Cloke, P., Clarke, N. and Malpass, A., 'Consuming Ethics: Articulating the Subjects and Spaces of Ethical Consumption', *Antipode*, Vol. 37, No. 1, 2005.

Barrientos, S. and Dolan, C., 'Transformation of Global Food System: Opportunities and Challenges for Fair and Ethical Trade', in S. Barrientos and C. Dolan (eds), *Ethical Sourcing in the Global Food System*, London, Earthscan, 2006.

Baudrillard, J., *Selected Writings*, Oxford, Polity Press, 1988.

Beck, U. and Gernsheim, E., *Individualisation*. London, 2001.

Belk, R., 'Possessions and the Extended Self', *Journal of Consumer Research*, Vol. 13, No. 3, 1988.

Berlant, L., 'Introduction', in L. Berlant, *Compassion: The Culture and Politics of an Emotion,* London, Routledge, 2004.

——, 'The Face of America and the State of Emergency', in *Disciplinarity and Dissent in Cultural Studies*, C. Nelson and D. P. Goankar (eds), Routledge, New York, pp. 397–440, 1996.

Bezençon, V. and Blili, S., 'Fair Trade Channels: Are We Killing the Romantics?', *International Journal of Environmental, Cultural, Economic and Social Sustainability*, Vol. 2, No. 1, 2006.

Biccum, A., 'Marketing Development: Live 8 and the Production of the Global Citizen', *Development and Change*, Vol. 38, No. 6, 2007.

Bourdieu, P., *Distinction: A Social Critique of the Judgement of Taste*, London, Routledge, 2000.

Bushman, R., The Refinement of America, New York, Knopf, 1992.

Cafédirect, 'Our Mission Statement', www.cafedirect.co.uk/our_business/fromourceo/ (accessed on 13 May 2009), 2009.

Callon, M., 'Introduction: The Embeddedness of Economic Markets in Economics', in Michel Callon (ed.), *The Laws of the Markets,* London, Blackwell, 1988.

Carrier, J., 'Gifts, Commodities, and Social Relations: A Maussian View of Exchange', *Sociological Forum*, Vol. 6, No. 1, 1991.

——, 'The Symbolism of Possession in Commodity Advertising', *Man* (n.s.), 25: 693–706, 1990.

The Co-operative 2010, *The Ethical Consumerism Report 2010: Ethical Shopping through the Downturn*, Manchester: The Co-operative Bank.

Cronin, A., 'Regimes of Mediation: Advertising Practitioners as Cultural Intermediaries?', *Consumption, Markets and Culture*, Vol. 7, No. 4, 2004.

Davies, I., Doherty, B. and Knox, S., 'The Rise and Stall of a Fair Trade Pioneer: The Cafédirect Story', *Journal of Business Ethics*, published online at http://ezproxy.ouls.ox.ac.uk:2101/content/d3757423873488m1/fulltext.pdf (accessed on 10 October 2009), 2009.

Dolan, C., 'Virtual Moralities: The Mainstreaming of Fairtrade in Kenyan Tea Fields', *Geoforum*, in press, 2009.

——, 'Market Affections: Moral Encounters with Kenyan Fairtrade Flowers', *Ethnos*, Vol. 72, No. 2, 2007.

Ericson, R., *The Conscious Consumer: Promoting Economic Justice through Fair Trade*, Washington, DC, The Fair Trade Resource Network, 2002.

Fairtrade Foundation, 'Fairtrade Mark is Top of Class in Superbrands Awards', www.fairtrade.org.uk/press_office/press_releases_and_statements/archive_2005/sept_2005/fairtrade_mark_is_top_of_class_in_superbrands_awards.aspx (accessed on 25 May 2009), 2005.

——, 'Fairtrade Flows Against the Tide', www.fairtrade.org.uk/press_office/press_releases_and_statements/april_2009/fairtrade_flows_against_the_tide.aspx (accessed on 4 June 2009), 2009.

FLO, Generic Standards for Small Farmers' Organisations, www.fairtrade.net/fileadmin/user_upload/content/Generic_Fairtrade_Standard_SF_Dec_2007_EN.pdf (accessed on 21 May 2009), 2007.

Foster, R., Coca-Globalization: Following Soft Drinks from New York to New Guinea, London, Palgrave Macmillan, 2008.

Fournier, S., 'Consumers and Their Brands: Developing Relationship Theory in Consumer Research', *Journal of Consumer Research*, Vol. 24, No. 4, 1998.

Freidberg, S., 'The Ethical Complex of Corporate Food Power, *Environment and Planning D: Society and Space*, Vol. 22, No. 4, 2003.

Gates, Kelly, 'Identifying the 9/11 "Faces of Terror": The Promise and Problem of Facial Recognition Technology', *Cultural Studies*, 20:4–5 (July/September): 417–40, 2006.

Goodman, M. K., 'Reading Fairtrade: Political Ecological Imaginary and the Moral Economy of Fairtrade Goods', *Political Geography*, Vol. 23, No. 7, 2004.

——, 'The Mirror of Consumption: Celebritisation, Developmental Consumption and the Shifting Cultural Politics of Fair Trade', Environment, Politics and Development Working Paper Series, 8, Department of Geography, King's College London, www.kcl.ac.uk/content/1/c6/03/95/42/GoodmanWP8.pdf (accessed on 29 May 2009), 2009.

Gorz, A., *L'immatériel*. Paris, Galilée, 2003.

Hearn, J., 'Meat, Mask, Burden: Probing the Contours of the Branded Self', *Journal of Consumer Culture,* Vol. 8, No. 2, 2006.

Hilton, M., *Consumerism in Twentieth-Century Britain: The Search for a Historical Movement*, Cambridge, Cambridge University Press, 2003.

Holt, D., 'Toward a Sociology of Branding', *Journal of Consumer Culture*, Vol. 6, No. 3, 2006.

——, 'Why Do Brands Cause Trouble? A Dialectical Theory of Culture and Branding', *Journal of Consumer Research*, Vol. 29, No. 1, 2002.

Klein, N., *No Logo*, London, Harper Perennial, 2005.

Kopytoff, I., 'The Cultural Biography of Things: Commoditzation as Process', in A. Appadurai (ed.), *The Social Life of Things*, Cambridge, Cambridge University Press, 1986.

Lee Potter, C., 'Can Celebrity Endorsement Save The Planet?', *New Statesmen*, www.newstatesman.com/200502280019, 2005.

Lury, C., (n.d.) *Brands: The Logos of the Global Economy*, London, Routledge, 2004.

Lyon, S. 'Migratory Imaginations: The Commodification and Contradictions of Shade Grown Coffee', *Social Anthropology*, Vol. 14, No. 3, 2006.

Mahmood, S., 'Ethical Formation and Politics of Individual Autonomy in Contemporary Egypt', *Social Research*, Vol. 70, No. 3, 2003.

Marshall, D., *Celebrity and Power*, Minneapolis, MN, University of Minnesota Press, 1997.

McCracken, G., 'Who Is the Celebrity Endorser? Cultural Foundations of the Endorsement Process', *Journal of Consumer Research*, Vol. 16 (December), 1989.

McNally, Gerri, Coffee: New Look for Cafédirect', Drinks Media Wire, 22 January 2007, available at www.drinksmediawire.com/afficher_cdp.asp?id=938&lnf=2, 2007.

Mintel, *Market Intelligence January 2009: Fair Trade Foods*, London, Mintel, 2009.

Moore, H., *A Passion for Difference*, Bloomington, Indiana University Press, 1994.

Nicholls, A., 'Fair Trade: Towards an Economics of Virtue', *Journal of Business Ethics, 2010*, forthcoming.

Paton, R., 'Fairtrade Matters', *The Money Programme*, available at: www.open2.net/money/briefs_20060310_fairtrade.html (accessed 21 June 2009), 2006.

Penaloza, L. and Price, L. 'Consumer Resistance: A Conceptual Overview', *Advances in Consumer Research*, Vol. 20, No. 1, 1993.

Polanyi, K., *The Great Transformation*, Boston, MA, Beacon Press, 1957.

Raynolds, Laura, 'Mainstreaming Fair Trade Coffee: From Partnership to Traceability', *World Development*, Vol. 37, No. 6, 2009.

Raynolds, L. 'Consumer/Producer Links in Fair Trade Coffee Networks', *Sociologia Ruralis*, Vol. 42, No. 4, 2002.

Renard, M-C, 'Fair Trade: Quality, Market and Conventions', *Journal of Rural Studies*, Vol. 19, No. 1, 2003.

Richey, L. A. and Ponte, S., 'Better (Red)TM than Dead? Celebrities, Consumption and International Aid', *Third World Quarterly*, Vol. 29, No. 4, 2008.

Rojek, C., *Celebrity*, London, Reaktion Books, 2001.

Rumbo, J., 'Consumer Resistance in a World of Advertising Clutter: The Case of Adbusters', *Psychology and Marketing*, Vol. 19, No. 2, 2002.

Sassatelli, Roberta, 'Virtue, Responsibility and Consumer Choice: Framing Critical Consumerism', in J. Brewer, and F. Trentmann (eds), *Consuming Cultures, Global Perspectives: Historical Trajectories, Transnational Exchanges*, Oxford, Berg, pp. 219–50, 2006.

Schickel, R., *Intimate Strangers: The Culture of Celebrity*, New York, Fromm International, 1986.

Schivone, G. M., 'An Interview with Noam Chomsky. On Responsibility, War Guilt and Intellectuals', *Counterpunch*, www.counterpunch.org/schivone08032007.html (accessed on 4 June 2009), 2007.

Schmelzer, M., 'Fair Trade – In or Against the Market?', Dreigliederung, Institut fur Soziale, www.threefolding.org/essays/2007–01–001.html (accessed on 1 June 2009), 2007.

Scholte, E., 'The Virtual Reality of Protestant Development Aid in the Netherlands', in P. Quarles van Ufford and A. Kumar Giri (eds.), *A Moral Critique of Development*, London, Routledge, 2003.

Smith, Adam, *A Theory of Moral Sentiments*, New York, Penguin, 2010.

Smith, D., *Moral Geographies in a World of Difference*, Edinburgh, Edinburgh University Press, 2000.

Smith, W. D., *Consumption and the Making of Respectability, 1600–1800*, New York, Routledge, 2002.

Soper, Kate, 'Re-thinking the "Good Life": The Citizenship Dimension of Consumer Disaffection with Consumerism', *Journal of Consumer Culture*, 2(4): 205–29, 2007.

Suchman, L., 'Anthropology as "Brand": Reflections on Corporate Anthropology', paper presented at the Colloquium on Interdisciplinarity and Society, Oxford University, 24 February, www.lancs.ac.uk/fass/sociology/papers/suchman-anthropology-as-brand.pdf (accessed on 22 May 2009), 2007.

Sznaider, N., *The Compassionate Temperament*, Lanham, MD, Rowman & Littlefield, 2001.

Trentmann, F., 'Before "Fair Trade": Empire, Free Trade, and the Moral Economies of Food in the Modern World', *Environment and Planning D: Society and Space*, Vol. 25, 2007.

Turman, Katherine, 'Fair Trade's Front Man', *Mother Jones*, www.motherjones.com/media/2004/01/fair-trades-front-man (accessed on 15 June 2009), 2004.

Yano, C., 'Charisma's Realm: Fandom in Japan', *Ethnology*, Vol. 36, No. 4, 1997.

Watson, M., 'Trade Justice and Individual Consumption Choices: Adam Smith's Spectator Theory and the Moral Constitution of the Fair Trade Consumer', *European Journal of International Relations*, Vol. 13, No. 2, 2007.

Whatmore, S. 'Dissecting The Autonomous Self: Hybrid Cartographies for a Relational Ethics', *Environment and Planning D: Society and Space*, Vol. 15, 1997.

Wilk, R., 'Bottled Water: The Pure Commodity in the Age of Branding, *Journal of Consumer Culture*, Vol. 6, No. 3, 2006.

Wilkinson, J., 'Fair Trade: Dynamic and Dilemmas of a Market Oriented Global. Social Movement', *Journal of Consumer Policy*, Vol. 30, No. 3, 2007.

Wright, C., 'Consuming Lives, Consuming Landscapes: Interpreting Advertisements for Cafédirect Coffees', *Journal of International Development*, Vol. 16, No. 5, 2004.

Zadek, S., Lingayah, S., Forstater, M., *Social Labels: Tools for Ethical Trade. Final Report*, Luxembourg, European Commission, 1998.

Falling foul of fair: The politics of supply chains

PETER LUETCHFORD

This chapter challenges popular representations of fair trade as an unquestioned good. While there is evidence that fair trade benefits participants, scholars have disputed its effectiveness in answering the problems it seeks to resolve. Studies of the fair trade supply chain have focused on such things as the way it is compromised by co-option by big business, the tendency for audit processes to diverge into governance and coercion, and the mismatch between Northern and Southern values. More serious with regard to this last point, is the charge that fair trade misses and even obscures the complexity of power relations between different parties at the production end as they engage with commodity markets.

Critics of the neoliberal economic project have noted how this market practice allows powerful interests to corner profits, often at the expense of primary producers and workers (Smithers and Smith 2009). A useful tool in documenting this process has been commodity chain analysis, pioneered by Gereffi and Korzeniewicz (1994), but since employed to show how and where value is extracted at different points as a commodity such as coffee moves from producer to final consumer (Daviron and Ponte 2005; Talbot 2004). Approaches in this vein identify contradictions and conflicts in the mechanisms established by fair trade, and the sufficiency or otherwise of those mechanisms to satisfy the aims and aspirations of activists and consumers in the North. It is argued, for instance, that fair trade is compromised by the need to compete in the market, and the requirement to monitor and regulate. Accordingly, the first part of this chapter focuses on the organizational side of fair trade and the contradictions and tensions encountered in the supply chain (Daviron and Ponte 2005; Dolan 2009; Fridell 2007; Jaffee 2007, Talbot 2004).

However, fair trade also draws upon an alternative economic model based on a foreshortened chain. Direct links are central to the fair trade imaginary since they are said to avoid intermediaries extracting profits and allow more of the commodity price to return to the producer. At the same time a social and moral relation of care and trust between producer and consumer is suggested (Whatmore and Thorne 1997; Raynolds 2002), articulated on the product label by photos and information on provenance (Luetchford 2011; Wright 2004). To interrogate such representations the second part of the chapter looks at experiences of fair trade in the South. Here falling foul of fair is less about the paradoxes and contradictions that ensue from profit-seeking, competition, and regulation in a commodity chain and more about the misfit between the social and moral aims of the movement and the realities of the political economies with which fair trade engages. Fieldwork data from Costa Rica is used to illustrate how conflicts and coercions occur along the chain as people pursue their economic interests. These conflicts and coercions are a necessary part of commodity production; they are not abolished simply because consumers and fair traders seek moral relations in the market economy (Luetchford 2008a).

The chapter therefore suggests three main ways in which fair trade may be compromised. First, it falls foul of the capitalist economy and the drive for profit, which undercuts moral and social values and replaces those values with purely economic considerations. Second, the process of certification, designed to implement the idea of fair trade, provides a reductive and depoliticized technical solution to social and economic problems. The implementation of the standards then demands compliance on the part of producers and producer groups, so certification is experienced in the south as a system of control, against which people can only manoeuvre and strategize. Lastly, to attract customers fair trade projects an image of producers and production that has only passing resemblance to the political economies in which the commodities are produced.

FAIR TRADE MARKETS, MOVEMENTS AND CERTIFICATIONS

There are a number of ways in which fair trade principles may be compromised by operating through markets (Talbot 2004: 207–10). There is, above all, an unresolved tension between downward pressure on the value of fair trade brands in a competitive market, as against the exclusivity of a product that commands higher prices and appeals to better off consumers buying into moral qualities. In effect, the market determines how much consumers are prepared to pay to 'internalize' social and moral considerations, as any fair trade product is indexed by price against other goods in that category.

The tension between profit and principles becomes more acute as supermarkets and transnational companies come to dominate the supply chain (Krier 2005). There is concern that big companies improve their public image by mimicking the practices and rhetoric of more committed fair traders, while undercutting smaller, specialist companies and NGOs, so devaluing fair trade. By engaging in mainstream markets fair trade inevitably becomes embroiled in competitive capitalism and profit-seeking. It is argued that companies like Starbucks, for example, can achieve a 'blue-washing' effect by certifying parts of their business as fair trade to gain kudos, while subsidizing it from their conventional operations and so undercutting the price of fair trade coffee (Talbot 2004: 209). Equally, higher volumes of sales allow bigger companies to work with smaller margins and cut prices. This leads to counter-intuitive encounters with fair trade products at knock-down prices or on special offer in my local supermarket. The pursuit of profit can also encourage less costly and rigorous corporate-friendly certification schemes, such as the Rainforest Alliance or Conservation International, which tend to emphasize environmental rather than social considerations and eschew minimum prices for products (Fridell 2007: 78–79). In this way, increasing competition in the sector puts downward pressure on prices and standards.

While competition and profit-seeking from fair trade threatens to undermine its economic value and moral integrity, market expansion could not have happened without certification. The certificate is what allows the fair trade good to circulate in the market; it guarantees authenticity and justifies the extra cost in monetary terms. That is, certification provides the mechanism for materializing and translating the politics of the movement into the commodity form. For this reason the inauguration of the first fair trade mark by Max Havelaar in Holland in the late 1980s can be seen as marking the onset of the mainstreaming process. Since then fair trade certification has been increasingly incorporated into commercial arenas. Today product certification is largely controlled by Fairtrade Labelling Organizations International (FLO), a group of 23 organizations, 19 of which are labelling initiatives such as The Fairtrade Foundation in the UK and Transfair USA (see FLO, www.fairtrade.net/our_members.html, accessed 22 May 2009). FLO owns the fair trade mark that 'guarantees a better deal to third world producers' by insisting upon commercial, social and environmental benchmark criteria. The mark is licensed out for use by companies on their products by the labelling initiatives in 23 consumer countries in Europe, North America, Australasia, and Japan. Alongside this are certification schemes with competing certification criteria, notably the Rainforest Alliance, which imposes standards but does not guarantee minimum prices.

As individual sovereign consumers make their choices in the supermarket aisles, substantive differences between fair trade products are erased by the common label, or the proliferation of labels and claims. How can one compare Tesco Fair Trade Colombian Roast Coffee (£2.69 for 227g) with Percol Fairtrade Colombia Arabica Ground Coffee (£2.89 for 227g), both certified by the Fairtrade Foundation and carrying the guarantee? In part it must boil down to price, and supermarkets aid comparison on that basis by labelling each product at a standardized cost per 100g. Similarly, how can shoppers distinguish between certifications by the Fairtrade Foundation (Cafédirect, Percol, and some Tesco coffee), the Rainforest Alliance (Kenco, other Tesco coffee), and Conservation International (Starbucks)? These tell us competing products all similarly offer a better deal to producers, leaving price as an important distinguishing feature for comparison and once again setting off competition on that basis.

But as Dolan (2009) has recently argued, certification may have more sinister effects than complicating choices in supermarket aisles. Monitoring is designed to ensure fair trade meets the aspirations of its advocates and retains credibility before its target audience, the citizen-consumer. Unfortunately the effect is that fair trade depoliticizes as it proceeds, making it reminiscent of the 'anti-politics machine' of development (Ferguson 1994). It does so in two ways. First, certification and audit provide purely technical solutions to complex economic, social and cultural problems. Trying to resolve things like inequalities between parties in an exchange, conflicting interests in labour relations in agriculture, or destructive interactions with the environment by implementing rational and neutral standards divorces certification processes from their political context. For example, certifying that producers receive a minimum price provides a technical solution to volatility in the coffee market without addressing the chronic cycles in supply and demand that generate price instability in the first place. The second way fair trade threatens to depoliticize is by relying upon and referring to the private conscience of western consumers and activists. This is not an innocent process. The displacement of responsibility for development onto individual ethical consumers and their choices renders it compatible with neoliberalism, and allows governments and organizations to escape responsibility for outcomes. In effect, through fair trade, inequalities and poverty become a matter for individual moral conscience, rather than the outcome of political and economic processes (Fridell 2007; Dolan 2009).

What happens when ideas about social justice and environmental protection pursued by northern consumers are implemented in the south through the technical rules and regulations of audit? The depoliticizing effect is revealed to be a mirage because, as in any power relation, accommodation and resistance ensue as producer groups negotiate their way around certification requirements or represent themselves in particular ways in order to access resources or enter valuable niche markets. For example, to be involved in fair trade they must present an image of highly democratic organizations made up of small farmers. To do so they are forced to gloss over such things as the way decisions are often made by individuals or small groups who make up administrative councils, and play down any variations in land ownership by members. Such strategizing indicates power relations and political processes are at work.

While compliance by producer groups is required, the door is left open for accommodation to cultural difference in the standards. An example is the case of gender. Under FLO regulations, producer groups must comply with minimum criteria of 'no official policies based on gender discrimination', combined with process criterion with 'evidence of some progress towards greater gender equity over time' (Fridell 2007: 207). Such demands are open to broad interpretation to accommodate social scenarios many Westerners used to women's involvement in public life would consider unduly patriarchal. In Latin America most farmers and workers are men, as are co-operative managers and local leaders. Women, on the other hand, usually work in the domestic and private sphere, and can be reticent about taking up public office. For example, during fieldwork in Costa Rica I witnessed women being proposed for positions of responsibility on development associations, but steadfastly refusing to take up these offices. Meanwhile, the local co-operative built and financed a restaurant to be run by women, a venture that failed partly because few women availed themselves of the opportunity. Co-operatives and associations can be seen to meet process criteria, but public spaces remain dominated by men.

A second area where we encounter accommodation and some resistance to imposed standards is the environment. There is a loose connection between fair trade, justice, and environmental sustainability, stemming from parallel aims in the minds of consumers, and a conflation under certification standards and in markets. For example, sustainability requirements clearly overlap with organic and shade grown coffee markets. While there may be common ground between the environmental aims of Westerners and the practices and goals of farmers, it can also be cause for contested interpretation (Lyon 2009). For example, farmers may refute the need for trees, or plant them as windbreaks to shelter their coffee and raise production, as much as to increase tree cover and develop habitats (Luetchford 2008a: 40). They may also contest the need to plant the diversity of trees laid down by the regulations, preferring a smaller range of fast-growing species. Practices that generate increased production, such as growing modern varieties in full sun, are at odds with Northern interests in shade diversity and song-bird habitats. Indeed, farmers' interests in organic seem to stem from the higher prices commanded in the quality coffee markets more than environmental considerations.

In this way, social and environmental criteria are demanded by certifiers and then interpreted, negotiated, and partially complied with by producer groups. In some cases visitors may be shown what they want to see on visits, such as traditional ethnic clothing, or poverty (Lyon 2009; Luetchford 2006). In other cases co-operative leaders may lobby and try to influence policy. In interviews with Costa Rican co-operative managers in 1998, a case was made for raising minimum prices and social premiums for fair trade coffee as these had not increased since 1989. As a result of pressure from producer groups, the minimum price for Arabica recently went from US $1.21 per pound to $1.25 and the social premium rose from $0.05 to $0.10 per pound. Despite this apparent victory, according to Juliane Reinecke who worked at FLO in the relevant period, Latin American co-operative managers had lobbied for larger increases (Reinecke 2009).

The argument presented so far is that there are contradictions and disjunctures between the social and environmental aims of Westerners involved in fair trade as a movement, and the market mechanisms and certification procedures through which it operates. In the next section I document how and why morally inspired initiatives do not translate into moral experiences at the production end. To the contrary, I present a polemical view that fair trade makes assumptions that obscures more than it reveals about supply chains. By relying on particular representations consumers are offered visions of 'ethicality' (Carrier 2008), which substitute for moral worlds that they wish to imagine; small farmers stand for an idealized economy, coral reefs become a pristine ecology. But in pursuing these ethical representations assumptions are made about the worlds they connect to. There is a need to interrogate those assumptions and to reveal what hides behind them.

VALUE CHAIN STRUGGLES: THE POLITICAL ECONOMY OF COFFEE PRODUCTION

I have said that fair trade presents a vision of ethicality, in which imagined worlds replace market relations that are then sold to consumers. I have two concerns about that process. First, the tendency is for fair trade to obscure the complexities of the political economy of commodity production. For example, differences between co-operative managers and farmers, larger landowners and smaller ones, women and men, workers and farmers, are hidden, often behind images like small farmers, or ideas, like partnership or community. At the same time, the capacity for different groups of people to benefit from fair trade, and the constraints they work under as they compete for contracts, are obscured.

The second assumption is that consumers and producers want the same thing. It is clear that in fair trade consumers are looking for and imagining some kind of social relationship with identifiable people in the south. This relationship is expressed either through a language of charity and patronage, which in itself obscures power relationships, or it is understood as a response to structural inequalities, reflecting the political concerns of activists. Producers and co-operative personnel on the other hand understand fair trade much more as a market relationship, with all that entails. To access the fair trade niche and get the higher prices on offer they are constrained to represent themselves and behave in particular ways. NGOs and co-operative managers play a crucial part in brokering the field in which economic imperatives and social considerations meet.

Such complications are little understood. Consequently there is a need to document how different people respond to the social, economic, and environmental opportunities and constraints set in motion by the fair trade agenda. We further need to interrogate the dynamics of a whole series of relationships and struggles down the supply chain. Conflicts in relations between different people are part of market relationships and it is the market aspect that is obscured in representations of fair trade. One source of conflict is processes of inclusion and exclusion, and the relative power of different actors. A second is the competition and strategizing required by the market. For example, in the case of Indian handicrafts, where prices and terms of contracts are dictated by fair trade buyers who can choose between different suppliers, manufacturers may not comply with certification standards in areas such as wage negotiations, union membership, or working conditions in order to cut costs and compete more effectively for contracts (Bulut 2009).

By way of example the remainder of this paper documents these conflicts and coercions as they are encountered by different actors at different 'levels' in the coffee chain in Costa Rica. Co-operative managers, landowners, and labourers all have distinct roles in the coffee industry, and there are important points of contestation between and within these groups to be understood. The information is based upon fieldwork carried out into coffee, co-operatives, and fair trade in 1998–99, and 2003. Although the data is specific to one country and a certain time period, it indicates the kinds of tensions and struggles that exist down the chain when there is a requirement to negotiate the economics of coffee markets, the ethical content of fair trade, and the social and political commitments of different parties.

The first distinct people involved with fair trade coffee in Costa Rica are co-operative managers. These are generally young or middle-aged professional men who live in rural areas close to the co-operatives that employ them. One part of their job is to improve production and ensure that wet processing of the coffee is carried out efficiently in the co-operative mill. This work is important; promoting and monitoring productive activities and improving processing facilities mean higher production and a better-quality product. The managers' second area of responsibility is marketing the coffee and the co-operatives. This requires business negotiations by phone, extensive national travel and some international travel. In this work the managers must negotiate specific contradictions between social values and the dictates of economy. Key concerns for these men are relationships with Northern Alternative Trading Organizations (ATOs), the level of participation of the different co-operatives in the consortium of Costa Rican fair trade co-operatives (Coocafé), and promoting the interests of the farmers in their co-operative.

These co-operatives portray themselves as a success. Beginning as disadvantaged producer groups, they have, since the 1980s, and with the help of Northern NGOs, developed rational technical and administrative processes. These have established strong institutions based upon sound economic management, implemented by professional business people (Ronchi 2002). However, this commercial relationship can conflict with the social aims of fair trade. We can consider how tensions between market rationality and social commitments are manifest in relations with Northern ATOs, in dealings with other producer co-operatives in their consortium, and in relations with farmers.

In the late 1990s managers complained that Northern ATOs were unwilling to listen to producers: they sent only junior staff to meetings with Southern co-operatives and dictated terms and conditions. So, while they valued their relations with some ATOs, they said that others wanted to deal only with poor and acquiescent coffee farmers. Managers contrasted this with their co-operative assemblies, in which, they said, open debate and an exchange of opinions is encouraged and policies are determined by members' votes. Perhaps mindful of this discontent, Northern Fairtrade organizations have tried to incorporate producers. For example, FLO says that it considers the participation of traders, producers and other stakeholders to be crucial. As a sign of this, the FLO Board currently has five members representing labelling initiatives, four representing producers, two representing traders and two representing outside bodies. That distribution reflects the concern to include the opinions of producer groups and so maintain the 'special relationship' promoted by fair trade (for details, see www.fairtrade.net/structure.html, accessed 25 May 2009).

However, negotiating deals in a complex coffee market is different from allowing producers' representatives to air opinions, and a key area of tension is participation in the fair trade market. While some producer groups, such as UCIRI of Mexico, routinely sell most of their coffee through the fair trade network (Fridell 2007: 192), others struggle to penetrate the fair trade market. In both 1999 and 2003, Costa Rican managers complained that Northern organizations had not managed to expand fair trade sales enough to absorb their co-operatives' production, much less the output of the 'unending queue' of producer groups joining the system. As a result, Coocafé's sales through fair trade fell from around 60% of total production in the 1990s to about 30% in 2003.

To participate in fair trade markets, organizations must tread a thin and contradictory line between being sufficiently advantaged to produce the kind of quality coffee required for specialty markets, while representing themselves as disadvantaged enough to require help. The economic imperative is competitive advantage, but the social requirement for access is deprivation. The aforementioned threat to Costa Rican co-operatives' participation in fair trade exemplifies that tension, as efficiency and the ability to provide a quality product in a competitive market destabilizes their self-representation as disadvantaged small farmers. The conflict between advantage and deprivation is enacted around processes of inclusion and exclusion, which is inevitably mediated by power relations.

The market imperative complicates relations between Northern and Southern partners, but there are also market tensions to be negotiated between the Coocafé co-operatives. As managers seek to maximize returns to their own co-operatives they have to negotiate participation in fair trade internally, within the Coocafé group. The problem is how to deal with shifts in prices, and resultant changes in the attraction of fair trade. Managers are keen to sell to fair trade when poor market conditions make the minimum price attractive, but as prices rise there is less commitment, especially from co-operatives with higher quality coffee to sell. Historically Coocafé has had more problems completing orders to fair trade markets when prices are high. As long as individual co-operatives in the Coocafé group wish to vary fair trade sales, then participation must be regulated. This can meet with varying degrees of success. The minor dispute between two co-operatives in the Coocafé consortium, Coopesanta Elena and Coopeldos, in which the former had attracted members away from the latter because it had secured higher sales to fair trade, was resolved by internal agreement of quotas (Coopeldos 2003). On the other hand, newer co-operatives joining the group have been excluded from fair trade markets (Smith 2007).

In addition to relations between co-operatives, we need to consider the range of interests and agendas in relationships between co-operatives and farmers. This required long-term fieldwork in a production zone, the area of El Dos, near the town of Tilarán in Costa Rica. Interviews were carried out with about 150 coffee farmers in different settlements. Most of these were men who take charge of commercial agriculture and the family farm. All were members of Coopeldos, a coffee producer co-operative that has supplied the fair trade market since the late 1980s. Other, more in-depth and repeated interviews were held in one settlement with landowners and local landless labourers. Some of these farmers grow coffee, some produce milk, and some keep beef cattle; many of them engage in a combination of these activities. The landless labourers mix more regular work, especially in the dairies, with casual employment in agriculture and the coffee harvest.

Farmers hold different kinds of relationships with the co-operative. Some are more active supporters, and these members are often involved in running Coopeldos. They tend to hold administrative positions on one of the different councils, they attend meetings regularly, and they are dedicated farmers who follow best practice guidelines set down by agronomists. Such members rarely criticize the co-operative or its policies; they give vocal support to the organization, see little or no contradiction between the social and the economic mission, and promote the co-operative to visitors. Beyond this 'inner circle' are a larger group of farmers who generally use the co-operative's facilities, but are not averse to seeking more advantageous outlets for their coffee, or expressing dissent at co-operative policy. Complaints and doubts were voiced frequently during private interviews, but they are also aired publicly during meetings between members and co-operative staff. A focus of dissatisfaction has been the disadvantaged position of growers as compared to processors in the division of profits.

Dissent towards processors and their capacity to swallow profits has a long history in Costa Rica (Acuña 1985, 1987; González 1987). The interests of the country's coffee oligarchy were, from the beginnings of the industry in the early decades of the 19th century, maintained by controlling processing and export, rather than production. In the wake of the 1948 civil war political interests were realigned as a professional middle class came to power under the leadership of José Figueres and the National Liberation Party (PLN). Thus began the long period of stable democratic government and the social welfare model for which Costa Rica is famous. More importantly, Figueres and his followers implemented policies to control the power of the dominant coffee interests and promote co-operatives (Cazanga 1987; Luetchford 2008a; Paige 1997; Winson 1989). In particular, Law 2762 sought to govern relations between coffee producers, processors and exporters. Regulating the industry was part of the package of social development, and has been described as a 'hymn of peace' that quelled unrest from producers at the extortionate practices of processors (Paige 1997). Ongoing dissent, especially in the co-operative sector, gives pause for thought on dominant representations.

Farmers complain, for example, that the co-operative and its employees 'eat the profits' and receive benefits, such as sick pay and holidays that farmers never enjoy. Such resentment is compounded by ideas about what constitutes work. To labour, for farmers, is to be involved in agriculture—in particular, working with one's hands to produce from nature. Farmers expressed this by asserting that administrators in the co-operative offices 'only shuffle papers and do not really labour'. Bureaucrats 'work least but earn most', and intermediaries in the supply chain 'make money without even handling the agricultural produce'. Criticism of bureaucrats and administrative systems goes deeper; some farmers suggested there was foul play, and urged me to investigate where 'missing money' owed to them had gone. To quell such accusations the co-operative boasts a policy of transparency, part of which is to reveal the financial accounting by which they arrive at final payments to producers. Producers are paid in retrospective instalments as the coffee is sold, except for the first instalment which can be claimed immediately to cover wages for labour. The final instalment, or *liquidación final*, is received by the producer almost a year after delivering the crop for processing.

At meetings paperwork is distributed to explain taxes, including the 9% profit guaranteed to the processor, a similar amount to cover processing costs, specific taxes on coffee of 3%, and income tax of 20%. The result is that an export price of US $125 for 100 lbs of green coffee results in a payment to the producer after deductions of around $87 (Coopeldos 1998).

Sometimes there are tensions between the core support of the co-operative and the peripheral, more critical members. One case was the selection of farmers to receive subsidies through the co-operative for conversion to organic production. The subsidies were designed to cover costs, including initial dramatic falls in production. This was a popular option with three times as many applicants as subsidies available. Organic promised to counteract the worst abuses of industrialized agriculture while resonating with farming systems before the green revolution, and to marry this with increased profits (Coopeldos 1995). While many farmers attempted conversion without subsidies, they found that yields fell so dramatically they were forced to return to applying chemicals. Only some of those who received subsidies were able to complete the conversion process and reap the rewards, leading to resentment. The greater profitability of organic was acknowledged by farmers during interviews in 2003; the price paid by Coopeldos for organic coffee was almost double that of the conventional product in the 2001–02 season (Icafé 2002).

Qualitative differences between farmers in their relation to the co-operative, and in prices they receive for different kinds of product are significant. However, variations in the amount of land owned, and coffee delivered for processing is of greater import. Figures show that 70% of Coopeldos members grow less than 40 *fanegas* of coffee, which is 30% of the total co-operative output. A *fanega* ('two double hectolitres' or 400 litres) is the unit used to measure the coffee cherries delivered by producers for processing. It is also the measure used when calculating the instalments paid by the co-operative to its members. By contrast, only six members produce more than 240 *fanegas*, making up 8% of total production (Coocafé 2009). Since 40 *fanegas* is a good return from 1 ha, the data ostensibly supports the association between coffee, fair trade, and small farmers.

But such data obscure issues around land and labour in the coffee industry; while informative about coffee production they say nothing about land distribution or income streams. The information collected from farmers in 1998 showed a significant minority of farmers had larger areas of land they dedicated to raising cattle, while cultivating small coffee plantations as a secondary source of revenue. For example, of 151 households in the area around El Dos, eight combined coffee with dairy farming on an average holding of around 20 ha, 19 had coffee and beef on farms of over 40 ha, and five engaged in all three activities with an average farm size nearer 200 ha. The 32 larger farmers who combine coffee with cattle need to be differentiated from the 57 coffee specialists who farm an average area of just under 2 ha. Likewise, a farmer with less than 1 ha is in a very different position to one with 2 or 3 ha, which in the El Dos area is the lower limit on which a family might survive on coffee alone. Those with smaller areas of land must supplement their incomes with wage labour or by running businesses. Small specialist coffee farmers working evenly distributed plots, as portrayed in advertising, were hard to find.

When we analyse incomes from coffee similar disparities emerge. The highest earning member of the co-operative in 1998–99 received about US $24,000 for their coffee, whilst the lowest earner received $40. Aggregate figures reveal that 9% of the 521 registered members earned over 1m. colones ($5,000), while 18% earned under 100,000 colones ($500). The remaining members either earned a figure between these amounts, or fell into the 10% who earned nothing at all. The figures are calculated at the then going exchange rate of 200 Costa Rican colones to the dollar. The highest earner received 4,858,700 colones, the lowest 8,050 colones (Coopeldos R.L. Departamento de Contabilidad 1999). Such differences undermine the representation of undifferentiated small family farmers, and since minimum prices and premiums are paid on coffee delivered for processing the disparities are exacerbated by fair trade payments. What is more, these data do not reveal income streams or strategies. For example, the figures do not demonstrate how farmers record all or part of their crop in the name of another family member for fiscal reasons, or how landowners divide their income by registering half the coffee in the name of the sharecropper who works their land.

Sharecropping practices are indicative of a final important area of differentiation and tension not entertained in representations of fair trade; that between landed and landless. Of the 151 households identified above, 44% are without land, though almost half of these engage in sharecropping agreements. Such *a medias* contracts resolve the labour problem for farmers and extend co-operative membership and access to the coffee market to the landless. They are illustrative of the kinds of ties that bind farmers and workers as patrons and clients into informal agreements to employ and supply labour. For more permanent residents such relations are more enduring. Contracted *peones* work on informal, semi-permanent contracts in the cattle and dairy industry which has regular labour requirements. For day labourers (*jornaleros*) employment is more sporadic and incomes more precarious. Though they can find casual labour in everything from cattle farming to building work, the main employer of temporary and casual labour is the coffee industry.

Variations in labour requirements in coffee cultivation are highly problematic for landowners, and many of those with more land use coffee to generate the capital to move into cattle husbandry. While a farmer can cultivate up to 2 ha of coffee alone much of the time, outside help is required for harvest. Family labour, particularly the 'reserve army' of wives, daughters and young sons is mobilized first. Their labour is then supplemented by local landless men and women. But as the harvest intensifies farmers rely on outsiders, mainly Nicaraguans, migrating into the area (Luetchford 2008b). Tensions arise between farmers and workers, particularly Nicaraguans. One area of conflicting interests is quality. As harvesters are paid piece rates, they want to maximize the amount picked to increase income. By contrast, to ensure quality the co-operative requires a high percentage of ripe red beans, rather than bitter green fruit and twigs. A system that imposes sanctions for poor quality ensures farmers monitor workers. A second problem is the reliability of Nicaraguans. While compliance of resident workers is generally guaranteed by their interest in maintaining social and economic ties, the same is not true of outsiders. They have no incentive to maintain longer-term relations, and move on in search of more rewarding work without warning. In keeping with their problematic status in Costa Rica, Nicaraguans are considered untrustworthy and are often reviled (Sandoval-Garcia 2004).

CONCLUSIONS

This chapter has identified contradictions down the fair trade supply chain by scrutinizing practices, processes and ideas at the consumption end through to production. It was argued that certification was required to mediate the problematic encounter between the movement and the market, but a technical fix with generic standards depoliticizes fair trade and obscures coercions at the production end. This contradicts the professed aims and desired outcomes of fair trade.

For consumers and consumer activists fair trade takes on the appearance of something that can negate or subvert the market. It does this through the presentation of ideas and images that correspond to current Western notions of what looks ethical. Part of that are forms, such as peasant production, that seem to have a foot outside the market. A related strand is a commitment to more direct relations between producer and consumer to mutual advantage. A third is the belief that social and environmental costs should and can be internalized in a politicized market. All these ideas raise contradictions in their encounter with the market. Products sold with costs internalized struggle to compete in a profit driven money economy as downward pressure is placed on standards and prices. The idea of the small farmer obscures differentiation. Likewise the evocation of the direct link between producer and consumer simplifies the chain and occludes sets of actors.

Accordingly, the second part introduced certain groups of people to reveal differences down the supply chain and explore tensions in relations within and between groups. Whereas consumers seem to enjoy fair trade as a hybrid of market and movement, co-operative administrators, farmers and workers have to subsume the fair trade market within formal economic roles and relationships since they experience it within that context. Consumers want fair trade to be a moral encounter, but producers, in as much as they consider it, relate to it as business, as usual.

BIBLIOGRAPHY

Acuña, V. H., 'Clases Sociales y Conflicto Social en la Economía Cafetalera Costarricense: productores contra beneficiadores 1921–36', *Revista de Historia*, Numero Especial: Historia, Problemas y Perspectivas Agrarias en Costa Rica, Heredia, Costa Rica, EUNA, 1985.

——, 'La Ideología de los Pequeños y Medianos Productores Cafetaleros Costarricenses, 1900–961', *Revista de Historia* 16: 137–59, 1987.

Bulut, T., 'Fair Trade – Says Who? A Study of Power Relations in the Fair Trade Supply Chain for Textiles and Accessories', paper presented at CRASSH workshop, *Fair Trade: a Moral Economy? Does Fair Trade Change the Rules of the Economic Game?*, Cambridge, 22 May 2009.

Carrier, J. G., 'Protecting the Environment the Natural Way: Ethical Consumption and Commodity Fetishism', Paper presented at the *Conservation and Capitalism Symposium*, University of Manchester, 9–10 September 2008.

Cazanga, J., *Las Cooperativas de Caficultores en Costa Rica*, Universidad de Costa Rica, San José, Editorial Alma Mater, 1987.

Coocafè R.L., 'Clasificaciòn de los Productores, cosecha 1998–99, Alajuela, Costa Rica, 2009.

Coopeldos, *Propuesta: Pequeñas Comunidades Organicas en Café*, Costa Rica, Coopeldos R.L., August 1995.

——, 'Liquidación al Productor para una Fanega de Café', *Charla Sobre Comercialización de Café*, Costa Rica, Coopeldos R.L. October 1998.

——, R.L. Departamento de Contabilidad, Sistema de Control de recibo de Café, 'Compras'. 12 March 1999.

——, *Memoria Annual 2002, Asamblea Ordinaria No. 44*, Costa Rica, Coopeldos R.L., 1 March 2003.

Daviron, B. and Ponte, S., *The Coffee Paradox: Global Markets, Commodity Trade and the Elusive Promise of Development*, London and New York, Zed Books, 2005.

Dolan, C., 'Virtual Moralities: The Mainstreaming of Fair-trade in Kenyan Tea Fields', *Geoforum*, doi: 10.1016/j.geoforum, 2009.

Ferguson, J., *The Anti-Politics Machine: Development, Depoliticization and Bureaucratic Power in Lesotho*, Minneapolis, University of Minnesota Press, 1994.

Fridell, G., *Fair Trade Coffee: The Prospects and Pitfalls of Market-driven Social Justice*, Toronto, University of Toronto Press, 2007.

Gereffi, G. and Korzeniewicz, M., (eds), *Commodity Chains and Global Capitalism*, Westport, CT, Praeger, 1994.

González, A., 'El Discurso Oficial de los Pequeños y Medianos Cafetaleros' (1920–40, 1950–61), *Revista de Historia* 16: 161–91, 1987.

Icafé, *Precio de Liquidación Final, Cosecha 2001–2002*, San José, Costa Rica, Icafé, 2002.

Jaffee, D., *Brewing Justice: Fair Trade Coffee, Sustainability and Survival*, Berkeley, University of California Press, 2007.

Krier, J.-M., *Fair Trade in Europe: Facts and Figures in 25 European Countries*, Brussels, Belgium, FINE, 2005.

Luetchford, P., 'Brokering Fair Trade: Relations between Coffee Cooperatives and Fair Trade Organisations: A View from Costa Rica', in Lewis, D. and Mosse, D. (eds) *Development Brokers and Translators: The Ethnography of Aid and Agencies*, Bloomfield, Kumarian Press, 2006.

——, *Fair Trade and a Global Commodity: Coffee in Costa Rica*, London, Pluto Press, 2008a.

——, 'The Hands that Pick Fair Trade Coffee: Beyond the Charms of the Family Farm', in De Neve, G., Luetchford, P., Pratt, J. and Woods, D. (eds), *Hidden Hands in the Market: Ethnographies of Fair Trade, Ethical Consumption, and Corporate Social Responsibility, Research in Economic Anthropology*, Vol. 28, UK, Emerald, 2008b.

——, 'Consuming Producers: Fair Trade and Small Farmers', in Carrier, J. and Wetchford P. (eds) *Ethical Consumption: Economic Value and Social Practice*, New York, Benghahn 2011 (forthcoming).

Lyon, S., '"What Good Will More Trees Do?": The Political Economy of Sustainable Coffee Certification, Local Livelihoods and Identities' in West, P. and Carrier, J. (eds), Surroundings, Selves and Others: The Political Economy of Environment and Identity', *Landscape Research*, Vol. 34, Issue 2, 2009.

Paige, J., *Coffee and Power. Revolution and the Rise of Democracy in Central America*, Cambridge, MA, Harvard University Press, 1997.

Reinecke, J., 'Beyond a Subjective Theory of Value and Towards a "Better Deal": Fairtrade Minimum Price Setting', paper presented at CRASSH workshop, *Fair Trade: A Moral Economy? Does Fair Trade Change the Rules of the Economic Game?*, Cambridge, 22 May 2009.

Raynolds, L., 'Producer Consumer Links in Fair Trade Coffee Networks', *SociologiaRuralis*, Vol. 42, No. 4:404–24, 2002.

Ronchi, L., 'The Impact of Fair Trade on Producers and their Organisations: A Case Study with Coocafé in Costa Rica', *PRUS Working Paper*, No. 11, Brighton, Institute of Development Studies, 2002.

Sandoval-Garcia, C., *Threatening Others: Nicaraguan Migrants and the Formation of National Identity in Costa Rica*, Athens, Ohio University Press, 2004.

Smith, J., 'The Search for Sustainable Markets: The Promises and Failures of Fair Trade', *Culture and Agriculture*, Vol. 29, Issue 2, pp. 89–99, 2007.

Smithers, R. and Smith, D., 'Tesco's Record Annual Profits: 3bn. South African Fruit Picker's Wage: £98 a month', *The Guardian*, 16 May, p. 15, 2009.

Talbot, J., *Grounds for Agreement: The Political Economy of the Coffee Commodity Chain*, Lanham, MD, Rowman and Littlefield, 2004.

Winson, A., *Coffee and Democracy in Modern Costa Rica*, Basingstoke, Macmillan Press, 1989.

Whatmore, S. and Thorne, L., 'Nourishing Networks: Alternative Geographies of Food', in Michael Watts and David Goodman (eds) *Globalising Food: Agrarian Questions and Global Restructuring*, London and New York, Routledge, 1997.

Wright, C., 'Consuming Lives, Consuming Landscapes: Interpreting Advertisements for Cafedirect Coffees', *Journal of International Development*, Vol. 16, No. 5, pp. 665–680, 2004.

Certification as governance: Current impacts and future prospects

GRAEME AULD

INTRODUCTION

More than 20 years ago, fair trade adopted certification and labelling as a new tool for promoting and extending fairer market dealings for some of the world's poorest producers. It was an unprecedented time, two facets of which were germane to this move. First, politically active consumerism was on the rise, with consumer polls reporting high-stated willingness to pay for environmentally friendly products and with high-profile consumer campaigns demanding the likes of dolphin-safe tuna, chlorine-free paper, and biodegradable plastics (Rice and Berlin 1990). Though boycotts were used before the 1980s (Friedman 1999), the decade saw much greater activity; there was even a biannual newsletter—the National Boycott News—that disseminated information about organized boycotts (Conklin 1991). Many efforts were undertaken to harness this new green enthusiasm. In the USA in 1988, the Council on Economic Priorities (CEP) released the first edition of *Shopping for a Better World*, a guide to thousands of products sold by hundreds of companies that ranked each on their ethical performance (Marlin *et al.* 1991). In the same year, a few UK environmental groups and companies organized a Green Consumer week to coincide with the launch of the *Green Consumer Guide* (Elkington and Hailes 1988), an equivalent to the CEP publication for the UK market (Urry 1988).

Second, the 1980s achieved little headway on development objectives, particularly in Africa (Michaels 1993; Brittain 1991), where foreign aid had been rising while conditions in many countries continued to decline (Lancaster 1999). Disquiet over the limited success of government-led efforts heightened, with questions raised about the efficacy of European development assistance meant to ameliorate famine in Ethiopia during the 1980s (Steele 1985; see also Bovard 1989) and about the appropriateness of US financial and military support for conservative governments in Central America (Financial Times 1983; Manuel 1985; Galen 1985). This discontent together with the growing consumer activism helped nurture efforts to circumvent the normal political channels and foreign assistance to instead buy directly from farmers to express solidarity with the oppressed and marginalized (Tallontire 2000, 2001; Goodman 2004).

Within this context interest heightened in expanding fair trade from charity shops, Alternative Trading Organizations (ATOs), and fair trade companies to the broader market. Although perspectives have long differed as to what labelling would and should involve, it represents an important development that has transformed the consumer landscape and, arguably, the fair trade movement. As this chapter will discuss, after the Dutch Max Havelaar Foundation launched its label to sell coffee from a co-operative in Mexico, the idea spilled over borders and products and now comprises a worldwide market worth nearly €3,000m. per annum. Yet, questions remain about the effectiveness of the tool. Debates within the fair trade community focus on what has been lost in the transition from fair trade organized around, and championed by, groups and companies entirely committed to fair terms of trade throughout their operations and fair trade that involves multinationals such as Starbucks, Nestlé, and McDonalds, which to date only sell a portion of their coffee under fair-trade terms (Vidal 2005; Sustainable Food News 2007; Godoy 2008). At the same time, there are concerns about the downside risk of not engaging mainstream corporations given the proliferation of alternative certification and labelling initiatives that are often criticized for watering down the high standards set by lead programmes including Fairtrade and organics (Conroy 2006: 250; Raynolds, Murray and Heller 2007; Bitzer, Francken and Glasbergen 2008; Murray and Raynolds 2000). With both of these concerns, one key question resonates: can and will advocacy-led certification transform global corporate practices?

With the aim of shedding light on this question, the remainder of the chapter proceeds in three parts. First, it reviews the origins and spread of certification and labelling for fair trade practices, documenting the quick expansion of the form across national borders and products. Second, it details the structures and functions of fair trade certification, offering some comparisons to other initiatives to identify certain unique facets of the fair trade form. Finally, the chapter turns to the issue of certification as governance and assesses the tool's current impacts across sectors where it has been applied and examines where fair trade labelling appears to be headed.

ORIGINS AND SPREAD OF CERTIFICATION AND LABELLING

A confluence of events facilitated the launch of fair trade certification and labelling. Principally, the growing activities of organic certifiers served as a salient model. As early as the 1920s, a coffee operation in Mexico, Finca Irlanda, began using biodynamic practices, and in the late 1960s it was the first coffee producer certified as organic (Giovannucci and Koekoek 2003: 45). This development would be influential for proponents of fair trade, which were, at the time, operating fair trade through ATOs, fair trade dedicated companies, and world shops, such as Ten Thousand Villages, and had been purchasing and promoting mainly handicrafts from small developing-world villages (Kochen 2003; Fridell 2007: 62; Davies 2007). However, the 1980s offered poorer market conditions for many developing countries (Michaels 1993), and it fostered a recognition within the alternative trade community that many of the producers they sought to help were farmers (Interview, Traidcraft Official, May 2007).

A shift in attention to crops such as coffee and tea soon followed. The Dutch Fair Trade Organization began selling fairly traded coffee in the early 1970s and by the late 1970s Traidcraft was established as a fair-trade mail order business and included coffee and tea in its catalogue in 1980 (Hockerts 2005) (see www.traidcraft.co.uk/temp/rad5E869.pdf). Yet, these efforts won minimal market share, and hence, there was an eagerness among producers to find further ways to increase demand for fair trade products (Giovannucci and Koekoek 2003). The European Fair Trade Association was formed in 1987 in an attempt to foster co-operation and information exchange among national fair trade associations and organizations (Bird and Hughes 1997); even still an interest to go further remained. With the growing acceptance of organic food and green consumerism noted above, certain fair trade proponents saw a window of opportunity to promote ethical labelling.

The first moves towards certification and labelling started in 1986 and involved collaboration between the Union of Indigenous Communities of the Isthmus Region (UCIRI) coffee co-operative in Oaxaca, Mexico (Interview, founder of Max Havelaar, February 2007) and Solidaridad, a Dutch development-aid organization (Kochen 2003; Jaffee 2007: 13; UCIRI 2005). The label (and the Max Havelaar Foundation) formed to offer UCIRI an alternative market channel that circumvented intermediaries and ensured more coffee could be exported under fair-trade terms than was possible through existing ATOs (Jaffee 2007: 13; Renard 2003).

The model quickly spread across countries and products. In 1991 Belgium created a Max Havelaar office, and in the UK a group, including Oxfam and Traidcraft, copied Max Havelaar with their own UK Fairtrade Foundation (see www.fairtrade.org.uk/about_us.htm). A year later, Switzerland established a Max Havelaar office and by 1994 France, Luxembourg, and Denmark were also part of the network (Bird and Hughes 1997; Max Havelaar, Switzerland 2006). By 1997 there were 14 national fair trade labelling initiatives (Linton, Liou, and Shaw 2004), which spurred interest in an international body to better co-ordinate their respective activities. In the spring of 1997 Fairtrade Labelling Organizations International (FLO) was formed for this very purpose (Raynolds 2000).

During this period, the suite of fair trade offerings also broadened. The Dutch Max Havelaar programme continued to be an important leader; it started work on cocoa in 1992 (Nelson and Galvez 2000), honey in 1994, and bananas in 1996 (FAO 1999; Murray and Raynolds 2000; Dankers and Liu 2003) (Interview, founder of Max Havelaar, February 2007). The German office of Transfair began work on tea in 1994, and by 1996 fair trade tea was available in Austria, Denmark, Germany, Japan, Luxembourg, Switzerland, and the UK (U.S. Department of Labor 1997). In addition to these goods,

FLO now endorses certification for fair trade production and exchange of cotton, flowers, several fresh fruits and juices, rice, spices and herbs, sports balls, sugar, and wine (see www.fairtrade.net/products.html).

FLO is now active in around 110 countries, with certified fair trade producers in 59 developing countries and sales of fair trade products in around 60 countries (Fairtrade Labelling Organization 2009a). For the 2008/09 fiscal year, sales of fair trade products were worth nearly €2,900m., with the UK being the largest single market worth just over €880m. The USA was a close second with a market of €758m. (Fairtrade Labelling Organization 2009a). There are now around 6,000 fair trade products available for purchase, and by the end of 2008 a total of 746 certified fair trade producers were enrolled with FLO worldwide (Fairtrade Labelling Organization 2009a).

STRUCTURES AND FUNCTIONS OF FAIRTRADE CERTIFICATION AND LABELLING

As a certification initiative, FLO has several distinct features. There are at least four key features to review: governance, standards setting and standards, accreditation and certification, and producer support.

Governance

FLO's governance structures are largely a product of its origins. Forming to co-ordinate existing national labelling initiatives (such as the various Max Havelaar and Transfair initiatives), broader membership was not initially considered. Instead, only the national labelling initiatives were granted voting rights; fair trade producers were given a voice through regional producer assemblies and the biennial fair trade forum (Zonneveld 2003; Slob and Oldenziel 2003). This choice was partly rationalized as a means to preserve the independence and objectivity of the certification process (Rice and McLean 1999). Nevertheless, by 1999 the Producers' Assembly was lobbying for voting rights (Rice and McLean 1999). It then took FLO seven years to change its constitution, and in May 2007 membership was granted to three producer networks: the African Fair Trade Network; the Coordination of Fairtrade Latin America and the Caribbean; and the Network of Asian Producers (Fairtrade Labelling Organization 2007) (see www.fairtrade.net/producer_networks.html).

The composition and selection of Board members has also undergone changes in FLO's 12-year life. An initial change in 2002 diversified the Board such that six representatives were from national labelling initiatives, four represented producer organizations, and two represented certified traders. Members were elected democratically for three-year terms (Zonneveld 2003; Taylor 2005). A more recent restructuring altered the make up to five representatives from national initiatives, four from producer networks (at least one from each of the three), two from certified traders, and three external independent experts (Fairtrade Labelling Organization 2009b).

One responsibility of the Board is to appoint representatives to three FLO committees addressing standards, finances, and nominations. The standards committee oversees the development of new and the revision of old standards; its members are representatives from producers, labelling initiatives and traders (Fairtrade Labelling Organization 2009b). The nominations committee is in charge of reviewing and recommending officials for consideration as Board and committee members, and it takes charge of evaluating these individuals' performance (Fairtrade Labelling Organization 2009b). Underneath the committees, FLO has a number of operational units, which are discussed further below.

Standard setting and standards

A key aim of FLO's progenitors was to rationalize and centralize standards development (Linton, Liou, and Shaw 2004; Raynolds 2000). Prior to this, the national labelling initiatives developed standards for new products which had high potential in their home market (Interview, FLO staff, February 2007). For instance, the German Transfair initiative began work on tea in the mid-1990s to tackle labour practices on Indian and Sri Lankan tea plantations and to offer an ethical option for German consumers (U.S. Department of Labor 1997). In other instances individual national initiatives worked on standards independently, which they later had to harmonize. The UK Fairtrade Foundation partnered with Sainsbury's and Co-op in the mid-1990s to promote fair trade flowers (Cowe 1996); it would take until 2004, however, before the first fair trade labelled flowers were sold in the UK market (Africa News 2004). During this time, Max Havelaar (Switzerland) also developed flower standards; the first labelled flowers were sold in 2001 (Max Havelaar, Switzerland 2006).

The unco-ordinated standards emerging from this approach presented challenges for fair trade as a whole. Yet, the shift to centralized standards setting was tricky since the system remained reliant on national initiatives' preliminary assessments of the marketability of new standards. During this time, control over the standards has also broadened. After the above-mentioned restructuring in 2002, producers, traders, ATOs, and other experts were able to serve on the standards and policy working group (Zonneveld 2003; Slob and Oldenziel 2003).

In terms of content, FLO's standards have a few key attributes. First, due to differences across sectors where fair trade labelling occurs, separate standards have been set for plantations, termed the 'hired labour standard', and co-operatives of small farmers, or the 'small-scale producer standard'. The former focuses on the conditions for plantation workers, whereas the latter focuses on social development of the farmer co-operative. In certain sectors, both standards apply (e.g. cocoa); whereas in others, only one does (e.g. only the small-scale producer standard is used for coffee). With both standards, FLO has developed generic standards over and above which crop-specific requirements apply. In all cases, the standards include minimum requirements, 'which all companies must meet from the moment they join fair-trade', and progress requirements, 'against which companies must demonstrate efforts towards long-term improvement and which should be developed according to a plan agreed by the company's management, some within a specific period of time' (Fairtrade Labelling Organization 2008).

Second, fair trade began in large part by offering producers more equitable terms of trade, and hence the standards centred on fair prices and pre-finance (Carpio 1993). Since, the standards have broadened to encompass specific social development objectives and environmental aspects of farming practices (Raynolds, Murray and Heller 2007). The standards now set requirements for labour conditions, including no forced or child labour, rights to unionization, fair wages, and safe working environment (see www.fairtrade.net/pdf/sp/english/Generic%20Standards%20SP%20version%20Jan03.pdf). Many of the economic requirements apply to companies trading in fair trade products. These are laid out in the trading standard, which stipulates that buyers pay prices sufficient to cover costs of sustained production, to support livelihoods, and to allow for investment in further development. Buyers are also meant to provide pre-financing credit to producers worth 60% of final harvest value and establish long-term contracts to allow for planning and sustainable practices (www.fairtrade.net/sites/standards/general.html).

Finally, the standards committee also determines the price premium for the different FLO products. Initially, the standards for tea production required a minimum premium rather than a minimum price; this changed in 2008 (U.S. Department of Labor 1997; Raynolds and Ngcwangu 2010). Price determinations are first handled by a division of FLO's standards unit, which then refers its analysis to the standards committee for decisions (Interview, FLO Staff, February 2007). This is a unique facet of fair trade certification. Other initiatives typically rely on the market to determine whether certified products garner a premium (Daviron and Ponte 2005; Muradian and Pelupessy 2005; Taylor 2005).

Certification and accreditation

Certification is another function that has changed since the FLO's launch. These were initially done in-house and often occurred as a joint support and monitoring activity (Slob and Oldenziel 2003; Courville 2003; Fairtrade Labelling Organization 1999). An in-house Certification Committee was initially in charge of certifying producers, and registering traders, processors, exporters, importers, roasters, and retailers. The FLO board appointed members of the committee, but had no other control over the decisions made regarding certification or registration (Slob and Oldenziel 2003). Fair trade emphasized the development aspect of its standards and considered farm-level visits opportunities to observe problems and offer consultation on how to improve. Although valuable as a system of assistance for the producers involved, with

FLO's growth a need to change became increasingly apparent. Consistency was one concern; credibility to outside observers was another. In 2002 FLO created an independent certification committee for making certification decisions (these were previously made by the Board). The committee included representatives for producers, traders, and national initiatives (Zonneveld 2003). Then, in September 2003, FLO delegated certification to an independent legal entity, FLO-CERT GmbH (Ltd) (Fairtrade Labelling Organization 2003), explaining that the move would increase the programme's credibility and protect it from liabilities associated with the commercial activities of certification.

This is another unique aspect of FLO. Other certification and labelling programmes typically use a stand-alone body to accredit outside auditors that then carry out the programme's certifications (Auld 2009). The International Federation of Organic Agriculture Movements (IFOAM) created the International Organic Accreditation Service in 1997 for the purpose of assessing organic auditors and endorsing their inspections as compliant with IFOAM requirements (International Organic Accreditation Service 2006). A similar body conducts accreditation for the Marine Stewardship Council and the Forest Stewardship Council. Although FLO did consider creating an accreditation programme, it opted for a single certifier partly because its mission is to serve the world's most marginalized producers. FLO officials explain that this means few commercial certifiers would be interested in accrediting with the programme, due to the market's small size (Information from presentations made by FLO staff at Biofach, Nuremburg, Germany, 2007).

Finally, while FLO controls the Fairtrade Mark, the existing national labelling initiatives remain in charge of licensing its use in their national markets. With the exception of the USA and Canada, all the fair trade labelling initiatives use the same fair trade label, which was introduced in 2003 (Zonneveld 2003). This posed challenges for FLO, since it meant no mechanism was in place to accommodate interest in fair trade from markets outside the network of national initiatives (Interview, FLO staff, February 2007). The eventual solution was to have FLO's head office oversee licensing in these countries. Another recent innovation was the creation of national marketing initiatives, which only promote fair trade labelling in a country and leave licensing to FLO. The South African initiative is the first such FLO affiliate (Fairtrade Labelling Organization 2009a, 2009b).

Producer support

As noted above, fair trade's initial certification activities mixed inspection and advice in the process of determining whether a producer group warranted listing on a given product's fair trade registry (Fairtrade Labelling Organization 1999). With the increased formalization of FLO's operations, such as through the creation of FLO-CERT and the adherence to ISO 65 norms, producer support evolved into a separate function (Fairtrade Labelling Organization 2003): the producer services and relations unit was formed in 2004. The new unit provides four key services: 'training in local languages'; 'guidance on certification requirements'; 'helping producers to gain access to new markets'; and 'facilitating relationships with buyers' (www.fairtrade.net/services_and_relations.html). FLO has five regional managers who work along with seven regional co-ordinators all for the purpose of assisting producers (www.fairtrade.net/support_for_producers.html).

ASSESSMENT: CURRENT IMPACTS

By weight, bananas are the most significant certified product; in 2008/09 just short of 300,000 tons were sold, with around a third having Fairtrade and organic certification and the other two-thirds just Fairtrade. This represents roughly 0.3% of world banana production (85,855,856 tons in 2007) (FAOSTAT, http://faostat.fao.org/, accessed 19 July 2009). For the same year, certified Fairtrade coffee totalled 65,808 tons, with a little under half (31,673 tons) also having received organic certification. For the previous year, FLO had certified 62,219 tons (62.2m. kg) of green coffee, or approximately 0.9% of the world coffee production using 2007 production values. Total production in 2007 was 116,212,000 bags (60 kg), which is equivalent to 6,972,720,000 kg (www.ico.org/prices/po.htm; see www.fairtrade.net/coffee.html for FLO coffee figures). Other significant crops by weight include sugar cane (56,990 tons in 2008/09), fruit juice (28,219 tons), fresh fruit (26,424 tons), tea (11,467 tons), and cocoa beans (10,299 tons) (Fairtrade Labelling Organization 2009a). As a percentage of total world production, Fairtrade's inroad in to these sectors remains small. With sugar cane, world production topped 1,600m. tons in 2007, meaning fair trade accounts for something around 0.003% of this total. Total production in 2007 was 1,590,701,770 tons, according to FAOSTAT (http://faostat.fao.org/, accessed 19 July 2009). With tea, Fairtrade has made a slightly bigger dent; total world production neared 3.9m. tons, of which around 0.3% were Fairtrade certified. Total production in 2007 was 3,887,308 tons, according to FAOSTAT (http://faostat.fao.org/, accessed 19 July 2009). Finally, with cocoa beans, Fairtrade accounted for around 0.25% of world production, which totalled nearly 4.2m. tons in 2007. Total production in 2007 was 4,161,631 tons, according to FAOSTAT (http://faostat.fao.org/, accessed 19 July 2009).

Despite the limited extent of fair trade's penetration into various markets, research does note the benefits for participating producers that accrue from pre-financing, the social premium, and the higher-than-world prices for crops including coffee (see e.g. Jaffee 2007; Bacon 2005, 2008; Raynolds 2002), tea (Dolan 2010), bananas (Shreck 2002, 2005; Murray and Raynolds 2000), cocoa (Nelson and Galvez 2000), among others (see Le Mare 2008, for review). If FLO receives any criticism on this front it is because the premiums are not high enough (Bacon *et al.* 2008: 360), the benefits available to producers are not spread to a large enough group of growers (Taylor 2005), or that the total premium does not make it back to the growers (Webb 2006; Shreck 2005).

More significant, however, are claims that the process faces deeper difficulties. First, research has identified unintended effects of certification processes as they interact with the customs and social practices of the communities being examined. Mutersbaugh (2008), for instance, documents tensions between organic-certification procedures and local customs and practices in coffee-growing communities, noting how standards-based assessments that use local farmers as on-the-ground guarantors of a co-operative's compliance made farmers act counter to norms guiding their customary role in the community. Doppler and Cabanas (2006) find similar tensions with fair trade. They point to FLO-CERT as part of the problem, conceding that it has improved 'the professionalization of fair trade', but that this has also 'made the system rather abstract, making it impersonal for the producers' organizations' (Doppler and Cabanas 2006: 54). In addition, the introduction of professionalized inspections came with fees for participating producers (Doppler and Cabanas 2006), something that formerly distinguished fair trade from other certification initiatives (Taylor 2005).

Even though the price premium might mean farmers are still ahead, the change does signify a different approach, and it gives evidence to FLO's critics who claim the initiative is not championing producers' interests. Overall, these authors feel the depersonalized approach is a shortcoming, discordant with the relationship-building aims of fair trade (see e.g. Jaffe and Bacon 2008; Taylor 2005). The balance FLO seeks is not an easy one. FLO must manage concern surrounding the credibility of its inspections (Weitzman 2006), while not going so far as to worsen perceptions that professionalizing inspections is alienating the producers the programme seeks to empower.

A second issue concerns whether those participating in fair trade are producers most in need of assistance. This applies to all voluntary certification and labelling initiatives: research shows that producers most able to meet standards are the most likely to participate (Auld, Gulbrandsen and McDermott 2008; Bernstein and Cashore 2007; Gulbrandsen 2009; Ponte 2008; Gullison 2003; Melo and Wolf 2007). Hence, the problems of key concern may remain unaddressed. For instance, Bray *et al.* (2008) suggest that Mexico dominates the organic coffee market because of 'pre-existing "social capital accumulation" in the Mexican countryside' (p. 238). Researchers examining fair trade have raised similar concerns about who participates and whether the most marginalized are well represented (Nigh 1997; Martínez-Torres 2008; Taylor 2005).

One way these concerns surface is in discussions over whether certification should apply to small-scale producers and plantations (see e.g. Besky 2008), a debate partly stemming from the various aims fair trade labelling established to address in separate national markets. Given the limited market for fair trade labelled products, some argue that the programme should focus on small producers exclusively. As an illustration, recall that Germany worked on tea standards to improve conditions for plantation workers (U.S. Department of Labor 1997). More recently, small-scale tea producers in African countries have been FLO certified, which has led to questions about whether they are unfairly disadvantaged relative to certified estates competing in the same markets (Raynolds and Ngcwangu 2010). With bananas as well, many producers in the Windward Islands of the Caribbean are small-scale operations unlike the larger-scale plantations dominating most of Latin America. Given the dismantling of special trading status with the EU, the lack of a fair trade label exclusively available for small-scale operators means banana producers from these countries are unlikely to remain viable (Moberg 2005; Smith 2006). What these developments illustrate is a tension surrounding what different fair trade supporters felt the labelling initiative ought to do. Because of the fragmented path of development, these different ideas are embodied in different aspects of the programme, creating what, to some, appear as contradictions and problems.

Having mainstream companies involved has intensified these debates as questions are raised about whether it is appropriate to have companies with poor ethical records gain an ethical veneer from selling a few branded products with the fair trade label (Davies 2007). For instance, when Nestlé released its fair trade labelled brand, it ranked very low on its overall ethical performance (Vidal 2005). To complicate things further, fair trade companies, smaller roasters and others entirely committed to fair trade practices, many of whom entered the market early, fear competition from the larger corporations (Benjamin 2007). With coffee, claims that the bigger roasters have been able to negotiate lower fees for licensing the fair trade label further stoke these fears (Sustainable Food News 2007), and lead analysts to foresee a retreat of core fair trade sellers back to a niche market distinguished from fair trade sold by mass-market operations (Davies 2007). A key question underlying this tension is how to expand the practice of fair trade while remaining true to core principles. Engaging the mainstream appears important for expanding the impacts of fairer trade; however, in doing so concerns can surface to undermine core support for FLO.

CONCLUSIONS: FUTURE PROSPECTS

As the discussion above has already indicated, FLO's market success has spurred the proliferation of other initiatives. Because fair trade along with organics are seen as high-bar standards (Bacon *et al.* 2008; Raynolds, Murray and Heller 2007), considerable attention is paid to whether the emergence of new programmes helps or hinders attempts to address social and environmental problems. One view warns that new programmes may foster regulatory competition leading to a 'race to the bottom' (Conroy 2006: 250; Raynolds, Murray and Heller 2007; Bitzer, Francken and Glasbergen 2008). Another view suggests that new initiatives might complement existing programmes and, therefore, help broaden the scope of issues addressed and the levels of participation (Auld 2007). A final view, based on research in the forest sector, notes the possibility that competition might ratchet up standards (Overdevest 2005; Cashore *et al.* 2007). If programmes can indeed be complementary or lead to upward pressure on standards, a key question is how to direct sector-level developments towards the alignment and coherence of activities.

Assessing differences across sectors where fair trade applies and the patterns of other programmes that have emerged offers initial insights into factors that influence the outcome of programme proliferation. A few trends stand out. First, sector-to-sector differences in market and regulatory structures seem to shape how easily fair trade principles garner support. Certain market characteristics constrain certification's transformative potential. With the former, Shreck (2005), examining bananas, explains that highly perishable crops require careful and sometimes capital intensive care throughout their production, transport and distribution. Hence, setting up a parallel trading system is costly and logistically challenging (see also Murray and Raynolds 2000). Riisgaard (2009) adds that in the cut flower market it has been considerably easier to promote adoption of ethical trading practices for flowers sold directly to supermarkets compared to those sold at auction. The distance between the perceived problems facing a sector and companies vulnerable to shame campaigns has also been shown to matter (Roberts 2003). With the latter, the intersection between certification and government institutions is considered by research as increasingly important (see e.g. Bitzer, Francken and Glasbergen 2008; Auld, Gulbrandsen and McDermott 2008; Potts 2008). For example, it appears to matter whether or not a crop has been previously regulated by an international commodity agreement. In sectors such as coffee, sugar and cocoa, dedicated commodity agreements were signed decades back, and although, by and large, they have lost their regulatory powers (Gilbert 1996), some continue to serve as venues in which to discuss sector concerns (see Potts 2008 for discussion of International Coffee Agreement). Other products—cut flowers, cotton, bananas, among others—lack such a focused international venue.

Second, certification's broader outcomes appear contingent on the specific constellation of programmes emerging in different sectors. In certain cases, the presence of an industry-wide initiative may be lessening concerns about downward pressure on standards. Within coffee, for instance, before the 4C (Common Code for Coffee Community) process was launched there was no common understanding of the minimum requirements certification initiatives should not fall below. The 4C code has provided some certainty in this regard even if there is disagreement as to whether it is exactly the right level (Down to Earth 2006; see also Tallontire and Greenhalgh 2005: footnote 46). Arguably, the 4C has allowed other standards to focus more on promoting and encouraging improvements at the upper end of the market. Although membership has fluctuated, before its formal launch, analysts noted that if fully implemented, it could affect the behaviour of 80% of the coffee sector (Muradian and Pelupessy 2005).

Similarly, the relationship among the different programmes is not equivalent across products. With coffee, certain observers consider the relationship between programmes complementary (Panhuysen and Weiligmann 2006), some programmes have publicly acknowledged their different roles (Max Havelaar, the Netherlands and Utz Kapeh 2006), and some have worked collaboratively to delineate commonly accepted standards (Courville 2008). By contrast, with bananas, the tension between the Rainforest Alliance and FLO was initially intense (Murray and Raynolds 2000; Taylor and Scharlin 2004). Indeed, Murray and Raynolds (2000) explain how a major Danish importer switched from Fairtrade to Rainforest Alliance bananas supplied by Chiquita, which meant a drop in Fairtrade sales. At least concerning labour standards, this has been viewed as a step backwards: 'The European retailer [appeared] to be trying to take advantage of the new market generated by the Fairtrade movement to sell bananas that would clearly not qualify for Fairtrade certification' (p. 71).

Still, it is difficult to ascertain whether removing other programmes would eliminate downward pressure on standards. The Chiquita example also highlights the different objectives pursued by various certification and labelling initiatives (Courville 2008; Raynolds, Murray and Heller 2007; Riisgaard 2009; Giovannucci and Ponte 2005; Hughes 2001; Big Grower 2008) and that these different objectives may still be assisting the producers involved. For instance, with coffee, a recent study by the Committee on Sustainability Assessment, surveyed 51 farms in six countries and found that 75% of participants felt certification with one or more of several coffee initiatives improved their overall condition (Giovannucci and Potts 2008). The assessment included: fair trade; organics; Rainforest Alliance; UTZ CERTIFIED; 4C; and Starbucks CAFE (Coffee and Farmer Equity) practices. Though based on a limited sample, the results suggest that participants are finding subjectively defined benefits from different certification initiatives.

Above all else, the committed work of ATOs and fair trade companies and the sustained ability of the entire movement to underscore why fair trade is different and important appear to be critical for continued progress. From Peace Coffee, a roaster in Minneapolis that distributes its roasted fair trade coffee by bike, hence reducing air and greenhouse gas emissions (www.peacecoffee.com/history.htm), and Day Chocolate Company that has given cocoa producers ownership stake in the company to ensure equitable distribution of benefits (Doherty and Tranchell 2005), to long-standing leaders such as Equal Exchange which continues to uphold fair trade principles, these organizations and companies provide a forward-looking facet of fair trade. They act as cutting-edge experiments of what is possible, and they portend what might become the demands for the mainstream market (see also Jaffe and Bacon 2008).

Having innovative facets of the sector taking the extra step to note what more there is to do, helps ensure that fair trade does not succumb to pressure to erode the gains it has already institutionalized in the certification and labelling field. This role is now further supported by the 2004 launch of the

Fair Trade Organization (FTO) Mark which is meant to give 'Fair Trade Organizations definable recognition amongst consumers, existing and new business partners, governments and donors who would like to support Fair Trade activities – providing wider market opportunities for producers'. Moreover, the hope is that the mark will be a 'means of identification' that 'sets organizations apart from other commercial businesses, making [recognizable] mission driven organizations whose core activity is Fair Trade' (www.ifat.org/index.php?option=com_content&task=view&id=3&Itemid=11). To qualify to use the label in promotional materials, an International Fair Trade Association member must undergo a self-evaluation with the addition of peer review and the possibility that their operations will be subject to external evaluation: approximately 5%–10% of the organizations are randomly audited (IFAT 2008). The standard covers social and environmental criteria, not unlike those of FLO; however, here the focus is on giving credit to fair trade organizations, not companies which carry fair trade labelled products. It will create another market segment, separate from the mainstream in which experimentation to further the aims of fair trade may transpire and push upward future expectations.

Of course, as noted above, the forward-pushing edge of the movement is only effective when fair trade is widely understood and recognized in the market. As it turns out, this is in fact the case. According to data reported by the European Fair Trade Association, by 2004 public awareness of the fair trade label was 63% in Luxembourg, 50% in the UK, 44% in Ireland, and 39% in Sweden (Krier 2005). More recent survey work has found still growing recognition and understanding of the fair trade label among consumers in various countries (Fairtrade Labelling Organization 2009a; Feinberg *et al.* 2008) (see http://www.scotland.gov.uk/Publications/2007/09/11091918/1). This high level of awareness, arguably, gives fair trade the ability to remain a front runner, pushing for ongoing change.

BIBLIOGRAPHY

Africa News, *Kenya; Foundation Rewards Flower Firm for Promoting 'Good Practice'*, (Newswire), 9 March 2004 (cited 29 July 2009), available from www.lexisnexis.com/.

Auld, G., 'The Origins and Growth of Social and Environmental Certification in the Coffee Sector', paper read at 48th Convention of the International Studies Association, 28 February–3 March, at Chicago, IL, 2007.

——, 'Reversal of Fortune: How Early Choices Can Alter the Logic of Market-based Authority', School of Forestry and Environmental Studies, New Haven, CT, Yale University, 2009.

Auld, G., Gulbrandsen, L. H. and McDermott, C., 'Certification Schemes and the Impact on Forests and Forestry' in *Annual Review of Environment and Resources* 33 (1): 187–211, 2008.

Bacon, C. M., 'Confronting the Coffee Crisis: Can Fair Trade, Organic, and Specialty Coffees Reduce Small-scale Farmer Vulnerability in Northern Nicaragua?', *World Development* 33 (3): 497–511, 2005.

——, 'Confronting the Coffee Crisis: Can Fair Trade, Organic, and Specialty Coffees Reduce the Vulnerability of Small-Scale Farmers in Northern Nicaragua?' in *Confronting the Coffee Crisis: Fair Trade, Sustainable Livelihoods and Ecosystems in Mexico and Central America*, C. M. Bacon, V. E. Mendez, S. R. Gliessman, D. Goodman and J. A. Fox (eds), Cambridge, MA, MIT Press, 2008.

Bacon, C. M., Mendez, V. E., Gliessman, S. R., Goodman, D. and Fox, J. A. (eds), *Confronting the Coffee Crisis: Fair Trade, Sustainable Livelihoods and Ecosystems in Mexico and Central America,* R. Gottlieb (ed.), *Food, Health, and the Environment*, Cambridge, MA, MIT Press, 2008.

Benjamin, A., 'Potential Banana Skin?: Is the Abundance of Ethically-labelled Products on our Supermarket Shelves Devaluing the Concept of Fair Trade and Leaving Customers Confused and Cynical, or is the Competition Good for Both Consumers and Farmers?', *The Guardian* (London), 7 March 2007, available from http://web.lexis-nexis.com, 2007.

Bernstein, S. and Cashore, B., 'Can Non-state Global Governance be Legitimate? An Analytical Framework' in *Regulation and Governance* 1 (4): 347–71, 2007.

Besky, S., 'Can a Plantation be Fair? Paradoxes and Possibilities in Fair Trade Darjeeling Tea Certification' in *Anthropology of Work Review* 29 (1): 1–9, 2008.

Big Grower, *Standards, Codes of Conduct, Certification ... What Does it all Mean to my Business?* [online article in Big Grower 3(1)]. Visions Group, February 2008 (cited 29 July 2009), available from www.biggrower.com/index.cfm&fuseaction=showArticle&appDirectory=bgr&articleID=8954.

Bird, K. and Hughes, D. R., 'Ethical Consumerism: The Case of "Fairly Traded" Coffee' in *Business Ethics* 6 (3): 159–68, 1997.

Bitzer, V., Francken, M. and Glasbergen, P., 'Intersectoral Partnerships for a Sustainable Coffee Chain: Really Addressing Sustainability or Just Picking (Coffee) Cherries?' in *Global Environmental Change* 18 (2): 271–84, 2008.

Bovard, J., 'Aid from the USA Often Hurts the Hungry' in *USA Today*, 24 November 1989 (cited 1 August 2008), available from www.lexisnexis.com/.

Bray, D. B., Sanchez, J. L. P., and Murphy, E. C., 'Social Dimensions of Organic Coffee Production in Mexico: Lessons for Eco-Labeling Initiatives' in *Confronting the Coffee Crisis: Fair Trade, Sustainable Livelihoods and Ecosystems in Mexico and Central America*, C. M. Bacon, V. E. Mendez, S. R. Gliessman, D. Goodman and J. A. Fox (eds), Cambridge, MA, MIT Press, 2008.

Brittain, V., 'UN Session will test the West's Commitment to Recovering Africa's Lost Decade' in *The Guardian* (London), 28 June 1991 (cited 7 August 2008), available from www.lexisnexis.com.

Carpio, I., 'The Netherlands: Dutch Promote Alternative Coffee Trade' (Newswire), IPS-Inter Press Service/Global Information Network, 2 July 1993 (cited 31 August 2005), available from www.lexis-nexis.com.

Cashore, B., Auld, G., Bernstein, S. and McDermott, C. L., 'Can Non-state Governance "Ratchet Up" Global Environmental Standards? Lessons from the Forest Sector' in *Review of European Community and International Environmental Law* 16 (2): 158–72, 2007.

Conklin, E. E., 'Consumer Activist Knows How to Say No and Make it Count' in LIVING: 131 LINES, Pg. C1, *Seattle Post Intelligencer*, 9 May 1991 (cited 27 January 2007), available from http://web.lexis-nexis.com.

Conroy, M. E., *Branded: How the 'Certification Revolution' is Transforming Global Corporations*, Gabriola Island, BC, New Society Publishers, 2006.

Courville, S., 'Social Accountability Audits: Challenging or Defending Democratic Governance?' in *Law & Policy* 25 (3): 269–97, 2003.

——, 'Organic and Social Certifications: Recent Developments from the Global Regulators' in *Confronting the Coffee Crisis: Fair Trade, Sustainable Livelihoods and Ecosystems in Mexico and Central America*, C. M. Bacon, V. E. Mendez, S. R. Gliessman, D. Goodman and J. A. Fox (eds), Cambridge, MA, MIT Press, 2008.

Cowe, R., 'Retailers Back Code for Third-World Suppliers' in *The Guardian* (London), 3 October 1996 (cited 29 July 2009), available from www.lexisnexis.com.

Dankers, C. and Liu., P., Environmental and Social Standards, Certification and Labelling for Cash Crops', Rome, Italy, Food and Agriculture Organization of the United Nations, 2003.

Davies, I. A., 'The Eras and Participants of Fair Trade: An Industry Structure / Stakeholder Perspective on the Growth of the Fair Trade Industry' in *Corporate Governance* 7 (4): 455–570, 2007.

Daviron, B. and Ponte, S., *The Coffee Paradox: Global Markets, Commodity Trade and the Elusive Promise of Development*, London and New York, Zed Books Ltd in association with CTA Wageningen, 2005.

Dickenson, N., 'Catering for the Ethical Shopper / A Look at a Growing Consumer Trend' [Management (Marketing and Advertising); p. 19], *Financial Times* (London), 15 April 1993 (cited 9 July 2007), available from http://web.lexis-nexis.com/.

Doherty, B. and Tranchell, S., 'New Thinking in International Trade? A Case Study of The Day Chocolate Company' in *Sustainable Development* 13 (3): 166–76, 2005.

Dolan, C. S., 'Virtual Moralities: The Mainstreaming of Fairtrade in Kenyan Tea Fields' in *Geoforum* 41 (1): 33–43, 2010.

Doppler, F., and Cabanas, A. A. G., 'Fair Trade: Benefits and Drawbacks for Producers' in *Latin American Relations Observatory*, www.obreal.unibo.it/File.aspx?IdFile=530, 2006.

Down to Earth, 'Coffee Code: Wide Agreement to Improve Industry Practice' in *Down to Earth: Science and Environment Online*, 6 December 2006 (cited 28 August 2008), available from www.downtoearth.org.in/full6.asp?foldername=20041215&filename=news&sec_id=4&sid=39.

Elkington, J., and Hailes, J., *The Green Consumer Guide: From Shampoo to Champagne, High-street Shopping for a Better Environment*, London, Victory Gollancz Ltd, 1988.

Fairtrade Labelling Organization, *Fair Trade: A Viable Alternative for Small Farmers* (Archived web pages), Fairtrade labelling Organizations International, 15 October 1999 (cited 6 October 2007), available from http://web.archive.org/web/20010619230548/www.fairtrade.net/coffee.html.

——, *Shopping for a Better World: Annual Report 03/04*, Bonn, Germany, Fairtrade Labelling Organizations International, 2003.

——, *Annual Report 2006 / 07 – Shaping Global Partnerships* (Web page), Fairtrade Labelling Organizations International 2007 (cited 7 August 2008), available from www.fairtrade.net/fileadmin/user_upload/content/Final_FLO_AR_2007_03.pdf.

——, Generic Fairtrade Standards for Hired Labour, Bonn, Germany, Fairtrade Labelling Organizations International, 2008.

——, *Annual Report 2008–09, Fairtrade: Leading the Way* (Web page), Fairtrade Labelling Organizations International 2009a (cited 19 July 2009), available from www.fairtrade.net/fileadmin/user_upload/content/2009/resources/FLO_ANNUAL_ REPORT_08–09.pdf. 2009a.

——, *How we're Run* (Web page), Fairtrade Labelling Organizations International 2009b (cited July 2009), available from www.fairtrade.net/how_we_are_run.html. 2009b.

FAO, 'The Market for "Organic" and "Fair Trade" Bananas' in *Intergovernmental Group on Bananas and on Tropical Fruits*, Gold Coast, Australia, Committee on Commodity Problems, Food and Agricultural Organization of the United Nations, 1999.

Feinberg, G., Leiserowitz, A., Auld, G. and Cashore, B., 'American and Canadian Consumer Attitudes toward Environmentally-Friendly Products and Eco-labeling' in *The GfK Roper / Yale Survey on Environmental Issues*, New Haven, CT, Yale School of Forestry and Environmental Studies, 2008.

Financial Times, 'El Salvador poses dilemma for US' (SECTION I; American News; p. 4), *Financial Times* (London), 21 January 1983 (cited 28 January 2007), available from http://web.lexis-nexis.com.

Fridell, G., *Fair Trade Coffee: The Prospects and Pitfalls of Market-driven Social Justice: Studies in Comparative Political Economy and Public Policy*, Toronto, University of Toronto Press, 2007.

Friedman, M., *Consumer Boycotts: Effecting Change through the Marketplace and the Media*, New York, Routledge, 1999.

Galen, M., 'Human Rights: American Senior Citizens "Vacation" in Nicaragua Coffee Fields' (Newswire), IPS-Inter Press Service, 20 February 1985 (cited 28 January 2007), available from http://web.lexis-nexis.com.

Gilbert, C. L., 'International Commodity Agreements: An Obituary Notice' in *World Development* 24 (1): 1–19, 1996.

Giovannucci, D. and Koekoek, F. J., *The State of Sustainable Coffee: A Study of Twelve Major Markets* (Report). ICO, UNCTAD and IISD, 2003 (cited 13 March 2006), available from www.iisd.org/publications/pub.aspx?pno=579.

Giovannucci, D. and Ponte, S., 'Standards as a New Form of Social Contract? Sustainability Initiatives in the Coffee Industry', *Food Policy* 30 (3): 284–301, 2005.

Giovannucci, D. and Potts, J., Seeking Sustainability: COSA Preliminary Analysis of Sustainability Initiatives in the Coffee Sector', Winnipeg, Canada, Committee on Sustainability Assessment, 2008.

Godoy, J., 'More Questions about Fair Trade Practices', Inter Press Service News Agency, 26 November 2008 (cited 28 July 2009), available from http://ipsnews.net/print.asp?idnews=44863.

Goodman, M. K., 'Reading Fair Trade: Political Ecological Imaginary and the Moral Economy of Fair Trade Foods' in *Political Geography* 23 (7): 891–915, 2004.

Gulbrandsen, L. H., 'The Emergence and Effectiveness of the Marine Stewardship Council' in *Marine Policy* 33 (4): 654–60, 2009.

Gullison, R. E., 'Does Forest Certification Conserve Biodiversity?' in *Oryx* 37 (2): 153–65, 2003.

Hockerts, K., 'The Fair Trade Story' (2nd place in oikos Sustainability Case Writing Competition 2005). Oikos sustainability case collection 2005 (cited 12 September 2006), available from www.oikos-foundation.unisg.ch/homepage/fairtrade.pdf, 2005.

Hughes, A., 'Global Commodity Networks, Ethical Trade and Governmentality: Organizing Business Responsibility in the Kenyan Cut Flower Industry' in *Transactions of the Institute of British Geographers* 26 (4): 390–406, 2001.

IFAT, *Monitoring: Building Trust in Fair Trade*, IFAT, 3 July 2008 (cited 7 August 2008), available from www.ifat.org/index.php?option=com_content&task=view&id=21&Itemid=68.

International Organic Accreditation Service, *History* (Web page). International Organic Accreditation Service, 21 March 2006 (cited 1 April 2006), available from www.ioas.org/WEBSITE/0410_History.htm.

Jaffe, R. and Bacon, C. M., 'From Differentiate Coffee Markets toward Alternative Trade and Knowledge Networks' in *Confronting the Coffee Crisis: Fair Trade, Sustainable Livelihoods and Ecosystems in Mexico and Central Amercia*, C. M. Bacon, V. E. Mendez, S. R. Gliessman, D. Goodman and J. A. Fox (eds), Cambridge, MA, MIT Press, 2008.

Jaffee, D., *Brewing Justice: Fair Trade Coffee, Sustainability, and Survival*, Berkeley, University of California Press, 2007.

Kochen, M., *History of Fair Trade* (Report). International Federation of Alternative Trade, December 2003 (cited 13 March 2006), available from www.worldshops.org/fairtrade/netw/2004_FinalHistory_of_FairTrade.doc.

Krier, J.-M., *Fair Trade in Europe 2005: Facts and Figures on Fair Trade in 25 European Countries* (Online report). Fair Trade Advocacy Office, December 2005 (cited 13 March 2006), available from www.worldshops.org/news/new/FairTradein Europe2005.pdf.

Lancaster, C., 'Aid Effectiveness in Africa: The Unfinished Agenda' in *Journal of African Economies* 8 (4): 487–503, 1999.

Le Mare, A., 'The Impact of Fair Trade on Social and Economic Development: A Review of the Literature' in *Geography Compass* 2 (6): 1922–42, 2008.

Linton, A., Liou, C. C. and Shaw, K. A., 'A Taste of Trade Justice: Marketing Global Social Responsibility via Fair Trade Coffee' in *Globalizations* 1 (2): 223–46, 2004.

Manuel, A., 'Human Rights: New Report on Nicaraguan Rebel Abuses', IPS-Inter Press Service, March 1985 (cited 28 January 2007), available from http://web.lexis-nexis.com.

Marlin, A. T., Schorsch, J., Swaab, E. and Will, R., *Shopping for a Better World*, New York, Council on Economic Priorities and Ballantine Books, 1991.

Martínez-Torres, M. E., 'The Benefits and Sustainability of Organic Farming by Peasant Coffee Farmer in Chiapas, Mexico' in *Confronting the Coffee Crisis: Fair Trade, Sustainable Livelihoods and Ecosystems in Mexico and Central America*, C. M. Bacon, V. E. Mendez, S. R. Gliessman, D. Goodman and J. A. Fox (eds), Cambridge, MA, MIT Press, 2008.

Max Havelaar, the Netherlands and Utz Kapeh, 'Fairtrade & Utz Kapeh: An Explanation about Two Leading Programs in Coffee Certification', Max Havelaar, the Netherlands and Utz Kapeh, 2006.

Max Havelaar, Switzerland, *The Max Havelaar Foundation (Switzerland)*, Max Havelaar, Switzerland, 1 February 2006 (cited 29 July 2009), available from www.maxhavelaar.ch/filemanager/publikationen/_backup/20080303/max_havelaar_portrait_en.pdf.

Melo, C. and Wolf, S., 'Ecocertification of Ecuadorian Bananas: Prospects for Progressive North-South Linkages' in *Studies in Comparative International Development (SCID)* 42 (3): 256–78, 2007.

Michaels, M., 'Retreat from Africa' in *Foreign Affairs* 72 (1): 93–108, 1993.

Moberg, M. 'Fair Trade and Eastern Caribbean Banana Farmers: Rhetoric and Reality in the Anti-Globalization Movement' in *Human Organization* 64 (1): 4–16, 2005.

Muradian, R. and Pelupessy, W., 'Governing the Coffee Chain: The Role of Voluntary Regulatory Systems' in *World Development* 33 (12): 2029–44, 2005.

Murray, D. L. and Raynolds, L. T., 'Alternative Trade in Bananas: Obstacles and Opportunities for Progressive Social Change in the Global Economy' in *Agriculture and Human Values* 17 (1): 65–74, 2000.

Mutersbaugh, T., 'Serve and Certify: Paradoxes of Services Work in Organic Coffee Certification' in *Confronting the Coffee Crisis: Fair Trade, Sustainable Livelihoods and Ecosystems in Mexico and Central America*, C. M. Bacon, V. E. Mendez, S. R. Gliessman, D. Goodman and J. A. Fox (eds), Cambridge, MA, MIT Press, 2008.

Nelson, V. and M. Galvez, 'Social Impact of Ethical and Conventional Cocoa Trading on Forest-Dependent People in Ecuador' in *Natural Resources and Ethical Trade Programme, Natural Resources Institute*, Chatham Maritime, University of Greenwich, 2000.

Nigh, R., 'Organic Agriculture and Globalization: A Maya Associative Corporation in Chiapas, Mexico' in *Human Organization* 56 (4): 427, 1997.

Overdevest, C., 'Treadmill Politics, Information Politics and Public Policy: Toward a Political Economy of Information' in *Organization & Environment* 18 (1): 72–90, 2005.

Panhuysen, S. and B. Weiligmann, Coffee Barometer 2006 – Certified Coffee in the Netherlands', Amsterdam, the Netherlands, Dutch Coffee Coalition, 2006.

Ponte, S., 'Greener than Thou: The Political Economy of Fish Ecolabeling and its Local Manifestations in South Africa' in *World Development* 36 (1): 159–75, 2008.

Potts, J., The International Coffee Agreement 2007: An Instrument for Building Sustainable Coffee Economy', Winnipeg, Sustainable Coffee Partnership, 2008.

Raynolds, L. T., 'Re-embedding Global Agriculture: The International Organic and Fair Trade movements' in *Agriculture and Human Values* 17 (3): 297–309, 2000.

——, 'Consumer/producer Links in Fair Trade Coffee Networks' in *Sociologia Ruralis* 42 (4), 2002.

Raynolds, L. T., Murray, D. and Heller, A., 'Regulating Sustainability in the Coffee Sector: A Comparative Analysis of Third-party Environmental and Social Certification Initiatives' in *Agriculture and Human Values* 24: 147–63, 2007.

Raynolds, L. T. and Ngcwangu, S. U., 'Fair Trade Rooibos Tea: Connecting South African Producers and American Consumer Markets', in *Geoforum*. 41 (1): 74–83, 2010.

Renard, M.-C., 'Fair Trade: Quality, Market and Conventions' in *Journal of Rural Studies* 19 (1): 87–96, 2003.

Rice, F. and Berlin, R. K., 'How to Deal with Tougher Customers', *Fortune* 122 (14): 38–45, 1990.

Rice, R. A. and McLean, J., Sustainable Coffee at the Crossroads. A White Paper', prepared for the Consumer's Choice Council, 15 October 1999 (cited 14 March 2006), available from www.greenbeanery.ca/bean/documents/sustainableCoffee.pdf, 1999.

Riisgaard, L., 'Global Value Chains, Labor Organization and Private Social Standards: Lessons from East African Cut Flower Industries' in *World Development* 37 (2): 326–40, 2009.

Roberts, S., 'Supply Chain Specific? Understanding the Patchy Success of Ethical Sourcing Initiatives' in *Journal of Business Ethics* 44 (2): 159–70, 2003.

Shreck, A., 'Just Bananas? Fair Trade Banana Production in the Dominican Republic' in *International Journal of Sociology of Agriculture and Food* 10 (2): 13–23, 2002.

——, 'Resistance, Redistribution, and Power in the Fair Trade Banana Initiative' in *Agriculture and Human Values* 22 (1): 17–29, 2005.

Slob, B. and Oldenziel, J., Coffee and Codes: Overview of Codes of Conduct and Ethical Trade Initiatives in the Coffee Sector', Amsterdam, SOMO, 2003.

Smith, A., 'The EU Banana Regime is Dead: Long Live the EU Banana Regime!' in *Banana Link*, 24 January 2006 (cited July 30 2009), available from www.ibc2.org// index.php?option=com_content&task=view&id=15&Itemid=14.

Steele, J., 'Trying to Stop the Famines of Tomorrow: Background Report on the Long-term Problems of Ethiopia', *The Guardian*, 16 July 1985 (cited 10 August 2007), available from www.lexisnexis.com.

Sustainable Food News, 'Critics Contend TransFair Cozying up to Big Coffee Buyers' in *Sustainable Food News*, 11 May 2007 (cited 27 July 2009), available from www.organicconsumers.org/articles/article_5322.cfm.

Tallontire, A., 'Partnerships in Fair Trade: Reflections from a Case Study of Cafédirect' in *Development in Practice* 10 (2): 166–77, 2000.

——, 'Fair Trade and Development' in *The Guide to Developing Agricultural Markets and Agro-Enterprises*, World Bank, 2001.

Tallontire, A. and Greenhalgh, P., Establishing CSR Drivers in Agribusiness, Final Report for Foreign Investment Advisory Service International Financial Corporation and World Bank', Natural Resources Institute, August 2005 (cited 20 August 2008), available from www.ifc.org/ifcext/economics.nsf/AttachmentsByTitle/CSR-FINAL+Report+on+CSR+Drivers+in+Agribusiness/$FILE/FIAS+CSR+drivers+final.pdf.

Taylor, J. G. and Scharlin, P. J., *Smart Alliance: How a Global Corporation and Environmental Activists Transformed a Tarnished Brand*, New Haven, CT, Yale University Press, 2004.

Taylor, P. L., 'In the Market but Not of It: Fair Trade Coffee and Forest Stewardship Council Certification as Market-based Social Change' in *World Development* 33 (1): 129–47, 2005.

U.S. Department of Labor, 'By the Sweat and Toil of Children', Washington, DC, U.S. Department of Labor, Bureau of International Labor Affairs, 1997.

UCIRI, UCIRI: Unión de Comunidades Indígenas de la Región del Istmo (Union of Indigenous Communities of the Isthmus Region), Paper read at The Second International Conference on Gross National Happiness: Rethinking Development: Local Pathways to Global Wellbeing, 20–24 June, at Antigonish, Nova Scotia, Canada, 2005.

Urry, M., 'Campaign To Put The Green Into Shopping', *Financial Times* (London), 12 September 1988 (cited 10 August 2007), available from www.lexisnexis.com.

Vallely, P. and McElvoy, A., 'Capturing the Flavour of Justice; Labelling, the Good Life' in *Spectrum*, Times Newspapers Limited, 19 July 1989 (cited 9 May 2006), available from www.lexis-nexis.com.

Vidal, J., '*Nestlé Launch of Fairtrade Coffee Divides Company's Critics*' in *The Guardian*, 7 October 2005 (cited 27 July 2009), available from www.guardian.co.uk/business/2005/oct/07/ethicalbusiness.fairtrade.

Webb, A., 'How Fair is Fairtrade?', BBC News, 9 March 2006 (cited 30 July 2009), available from http://news.bbc.co.uk/2/hi/business/4788662.stm.

Weitzman, H., 'The Bitter Cost of "Fair Trade" Coffee' in *Financial Times* (London), 8 September 2006 (cited 30 July 2009), available from www.ft.com/cms/s/2/d191adbc-3f4d-11db-a37c-0000779e2340.html.

Zonneveld, L., *2001–2002: The Year in Review*, Fairtrade Labelling Organizations (FLO) International, February 2003 (cited 28 July 2008), available from http://web.archive.org/web/20030220131324/www.fairtrade.net/sites/news/onetonine/two.htm.

Fair trade and development: A changing paradigm

Daniel Jaffee

By the time the fair trade movement celebrated the 20th anniversary of its founding in 2008, it had been transformed virtually beyond recognition. From a marginal European movement characterized by small ethical companies, non-profit charities, solidarity groups and alternative trading organizations (ATOs) selling coffee and handicrafts to a small group of politicized consumers through alternative world shops, fair trade has become an international market system with annual sales of nearly US $5,000m. (€3,500m.) (FLO 2010), reaching mass audiences of mainstream shoppers across the global North with a wide range of food and non-food products originating from both small producer co-operatives and large agribusiness plantations in nearly 60 nations. Some of the largest transnational food corporations now sell fair trade labelled products, in addition to thousands of smaller companies, and fair trade enjoys widespread consumer recognition in many countries. The fair trade system has also become institutionalized, with a large international certification and co-ordinating body establishing and enforcing generic and product-specific standards, as well as national certification and licensing bodies in 20 countries.

How do the concrete realities of the fair trade movement at 21 years square with the original visions and aspirations of the movement's founders? Does fair trade's success in sales and marketing terms correspond to an equal degree of effectiveness in transforming the material socio-economic (and ecological) conditions of life and work for the movement's intended beneficiaries? And has it succeeded, even if marginally, in altering the highly inequitable terms of global trade for specific primary commodities, or the rules of global trade more generally?

It is instructive to take a brief look at a few of the early conceptualizations of fair trade's aims. Many of the pioneering movement activists vocalized a vision of fair trade that involved the creation of an alternative to the capitalist market system, with distinct institutions that would operate alongside the structures of the deeply inequitable global market. Michael Barratt Brown, the founding chair of the ATOs TWIN and TWIN Trading in the United Kingdom, and author of the first book on fair trade, describes the movement as operating both 'in and against the market' (1993: 156). Brown's analysis, according to author Gavin Fridell, was informed by the insights of radical dependency theorists; he saw fair trade as an approach that could combat structural underdevelopment in the global South by creating an alternative to the 'unequal exchange' that plagued export commodity-dependent farmers and nations. Brown's vision was that of a parallel market, operating on the basis of mutual solidarity between Northern consumers and Southern producers, the latter of whom would be protected from the noxious effects of commodity speculation by guaranteed base prices. However, he also strongly believed that strict market regulation by interventionist states was essential to achieving this vision of a fair market (Fridell 2007: 42–46). Pauline Tiffen, another British movement pioneer, described an early fair trade conference organized by TWIN in the 1980s, in which 'the choice of [the term] *fair* was a deliberate decision to broaden a concept that for us was quite anti-capitalist. Like alternative as in alternative system, a parallel system to the market, a challenge to the capitalist system' (Tiffen 2005). As fair trade began to become institutionalized, however, beginning in the late 1980s with the creation of the Max Havelaar certification for coffee, this challenge to the market underwent a substantial deradicalization, in a conscious strategy to increase the volume of fair trade sales through mainstream retail venues and under existing commercial brands. Fridell asserts that in this process, fair trade became compatible with—rather than antithetical to—the neoliberal economic policies that were dramatically undermining living conditions for the rural (and urban) poor across the global South (Fridell 2007: 53). However, a concern with working to change the terms of the broader unjust global trading system remained for many participants. In 2001 four key fair trade organizations—grouped under the acronym FINE—agreed upon a common definition of fair trade, describing it as:

> a trading partnership, based on dialogue, transparency and respect, that seeks greater equity in international trade. It contributes to sustainable development by offering better trading conditions to, and securing the rights of, marginalized producers and workers – especially in the South. Fair Trade organizations (backed by consumers) are engaged actively in supporting producers, awareness raising, and in campaigning for changes in the rules and practice of conventional international trade.
>
> (FINE 2001: 1)

Even more germane to this chapter, the FINE definition goes on to elaborate a series of instrumental goals. 'Fair Trade's strategic intent', the authors write, is:

— deliberately to work with marginalized producers and workers in order to help them move from a position of vulnerability to security and economic self-sufficiency;
— to empower producers and workers as stakeholders in their own organizations;
— actively to play a wider role in the global arena to achieve greater equity in international trade (FINE 2001: 2).

FAIR TRADE'S DEVELOPMENTAL GOALS: FIVE VISIONS

Is fair trade meeting the developmental vision established by its founders? In attempting to answer this seemingly straightforward question, one encounters a basic problem: there has never been full agreement within the movement on what these goals are, and any partial consensus that may have existed at the outset has long since broken down. Rather, a series of distinct visions, often not explicitly expressed by the actors who hold them, exist side by side.

The five approaches outlined below are not an exhaustive list of the approaches to fair trade; however, they roughly indicate the range of positions within the movement regarding its developmental and political-economic impact. While they are not all incompatible, as the quote from FINE above indicates, some are arguably indeed contradictory. Participants in the international fair trade networks variously conceptualize the primary role of fair trade as: a method of poverty alleviation and successful market integration; a means of empowering producers; a device for redistributing wealth between the global North and South; an approach that can internalize the social and ecological costs of conventional trade and commercial practices; or a tool for leveraging greater corporate accountability and thus social and economic justice. These positions, in turn, reflect a deeper divergence in participants' understanding of the relationship between fair trade and the global market, a topic I address in the following section.

The first set of narratives describes fair trade primarily as a device for ameliorating severe rural poverty in the global South, as well as achieving other essential livelihood improvements denied to small farmers by the inequitable terms of global trade, such as debt reduction, food security, better housing conditions and greater educational opportunities. Fridell refers to this as the 'shaped advantage' approach, in which fair trade 'is viewed as shielding its participants from the worst effects of neoliberal globalization by providing a non-governmental approach to price subsidies and a degree of social welfare in the wake of the death of the "developmental state"' (Fridell 2007: 85). Examples of this framing of fair trade abound. Authors Alex Nicholls and Charlotte Opal describe fair trade as 'a development tool that uses existing capitalist supply chains to return more income to producers' (2005: 32). A declaration by fair trade representatives to the 2004 United Nations Conference on Trade and Development (UNCTAD) stated that fair trade 'represents a more effective mechanism for alleviating poverty than aid or macro-institutional economic intervention' (Asarbolsem *et al.* 2004). The pioneering US coffee roaster Equal Exchange promised consumers in a promotional flyer that by supporting fair trade, 'our trading partners have a chance to break the cycle of poverty and can make the economic choice to farm their land sustainably' (Equal Exchange 2002). In this understanding of fair trade, along with poverty reduction, the successful insertion of small producers into the global market becomes a primary consideration, and the higher minimum price is viewed as the primary tool for achieving this outcome. Diana Gayle of the

UK fair trade certifier Fairtrade Foundation describes fair trade as being 'about working with marginalized producers ... building their sustainability, their understanding of selling and trading and allowing them to survive ... so it's about empowerment and the growth of output and quality for the groups and to get to a point where they no longer need to engage with the fair trade relationship' (cited in Nicholls and Opal 2005).

While until recently comprehensive empirical research on the socio-economic benefits of fair trade was virtually non-existent—especially work comparing producers accessing fair trade markets and similar producers selling to conventional markets—the past few years have seen the publication of a number of case studies confirming that fair trade is associated with real and significant material benefits for small producers. These include higher household incomes and lower rates of indebtedness, greater food security, improved housing, higher rates of educational attainment, and greater use of environmentally sound agricultural practices (e.g. Bacon 2005; Jaffee 2007; Lewis and Runsten 2008; Ruben 2008). On the other hand, various observers (including many of these same authors) have noted the multiple limitations of such benefits: the fact that most producer groups are only able to sell a small portion of their total production at fair trade prices, thereby diluting their effect; the deteriorating real value of fair trade minimum prices themselves; the greatly increased labour demands and costs borne by co-operatives and individual producers to meet fair trade and organic certification requirements and buyers' quality standards; the reduced attractiveness of fair trade for some farmers when conventional prices are high; and the tendency toward intensification (and away from diversification) that can accompany market success for the most efficient producers (see Murray *et al.* 2006; Renard and Perezgrovas 2007; Bacon *et al.* 2008; Jaffee 2008; Mutersbaugh 2008).

The declining purchasing power of the minimum prices for coffee in particular is cited repeatedly by producer organizations and their progressive roaster and NGO allies in the North as a major obstacle to realizing even the poverty reduction promise of fair trade. According to researcher Christopher Bacon, the fair trade base price for organic coffee (which was US $1.41 from the movement's inception until it was raised in 2008 by FLO to $1.55 per pound), has lost over 41% of its value, using only the lower US inflation rate; despite the recent boost, it would need to be over $2.29 per pound today to recoup its former value to producers. Many coffee organizations claim that their members can no longer break even, despite receiving the full fair trade organic price (Bacon *et al.* 2006; Jaffee 2007; Bacon 2010). Yet the nature of price-setting process at the FLO level—essentially, a political impasse between retailers and producers—has impeded the restoration of the minimum prices to levels adequate to provide farmers a sufficient margin. 'Fairtrade's efficacy as a safety net', write Holt-Giménez, Bailey and Sampson, 'is eroding because it is based on a premium price that no longer provides a living wage' (2007: 19).

Of course, all of this ignores other key practices that were originally central to the fair trade model—particularly the maintenance of long-term trading relationships between buyers and producers, and provision of pre-harvest credit. Many fair trade consumers are surprised to learn that neither of these practices is now consistently honoured, especially by the larger transnational firms participating in the fair trade market (see Reed 2009).

Nevertheless, even if fair trade were far more effective at ameliorating rural poverty for participants, this is a meagre goal, a neoliberal goal, compared to the original transformative vision of most movement pioneers. Indeed, the World Bank has for several years embraced fair trade as consistent with its programmes (Farnsworth and Goodman 2006; World Bank 2008). 'The neoliberal position that markets in and of themselves are sufficient to reduce poverty, end hunger, and promote sustainable development', write Holt-Giménez, Bailey and Sampson, 'is a notion that has been refuted by two decades of disastrous corporate-led globalization' (2007: 18).

A second view frames fair trade as primarily a means of empowering small producers—and in some cases, waged labourers—as the second strategic goal in the FINE definition above indicates. Does fair trade empower? An obvious question is, empower whom? That is, who are the intended beneficiaries of fair trade? The movement was founded explicitly as an alternative market for the products of highly marginalized small peasant farmers and producers of tropical commodities such as coffee, cacao, bananas and tea, who were expected to organize collectively in order to access the fair trade market. The general thrust of the critique by early fair traders of the unjust terms of global trade focused squarely upon the impoverishment generated by the triple burden of miserably low crop prices for peasant farmers (along with the resultant cycle of debt), the volatility of commodity speculation, and the predatory role of local and international intermediaries. Thus, creating shorter, more direct, and less exploitative trading relations was seen as the route to achieving higher and more stable prices and greater economic justice for farmers. However, particularly in the past five years, the FLO system has made a dramatic expansion into crops produced not by small farmers but by waged workers on plantations and estates. The fair trade standards in this newer 'plantation modality' are distinct: they stipulate payment of national minimum wages (though not necessarily a living wage); respect for the right to organize (though not a requirement for the presence of an independent labour union); adherence to minimum ILO labour standards; a prohibition on the use of the worst agrochemicals; and payment of the fair trade social premium into a fund to be administered by a 'joint body' composed of both labour and management. While they initially represented a negligible share of total fair trade volume (primarily for crops such as tea, where smallholder co-operative production was temporarily insufficient to meet consumer demand), plantation crops in the past five years have come to represent a steadily increasing proportion of fair trade certified products. Virtually all of the new products introduced by FLO—key among them cut flowers, tropical fruits and fruit juices, and wine—are produced primarily or exclusively on plantations, rather than by small producers, and may well come to represent the majority of fair trade volumes in the near future (Dickinson 2004). This is a significant shift, one opposed by the overwhelming majority of small producer representatives to FLO, as well as many Northern fair trade NGOs and retailers. The US fair trade coffee roaster Equal Exchange publicly stated its 'belief that the very nature of plantations is antithetical to the goals of fair trade … [t]he company believes that "fair trade" needs to mean "small farmer"' (Equal Exchange 2009).

Thus, the question of whether fair trade empowers is not as straightforward as it might appear. Furthermore, it depends which aspects of fair trade are viewed as empowering; the premise that the economic benefits alone empower farmers is controversial. Holt-Giménez, Bailey and Sampson write that marketers who 'claim that Fairtrade "empowers farmers" are in essence claiming certification is the small adjustment needed to make good on the neoliberal promise' (2007:18). However, several empirical studies do point to important, less quantifiable processes of personal and collective transformation that take place for producers when they organize and begin to engage with value-added markets such as fair trade, aided both by the power of numbers and by the greater transparency and consistency these markets can offer. Others describe important dynamics of gender empowerment in which women are able to assume key decision-making roles through their co-op membership that were formerly closed to them; still other studies cite the greater ability of co-operative members to demand and obtain services and financial resources from state entities in some contexts (e.g. Shreck 2002; Jaffee 2007; Bray *et al.* 2008). If small producers are organized in democratic co-operative organizations, then, the response to whether fair trade empowers is a qualified yes.

If the fair trade participants are waged labourers on certified plantations, on the other hand, the answer is less clear. Several observers have raised questions about whether the higher fair trade prices and premiums actually translate into material improvement for workers. A recent story in the *Times* of London claimed that workers on some Indian fair trade tea plantations had experienced no benefits at all from certification (Bahra 2009); other reports indicate that unionization is non-existent on any fair trade certified flower plantations in notoriously union-hostile Colombia. Bama Athreya, the executive director of the NGO International Labor Rights Forum, stated that '[w]e wonder if Transfair [USA] is equipped to deal with worker-rights violations, especially as they expand and get into more complex supply-chain industries' (Goigoi 2008).

A third approach views fair trade as a tool for redistributing wealth. The worsening terms of trade for primary commodities for Southern nations and producers, a trend underway for much of the 20th century but especially pronounced since the 1970s, were central to the analysis of fair trade's founders. Their work was infused with a strong moral thread, which stressed the imperative of achieving greater distributive justice for marginalized small farmers who were trapped in a cycle of low farm prices and recurring debt. Coffee producing nations currently retain less than 10% of the retail price of

coffee, down from approximately one-third in the era of the International Coffee Agreement, a supply management pact which was in effect from the 1960s until 1989. The obscene differences between farmgate prices and retail prices—for example, conventional small coffee farmers can receive as little as 1% of the purchase price of the beans they grow—focused the early fair traders' attention on the composition of the supply chain and the necessity of eliminating exploitative intermediaries, thereby shortening the distance between producers and consumers and freeing up extra capital that could flow to farmers in the form of a fairer price.

And fair trade has indeed succeeded in redistributing capital. The national certifier Transfair USA calculates that from US consumer purchases alone, fair trade has transferred more than US $148m. above prevailing market prices into the pockets of farmers since 1998 (Transfair USA 2009). Yet while this does constitute a distinct and more remunerative market, these amounts alone are obviously inadequate to alter the scale of the structural injustice affecting small producers. Moreover, the fair trade prices and premiums still represent a very small portion of the value to be realized along the commodity chain—for example, the fair trade farmgate prices (the amount that actually reaches farmers, as opposed to their organizations) are only between 5% and 15% of the retail price of coffee. (Because green coffee loses weight in the roasting process, this relationship is not exact; however, it does serve as a useful benchmark for comparison). The majority of the profit is captured in the North, in processing, packaging and retailing—activities in which only a handful of producer organizations hold any stake. Equal Exchange co-founder Jonathan Rosenthal asserts that 'one of our biggest challenges is that fair trade … isn't particularly fair. It's much better, and it can be very powerful relative to what the alternative is—business as usual. But if I look at the way that I live, and the way a coffee farmer lives in Nicaragua, say—what's fair about their life compared to my life? How can you say this is *fair* trade, almost as if it's enough?' (Rosenthal 2005). Add to this the problem of stagnating real fair trade minimum prices, and the challenges to realizing the premise of meaningful distributive justice through fair trade appear fairly daunting.

A fourth conceptualization of fair trade is that of a tool for internalizing the social and environmental costs of conventional trade and business practices. Because of the existence of uniform labour standards and independent third-party licensing, fair trade certification at least theoretically poses a barrier to the extreme exploitation of small farmers and waged labourers by large commercial firms and estate owners; firms that want to participate will face greater constraints on their behaviour, and thus potentially reduced profits. In the same way, the ban in FLO standards on the use of the worst agrochemicals, and the synergy between fair trade and organic certifications (especially considering the ecosystem-protecting services rendered by organic practices) would seem to constrain firms' ability to externalize environmental costs. 'At present', write Nicholls and Opal, 'the vast majority of businesses do not

internalize the costs of their social and environmental impacts. By contrast, the fair trade movement believes that in order for trade to be sustainable, and not to distort markets, the full social, environmental and economic costs of goods and services must be taken into account' (2005: 27). The Equal Exchange promotional flyer quoted above claims that fair trade allows farmers the economic freedom to engage in sustainable agricultural practices (Equal Exchange 2002).

To what extent are such claims valid? Fair trade clearly does increase producer incomes in many cases, directing additional capital to farmers and their communities in the form of higher prices as well as social premiums that can fund infrastructure or other projects at the household or village level. When combined with organic production practices, fair trade is also associated with more ecologically beneficial farming practices (and in many case with higher farmgate prices), although these practices also frequently involve higher labour costs as well. On the other hand, some current developments in the fair trade system threaten to undermine these potential benefits. The first is the dramatically increased participation of large mainstream commercial firms, some of them transnational corporations, in the fair trade market. The most notable cases are in the coffee market, where the specialty coffee giant Starbucks, along with the dominant mass marketers Procter & Gamble, Sara Lee, Nestlé and even Coca-Cola have received certification for individual lines of fair trade coffee. While this development has greatly increased total fair trade coffee volumes (Starbucks alone accounted for over one-quarter of the certified beans purchased in the USA in 2008, according to Transfair USA 2009), it also permits these firms to dabble in the fair trade market at a miniscule proportion of their total purchases (in the cases of the other four firms listed above, less than 1% of overall volumes). In this situation, participating in fair trade does not ameliorate the negative social or environmental externalities caused by these firms, except for the small proportion of their production that is actually fair trade certified. Second, the increase in the proportion of certified goods coming from agribusiness plantations—which places the fair trade imprimatur upon crops produced using many of the worst conventional agricultural and labour practices, with only minimal changes—further weakens the claim that the fair trade seal connotes an assurance of sustainability. Finally, the structural nature of the market economy limits the extent of internalization that is possible, even for the most ethical companies. Fair trade products have to compete on the basis of price with other comparable products for consumers. While in some cases shoppers are willing to pay slightly higher prices for fair trade goods, and the shorter fair trade supply chains (bypassing some traditional intermediaries in some cases) do allow the freeing up of additional capital to producers, there are also very real limits to this flow of value, unless producers are able to obtain an equity stake in the retailing of their products in Northern markets. It is also worth noting that for large corporate retailers, selling fair trade goods in no way implies that their detrimental labour or environmental practices in the country of sale have

been altered. This allows Walmart, for example, to sell fair trade certified coffee for US $5.99 per pound, undercutting its competitors by subsidizing the price precisely because it can externalize social and ecological costs for the vast majority of its other products.

A fifth and final conceptualization of fair trade is that of a device for leveraging greater corporate accountability. As large corporations have entered the fair trade certification system, they have caused dramatic volume growth, but also generated substantial tensions and contradictions, partly discussed above. However, this approach views corporate involvement as a valuable opportunity to change the overall behaviour of large firms that have in some cases earned a reputation as 'bad actors'. Nestlé, for example, was for two decades the target of NGO campaigns excoriating the corporation for its destructive infant formula marketing practices in the global South. Is fair trade a mechanism that can effect changes in these damaging practices, holding firms accountable for their overall corporate behaviour? Or does the fair trade seal instead serve as window-dressing for companies' image-enhancement efforts regarding their corporate social responsibility—a 'fig leaf' allowing them to 'fair-wash' their larger record (see, for example, Renard 2005; Fridell 2007; Reed 2009)? The movement is deeply divided over this question. When Nestlé received certification in 2005 for its Partners Blend coffee line (comprising less than 0.2% of its coffee supply), Harriet Lamb, the director of the UK certifier Fairtrade Foundation, declared that 'it's an incredible step for Nestlé, one of the four biggest companies, to recognize the values of fair trade'. However, much of the reaction from within the movement was negative. One Latin American coffee producer representative asked: 'We thought this fair trade would help us escape the practices of companies like Nestlé. How can it be that they are now a fair trade company, buying a tiny amount, while their practices on the whole remain as exploitative as ever?' (both quoted in Tucker 2006: 7). Such 'dabbling' is possible because neither the FLO system nor the national certifiers stipulate a minimum percentage level for entry into the fair trade market, nor do they mandate an increase in volumes over time. When a firm can receive fair trade certification (and the highly valuable accompanying public relations benefits) for less than 1% of its total supply chain, with its social and environmental practices unchanged for the remainder, the framing of fair trade as a corporate accountability device is a questionable one. On the other hand, if certifiers were to pursue more zealously the regulatory function with which they are charged—for example, if they required steadily increasing volume levels over time, or conditioned certification upon an evaluation of companies' overall practices—fair trade might be able to serve as a wedge to force greater accountability. However, the certifiers insist that these concerns are beyond their purview. Paul Rice, the CEO of Transfair USA, says that 'we feel like rather than taking a regulatory, or even a punitive, approach to this whole question, the best thing we can do is engage the best we can with the industry around expectations and commitments to growth' (Rice 2005). The certifier's

'Corporate Engagement Guidelines' state that 'Transfair's certification and audit system focuses on Fair Trade Certified products, not a company's overall business practices ... It is beyond the scope of Transfair's certification model to try to address these concerns or to provide a comprehensive corporate social responsibility (CSR) rating' (Transfair USA 2008). Thus, while fair trade does have the potential to serve a role in creating greater corporate accountability, its key institutions have opted not to exercise this power.

It is important to note that none of the five perspectives discussed above directly addresses a key element prominent in the vision of most of the founders of fair trade, one which is summarized by the call in FINE's definitional document to 'play a wider role in the global arena to achieve greater equity in international trade' (2001: 2). The following section takes on this question more explicitly.

THE ROLE OF FAIR TRADE VIS-À-VIS THE GLOBAL MARKET

The disjunctures described in the previous section owe their existence to a deeper and more fundamental set of divergences within fair trade over participants' understanding of the relationship between this alternative movement and the larger market—that is, over the question of whether fair trade functions principally within the logic of global capitalism or whether it presents a distinct challenge to that system. Owing in part to the split origins of the movement, which emerged both from radical solidarity activist organizations with a deep critique of international capitalism on the one hand, and from liberal religious charities and secular development NGOs on the other, fair trade has been characterized since its inception by multiple diagnoses of the core problems, as well as multiple prescriptions for action. The range of positions within the movement has also shifted and broadened over the past two decades as the fair trade market has grown dramatically, the certification system has become institutionalized, transnational companies have entered fair trade, and the perspectives of these larger commercial firms—along with more reformist NGOs, international financial institutions and other actors—are added to the mix.

Underlying the original vision of fair trade's pioneers was a profound conviction that the global market is fundamentally broken—that it works to harm, rather than benefit, small peasant producers. Markets, to paraphrase the argument of the influential Hungarian economic historian Karl Polanyi, had traditionally been 'embedded' within systems of social and moral obligation and reciprocity, but beginning with the industrial revolution they became the organizing principal of the entire economy and society, wreaking severe social and environmental damage. Polanyi viewed the broad range of social and labour movements, and the resulting creation of welfare states in Europe, North America and elsewhere, as 'movements of self-protection' that by the post-Second World War period had succeeded in taming and reregulating markets—'re-embedding' them to once again serve society (Polanyi 1944).

However, the revival since 1980 of the doctrine of unfettered markets and free mobility for capital—and the accompanying neoliberal policies of structural adjustment, debt management and export-led development that have been applied across the global South by Northern financial institutions and governments—have notably deepened the immiseration of both Southern states and citizens. Several observers of fair trade have applied a Polanyian framework to the fair trade movement, asking whether it does or can succeed in re-embedding economic exchange (e.g. Raynolds 2000; Hudson and Hudson 2004; Mutersbaugh 2005; Fridell 2007; Jaffee 2007).

While many current fair trade participants might answer that general question in the affirmative, there has long been a lack of consensus within the movement on the tactical and strategic questions of how such re-embedding might be achieved. This divergence predated the entry of transnational corporations into the fair trade system, and has been sharpened by their participation. One of the axes of tension—particularly pronounced in the US context—is between two distinct groups of fair trade retailers: on the one hand, small and medium-sized companies selling largely or entirely fair trade certified products, most with long histories of collaboration with producer groups and communities, and on the other, the large publicly-traded corporate firms that account for an increasingly large proportion of fair trade sales volumes. The divergence between these movement-oriented and profit-oriented firms has in turn given rise to another set of tensions, pitting progressive movement-oriented NGOs and membership-based fair trade groups against FLO and some national certifiers, along with a more moderate group of NGOs. These differences emerge in concrete form around practical questions of policy, standards formulation, and governance in the FLO system. The most contentious of these have been described above: the desirability of transnational corporate participation (and under which conditions); the appropriateness of increased fair trade production from agribusiness plantations; and the level of the minimum prices and the process for adjusting them. The decisions by the US and UK certifiers to license Starbucks and Nestlé, respectively, generated especially virulent controversy between these various constituencies.

Yet beneath these policy battles lies a deeper set of differences between various participants over the nature of the relationship between fair trade and the 'unfair' global market. Is fair trade principally an adjunct to the dominant market that can ameliorate some of its harshest features for a small subset of farmers and labourers? Does it constitute a set of genuinely alternative trading structures that have the potential to reform the functioning of global markets, thereby tipping the balance in favour of small producers? Or does it represent a means of radically transforming the global capitalist economy, altering the basic functioning of international trade and moving toward a genuinely equitable global economy? Another, subsidiary, set of questions flows from these. How does fair trade relate to (and how is it affected by) the rules, policies and institutions of international trade, especially those of the global economic managers—the World Trade Organization, the

International Monetary Fund, and the World Bank? And how does the concrete purchasing of fair trade certified commodities relate to broader movements and projects that aim to achieve greater trade and economic justice?

Examining the record of the fair trade movement to date can help indicate which of these three descriptions is in fact closest to reality. The previous sections have considered the policy developments within fair trade around four key issues: the issue of mainstreaming and corporate entry; the conditions for ongoing corporate participation; the level and real value of minimum prices; and the role of plantations in fair trade. Other contentious issues within the movement include: struggles over formal producer representation within the FLO governance structure (their numbers have increased, but still constitute a minority) (Renard 2006); the extent to which corporate participation has actually weakened or diluted the standards underpinning fair trade (see Thompson and Coskuner-Balli 2007; Fridell *et al.* 2008; Jaffee and Howard 2010); and the process—by now well advanced—of harmonizing the FLO standards with other global standards regimes, such as those of the International Standards Organization and the WTO (Mutersbaugh 2005).

Examining the evidence, it seems clear that the fair trade movement has since its early days moved away from its foundational aspirations of market transformation and/or market reform. At the start of its third decade, fair trade functions largely as an adjunct to the market— a tool primarily for achieving market access and poverty amelioration—rather than constituting a truly alternative set of trading institutions or presenting a fundamental challenge either to the overall terms of global trade or to prevailing industry practices. There are, of course, noteworthy exceptions to this broad generalization. At the same time, the fair trade system has in the same two decades grown substantially, reaches large numbers of mainstream consumers, and increasingly generates real (and sometimes significant) material benefits for producers, in large part because of this very process of deradicalization. This paradox may be cold comfort for advocates of a vision of fair trade as a more holistic, more transformative economic social movement. However, it is precisely because fair trade *does* have the potential to force far more substantial changes—possibly even becoming a force capable of reforming global markets (that is, if there were substantial internal policy reforms)—that such advocates might do well to consider continuing to work to change the system, either from the inside and/or outside.

THE FUTURE OF FAIR TRADE

What awaits the fair trade movement? Is it possible to extrapolate from current trends to imagine the state of the movement in the medium-term future, say a decade from now? I take two different approaches to addressing these questions, examining some qualitatively new developments that may take fair trade in unanticipated directions, and looking at the issue of the growth of the formal certification system.

Within the past several years, fair trade activists have begun to extend the traditional South-North model in some intriguing new directions. The first of these is the advent of domestic fair trade. As the limitations to the capacity of international fair trade markets to absorb the production of small producer organizations became more apparent in the 1990s (the average fair trade coffee co-operative on the FLO register can only find buyers at fair trade prices for less than 25% of its harvest), and as organized producers of other crops (those without certification or unable to meet international quality demands) were shut out from value-added markets entirely, some producer groups and NGO allies in the South began to apply the international fair trade model to a domestic context. Beginning in Mexico with the NGO Comercio Justo Mexico (Fair Trade Mexico), these advocates created a national certification system for the products of small producer co-operatives, seeking to build markets among domestic consumers by appealing to values of social solidarity with marginalized peasant and indigenous farmers. These efforts soon expanded to Brazil and South Africa, both of which have seen the state take an active role in fomenting demand for national fair trade products. These efforts dovetail with the growing 'solidarity economy' movement, which is particularly strong in South America (Renard and Perezgrovas 2007; Wilkinson and Mascarenhas 2007). In a distinct but analogous development, groups of family farmers and progressive NGOs in the USA have also experimented with creating domestic fair trade initiatives, linking economically-struggling dairy, fruit and nut farmers with urban consumer markets under several new labelling initiatives. A set of domestic fair trade standards has also been developed by a coalition of farmworker justice and agriculture and trade policy groups, with certification predicated upon living wages for labourers and a fair price for farmers; these products recently made their debut in some regions of the USA (Jaffee, Kloppenburg and Monroy 2004; Agricultural Justice Project 2008).

The other innovation with the potential to alter the trajectory of fair trade is the creation of fair trade companies with direct producer equity co-ownership. As of this writing, at least two such firms exist: Cafédirect, a sizeable ATO with a one-third share of the UK coffee and tea markets (Nicholls and Opal 2005: 122), which is at least 5% owned by its producer co-operative members; and the Day Chocolate Company, which sells its Divine Chocolate products in both the UK and USA, in which the Ghanaian producer group Kuapa Kokoo holds a 45% equity stake. Further extension of this model of capturing added value, which Doherty and Tranchell (2007) term 'radical mainstreaming', could go a long way toward redressing the serious limitations on the flow of capital to producers under the conventional fair trade model.

A second major issue is the growth of fair trade. That the market for fairly traded products will continue to grow is highly likely, but what kind of growth will it be? This is a question of means and ends, one which encapsulates many of the intra-movement splits discussed in the previous sections. The international fair trade movement and system are divided over what model of growth to pursue. One vision involves volume growth as the preeminent movement goal, to be achieved by any means possible in order to benefit the greatest number of producers and organizations. In this view, the increasing certification of agribusiness plantations is seen as a logical route to rapid growth, because they are most capable of meeting retailers' demand for high volumes and new certified products efficiently. Yet this approach is controversial. 'The fair trade movement has grown so fast', says former CEO of certifier Max Havelaar Switzerland and former FLO board member Paola Ghillani, 'but has forgotten to invest enough in growth management like normal companies' (quoted in Bahra 2009). Transfair USA's CEO Paul Rice, dismissing criticism that further certification of plantations would harm small producers of the same crops, responded that '[t]he disadvantaged majority would be locked out of the market if I were to look only for small farms for bananas and tea' (quoted in Goigoi 2008). The other approach is diametrically opposed: a vision of intentionally slower market growth, with increased attention paid to retaining the movement's foundational values and principles. The FLO system is 'trying to increase the number of people in the fair trade movement', says pioneer Michael Barratt Brown, 'but at the expense, I fear, of some of the principles' (Brown 2004). In one concrete example of this divergence, all of the fair trade coffee producer organizations joined forces in 2004 to mount fierce resistance to FLO's proposal to allow plantation certification for coffee, a plan which was defeated and is currently dormant. Likewise, three other products remain closed to plantation certification—cacao, honey and cotton—but these four crops are likely to be the only exceptions to fair trade's expansion into the waged labour sector at the expense of small farmer co-operatives.

CONCLUSIONS

This chapter has attempted to assess the current state of the politics of the fair trade movement, and address whether fair trade has met the developmental and political-economic visions set out by its founders. But in order to come to any meaningful conclusions about fair trade's efficacy, one needs to answer a key question: what constitutes success? Given that fundamental divergences have riven the movement over basic goals and policy choices, is agreement on what it would look like even possible? With different groups of advocates passionately defending metrics of success that range from rapid sales volume growth and increased corporate engagement and expansion of the plantation sector, to 'deep fair trade', characterized by slow growth, the exclusive participation of small producers and an emphasis on building truly alternative commercial models and institutions, there often seems to be little common ground. While very few participants have left the formal certification system over these divisions so far, there is evidence of growing strains in holding the fair trade coalition together. Many movement 100% fair trade retailers—particularly in the USA—have opted to leave the FLO certification system and switch to the new 'Fair For Life' seal administred by the certifier IMO, and the organized producer assemblies within FLO have expressed great dissatisfaction with the stagnating minimum prices and increasing certification of plantations; on the other hand, some commercial firms insist that they are paying too much for fair trade goods. Whether the FLO system is capable of resolving these tensions to the satisfaction of most or all parties is far from certain.

What will the fair trade label signify in the future? With the movement currently undergoing a struggle over the soul of the seal, it is possible to imagine a few distinct alternative paths. One scenario, based on current trends, involves the proliferation of new fair trade plantation products, an ever-larger role for large companies, and further marginalization of small farmer groups (in most or all products) and mission-oriented retailers. Another potential route could involve FLO acknowledging the need to accommodate the concerns of small farmers and small retailers, and undertaking a modest restructuring of the initiative's governance to provide these groups greater representation and defuse tensions. A third possibility might be that the large commercial firms in the system opt to focus more upon their own first-party corporate social responsibility initiatives—over which they can exert far more control than the fair trade standards—and begin to reduce their participation in the fair trade market, leaving the niche to a growing number of small and medium-sized firms. A corollary to this might be the marginalization of fair trade by an increasing number of alternative eco-labels, with consumers confused by the welter of competing claims.

Ultimately, however, all of these debates over contending policy options and models of growth within the fair trade system encounter the same fundamental problem: market- and consumption-based approaches alone will not render the global economy fair. The formal fair trade system and movement would do well to explore how to fuse the concrete commodity certification initiative with deeper and broader social movements for economic and environmental justice. Particularly during the current economic crisis, in which the deeply flawed nature of neoliberal economic dogma has finally been revealed to large numbers of people as well as governments worldwide, the fair trade movement should also recognize that without substantially increased state and supra-state (re-)regulation of global capital, there will be little chance of achieving a fundamentally more just global economy.

Finally, fair trade could benefit greatly from returning as much as possible toward the loose consensus vision of its founders. This would involve working to ensure that fair trade becomes not merely bigger but fairer for its intended beneficiaries, and striving to make it truly a countervailing force to the unjust terms and structures of global economic exchange. It means building, in other words, a more moral economy.

BIBLIOGRAPHY

Agricultural Justice Project, *Social Stewardship Standards in Organic and Sustainable Agriculture: Full Standards Document*. Minneapolis, MN, Agricultural Justice Project, 2008.

Asarbolsem *et al.*, 'Fair Trade Declaration – UNCTAD XI – Sao Paulo', http://fairtrade-advocacy.org/images/stories/publications/ft_declaration_unctad11_jun04.pdf, accessed 20 June 2009. 2004.

Bacon, C., 'Confronting the Coffee Crisis: Can Fair Trade, Organic, and Specialty Coffees Reduce Small-Scale Farmer Vulnerability in Northern Nicaragua?' in *World Development* 33(3): 497, 2005.

Bacon, C., 'Who Decides What is Fair in Fair Trade? The Agro-environmental Governance of Standards, Accesss, and Price. *Journal of Peasant Studies* 37: 111–147, 2010.

Bacon, C., CAFENICA and C. Coordinadora Latinoamericana y del Caribe de Pequenos Productores de Comercio Justo, *Estudio de Costos y Propuesta de Precios para Sostener el Café, las Familias Productores y Organizaciones Certificadas por Comercio Justo en America Latina y el Caribe*: Coordinadora Latinoamericana y del Caribe de Pequenos Productores de Comercio Justo, CLAC, 2006.

Bacon, C., Ernesto Méndez, V., Gómez, M. E. F., Stuart, D. and Flores, S. R. D., 'Are Sustainable Coffee Certifications Enough to Secure Farmer Livelihoods? The Millenium Development Goals and Nicaragua's Fair Trade Cooperatives' in *Globalizations* 5(2): 259–74, 2008.

Bahra, P., 'Tea Workers Still Waiting to Reap Fairtrade Benefits' in *The Times* (London), www.timesonline.co.uk/tol/news/uk/article5429888.ece, accessed 8 January 2009, 2009.

Bray, D. B., Plaza Sánchez, J. L. and Contreras Murphy, E., 'Social Dimensions of Organic Coffee Production in Mexico: Lessons for Eco-Labeling Initiatives' in *Confronting the Coffee Crisis: Fair Trade, Sustainable Livelihoods and Ecosystems in Mexico and Central America* in C. Bacon, V. E. Mendez, S. R. Gliessman, D. Goodman and J. Fox (eds), Cambridge, MA, MIT Press: 237–60, 2008.

Brown, M. B., *Fair Trade: Reform and Realities in the International Trading System*, London, Zed, 1993.

Brown, M. B., Founder and Director, TWIN Trading; Co-founder, Cafédirect. Personal Communication. Madison, WI, 28 July 2004.

Dickinson, R., Co-Director, Equal Exchange Coffee. Personal Communication, Canton, MA, 25 May 2004.

Doherty, B. and Tranchell, S., '"Radical Mainstreaming" of Fairtrade: The Case of The Day Chocolate Company' in *Equal Opportunities International* 26(7): 693, 2007.

Equal Exchange, 'Our Mission' (www.equalexchange.com/intro/eeintro5.html), accessed 7 September 2002.

——, 'Equal Exchange Joins Critique of Fair Trade Plantations: Tea Estate Workers Voice Skepticism Over Ethical Claims' (www.equalexchange.coop/equal-exchange-joins-critique-of-fair-trade-plantations), accessed 3 March 2009.

Farnsworth, C. and Goodman, M., *Growing Ethical Networks: the Fair Trade Market for Raw and Processed Agricultural Products: Background Paper for the World Development Report 2008*, Washington, DC, World Bank, 2006.

FINE, 'Fair Trade Definition and Principles', FINE, 2001.

FLO, *Growing Stronger Together: Annual Report 2009–10*. Bonn, Germany, FLO, 2010.

Fridell, G., *Fair Trade Coffee: The Prospects and Pitfalls of Market-Driven Social Justice*, Toronto, University of Toronto Press, 2007.

Fridell, M., Hudson, I. and Hudson, M. 'With Friends Like These: The Corporate Response to Fair Trade' in *Review of Radical Political Economy* 40(1): 8–34, 2008.

Goigoi, P., 'Is Fair Trade Becoming "Fair Trade Lite"?' *Business Week*, 18 June 2008.

Holt-Giménez, E., Bailey, I. and Sampson, D., *Fair to the Last Drop: The Corporate Challenges to Fair Trade Coffee*. Oakland, CA: Food First, 2007.

Hudson, M. and Hudson, I., 'Justice, Sustainability, and the Fair Trade Movement: A Case Study of Coffee Production in Chiapas', in *Social Justice* 31(3): 130, 2004.

Jaffee, D., *Brewing Justice: Fair Trade Coffee, Sustainability, and Survival*, Berkeley, California, University of California Press, 2007.

——, '"Better, But Not Great": The Social and Environmental Benefits and Limitations of Fair Trade for Indigenous Coffee Producers in Oaxaca, Mexico' in *The Impact of Fair Trade*, R. Ruben (ed.) Wagenigen, Netherlands, Wagenigen Academic Publishers: 195–222, 2008.

Jaffee, D. and Howard, P. H., 'Corporate Cooptation of Organic and Fair Trade standards' in *Agriculture and Human Values* 27(4): 387–399, 2010.

Jaffee, D., Kloppenburg, J. R. and Monroy, M. B., 'Bringing the "Moral Charge" Home: Fair trade within the North and within the South' in *Rural Sociology* 69(2): 169–96, 2004.

Lewis, J. and Runsten, D., 'Is Fair Trade-Organic Coffee Sustainable in the Face of Migration? Evidence from a Oaxacan Community' in *Globalizations* 5(2): 275–90, 2008.

Murray, D. L., Raynolds, L. T. and Taylor, P. L., 'The Future of Fair Trade Coffee: Dilemmas Facing Latin America's Small-Scale Producers' in *Development in Practice* 16(2): 179–92, 2006.

Mutersbaugh, T., 'Fighting Standards with Standards: Harmonization, Rents, and Social Accountability in Certified Agrofood Networks' in *Environment and Planning A* 37(11): 2033–51, 2005.

——, 'Serve and Certify: Paradoxes of Service Work in Organic Coffee Certification' in *Confronting the Coffee Crisis: Fair Trade, Sustainable Livelihoods and Ecosystems in Mexico and Central America*, C. Bacon, V. E. Mendez, S. R. Gliessman, D. Goodman and J. Fox (eds), Cambridge, MA, MIT Press: 261–88, 2008.

Nicholls, A. and Opal, C., *Fair Trade: Market-Driven Ethical Consumption*, London, Sage, 2005.

Polanyi, K., *The Great Transformation*, Boston, Beacon Press, 1944.

Raynolds, L. T., 'Re-Embedding Global Agriculture: The International Organic and Fair Trade Movements' in *Agriculture and Human Values* 17(3): 297–309, 2000.

Reed, D., 'What do Corporations have to do with Fair Trade? Positive and Normative Analysis from a Value Chain Perspective' in *Journal of Business Ethics* (86): 3–26, 2009.

Renard, M. C., 'Quality Certification, Regulation and Power in Fair Trade' in *Journal of Rural Studies* 21(4): 419–31, 2005.

——, 'Recomposición de la Gobernancia en el Comercio Justo', paper presented at Coloquio ALTER 2006, Baeza, Jaén, Spain, 18–21 October 2006.

Renard, M. C. and Perezgrovas, V., 'Fair Trade Coffee in Mexico: At the Center of the Debates' in *Fair Trade: The Challenges of Transforming Globalization*, L. T. Raynolds, D. Murray and J. Wilkinson (eds), New York, Routledge: 138–56, 2007.

Rice, P., CEO, Transfair USA, Personal Communication, Seattle, WA, 16 April 2005.

Rosenthal, J., Director, Just Works; Co-founder, Equal Exchange Coffee, Personal Communication, Boston, MA, 27 May 2005.
Ruben, R. (ed.), *The Impact of Fair Trade*, Wagenigen, Netherlands, Wagenigen Academic Publishers, 2008.
Shreck, A., 'Just Bananas? Fair Trade Banana Production in the Dominican Republic' in *International Journal of Sociology of Agriculture and Food* 10: 11–21, 2002.
Thompson, C. J. and Coskuner-Balli, G., 'Countervailing Market Responses to Corporate Co-optation and the Ideological Recruitment of Consumption Communities' in *Journal of Consumer Research* 34: 135–52, 2007.
Tiffen, P., Independent Consultant, Personal Communication, Madison, WI, 4 March 2005.
Transfair USA, 'TransFair USA Corporate Engagement Guidelines' (www.transfairusa.org/content/Downloads/resources/TFUSA_Engagement_Guidelines.pdf, accessed 12 May 2009), 2008.
——, *Almanac: 2008*, Oakland, CA,Transfair USA, 2009.
Tucker, A., 'Fair Enough?' in *New Internationalist* 395: 7, 2006.
Wilkinson, J. and Mascarenhas, G., 'Southern Social Movements and Fair Trade' in *Fair Trade: The Challenges of Confronting Globalization*, L. T. Raynolds, D. Murray and J. Wilkinson (eds), New York, Routledge: 125–37, 2007.
World Bank, *World Development Report*, Washington, DC, World Bank, 2008.

Case studies

Handicrafts

PATRICK C. WILSON

While the current fair trade movement is tied and reacting to the dominance of neoliberal globalization since the 1980s, its historical roots are diverse and include the co-operative movement of the late 19th century (Moore 2004), a concern with exploitative colonial relations of production (Redfern and Snedker 2002), and attempts to combat plummeting prices for primary commodities in the inter-war period (Fridell 2004). The historical developments that most closely resemble the fair trade movement, however, are tied to the formation of Alternative Trading Organizations (ATOs) engaging in 'charity trade' following the end of the Second World War to provide relief to war refugees and marginalized populations. One pioneering project grew out of the charity work of Edna Byler, a layperson for the Mennonite Church. In 1946 she visited a project by volunteers of the Mennonite Central Committee working in Puerto Rico, and began selling the embroidery produced by students in this project from her home through the distribution of mail order catalogues (Redfern and Snedker 2002). Calling her initiative 'SELFHELP: Crafts of the World', successful sales led her to expand to include cross-stitch needlework produced by Palestinian refugees and hand-carved wooden goods produced by Haitians (Witkowski 2005; Redfern and Snedker 2002). Her work eventually became institutionalized under the Mennonite Central Committee and led to the creation of the first alternative trade store in North America, also called SELFHELP, in 1972. SELFHELP was later renamed Ten Thousand Villages in 1996, which now is the largest chain of fair trade retail stores in North America. Also around the end of the Second World War, another ATO, Sales Exchange for Refugee Rehabilitation (SERVV), was formed out of the Church of the Brethren to sell German cuckoo clocks to aid in refugee relief (Low and Davenport 2005). Similarly, in the United Kingdom, Oxfam was formed in 1942 to aid war refugees in Greece.

The institutionalized concept of alternative trade, then, is a product of these developments during and following the Second World War, and the growth of the idea of handicraft production as an alternative means of economic support for marginalized communities grew out of these early initiatives. For example, Oxfam's refugee relief was initially primarily funded through the establishment of charity shops— second-hand stores that would generate revenue for relief efforts. However, by the early 1950s Oxfam began including handicrafts produced by refugees alongside second-hand goods in their stores (Low and Davenport 2005), and the concept of 'alternative trade' became formalized in Great Britain in 1964 when Oxfam UK was officially formed as an 'Alternative Trade Organization' (Witkowski 2005). Similarly, in 1959 an alternative importing organization, SOS (now Fair Trade Organisatie), was established in the Netherlands and the first alternative trade retail store was opened there in 1961 (Witkowski 2005).

In the 1950s and 1960s these early organizations facilitated import sales through mail-order catalogues, and by the 1970s retail outlets, such as SELFHELP, drove alternative trade in handicrafts through a model that focused on politically-motivated solidarity with Third World producers (Tallontire 2000). This represented a continuation of the motivations driving refugee relief work during and following the Second World War, but was now expanded to address concerns of the social and economic conditions of Third World producers, broadly conceived. Alternative trade through retail shops attempted to address questions of social and economic justice through direct relationships (a sense of 'connectivity') with Third World producers and the purchase of their products at a 'fair price' (Bryant and Goodman 2004). The solidarity model revealed the politicized nature of consumption and posited that consumptive practices could, in fact, be transformative in terms of economic and social justice.

The 1970s and early 1980s represented a period of growth for alternative trade in handicrafts, burgeoned by the radical politics of the late 1960s and early 1970s and the rise of dependency theory that illustrated global interconnectedness and the enduring negative political, economic and social consequences of European colonialism. By the early 1990s Oxfam had 625 retail shops in the UK; by 2000 there were approximately 2,700 'world shops' in Europe and 7,000 in the USA and Canada, and the percentage of mail order sales to total fair trade sales had dropped to less than 10% (Moore 2004). Yet the growth of fair trade stores was not an accurate reflection of trends within the fair trade handicraft market. While overall fair trade continued to grow rapidly through the 1990s and into the 2000s, this growth was almost entirely in the food sector; in contrast, by the late-1980s handicraft sales had levelled off, and many of the ATOs dealing in artisan products found themselves in a financial crisis.

There are multiple factors that contributed to the stagnation of the fair trade handicraft market. As previously mentioned, fair trade ATOs were built on a model of solidarity with Third World producers. As the political climate in the global North became more conservative in the late 1980s, the solidarity model was less tenable (Tallontire 2000). Additionally, the quality of fair trade handicrafts was often substandard, but ATOs, due to their adherence to principles of solidarity, purchased these goods to protect small producers from their vulnerability to market forces (Redfern and Snedker 2002). The high prices for lower quality goods, however, deterred many potential consumers from purchasing them. At the same time, the rise of neoliberalism in the 1980s spurred the dismantling of trade barriers and facilitated the growth of conventional markets for imported crafts and other 'exotic' goods. By the late

1980s large-scale retail competition grew from the likes of Pier One Imports and Bombay Trading Company, which sold goods at lower prices than the ATO shops, and cut into the market niche previously held by the ATO sector (Low and Davenport 2005). Finally, the ATOs and the alternative trade model more generally suffered from structural limitations that rendered growth difficult beyond its early niche market. The ATO shops were not high volume retail stores, and artisan crafts, themselves, are typically purchased in smaller volumes and not as likely to receive repeat purchases as foodstuffs.

These structural limitations largely remain in place for fair trade handicrafts, and while no reliable figures exist for the percentage share of the fair trade marketplace commanded by handicrafts, it is estimated that handicrafts may represent 20% of that market, mostly through sales in 'world shops' (Moore 2004). Unlike food commodities, handicrafts are less likely to possess the potential for mainstreaming through product placement in conventional retail outlets, and producers remain reliant on fair trade stores like Ten Thousand Villages or Oxfam, smaller solidarity shops, and increasingly e-commerce for the sale of their products. Furthermore, the prospects for generating domestic markets for fair trade handicrafts in order to control dependence on international consumers of fair trade goods have, thus far, been limited. For example, Comercio Justo México has made progress in creating a market for locally-produced fair trade food commodities in Mexico, complete with a set of certification standards based on international standards and educational outreach programmes (Jaffe *et al.* 2004), but similar results for the commercialization of artisan crafts have been elusive (but see the case study discussed below).

Recently, and in response to shrinking sales and the economic losses suffered by many ATOs at the end of the 1980s and beginning of the 1990s, some ATOs began shifting towards a more interventionist approach to handicraft production, demanding higher quality products and making purchasing dependent on the marketability of the goods being produced (Fridell 2004). Ensuring quality standards has become central to fair trade marketing, through a variety of certification labels attached to commodities. Certification allows for product standardization, thereby guaranteeing high quality products for the consumer (Renard 2003). While certification standards currently exist for a range of fair trade food products and selected other commodities, no universal standards exist for artisan handicraft production. Therefore, the standards used to govern quality in handicraft production are typically established by the NGO or ATO purchasing the crafts, and on a case-by-case basis. Lynn Stephen (2005), for example, recounts how an NGO refused to purchase weavings by a Zapotec weaving co-operative when those goods did not comply with the patterns and colour-schemes requested by the NGO. This move towards ensuring quality standards represents a partial departure from the solidarity model of earlier decades, where ATOs are now attempting to balance the need for profitability with the ideal of solidarity with 'southern' producers. While this may not fully address issues associated with the limited economy of scale for handicrafts, it does signal greater concern with the economic viability and competitiveness of the ATOs.

Handicraft fair trade is regulated according to the principles of fair trade developed by the World Fair Trade Organization (WFTO, formerly IFAT) and Fairtrade Labelling Organizations International, now abbreviated to Fairtrade International (FLO). This includes standards governing labour practices, child labour, gender equality and environmental sustainability, as well as those designed to ensure higher prices for producers. In one estimate (Littrell and Dickson 1997), handicrafts produced through fair trade relationships earned 40% of the retail value of their products, while conventional markets only returned about 10% of the retail value to the producer. Most ATOs distributing and selling handicrafts are members of the WFTO (Raynolds and Long 2007); while there are no existing certification standards for artisan crafts, the WFTO is currently drafting a certification standard that will apply to handicraft producers known as the Sustainable Fair Trade Management System (SFTMS). The SFTMS, like the monitoring system currently in place by the WFTO, will be a voluntary programme. Departing from the existing certification system, however, which is largely based on self-assessment and voluntary adherence to the '10 Principles of Fair Trade', the SFTMS will include third-party evaluation (WFTO 2009), thereby adding a component of external regulation similar to the FLO-CERT system. At the same time, it will be more flexible than the FLO certification standards to accommodate the diverse products and corresponding variation in production techniques and organization of labour common in artisan activities.

GOALS AND CHALLENGES OF HANDICRAFT FAIR TRADE: A CASE STUDY FROM BOLIVIA

A number of studies have illustrated the potential that handicrafts possess for enhancing the domestic economy of small producers. These studies emphasize the creativity and flexibility of handicraft production and labour (Chibnik 2000), the potential that such production in alternative markets or co-operative movements has for resisting the deepening of neoliberalism and its damaging impacts for small, Third World producers (Stephen 2005), and the capacity of these productive activities to ameliorate social marginalization and gender inequality (Nash 1993). From a different vantage point, some researchers have argued that fair and alternative trade in handicrafts has done little to address the core causes of social and gender stratification in society, has contributed to enhancing socio-economic differentiation within communities or productive co-operatives, and often fails to deliver on promises of greater economic prosperity for those engaged in handicraft production (Scrase 2003; Cohen 1998). This divergence in perspectives and analysis points to the unevenness of development outcomes, fair trade or otherwise, and the need to examine not simply a series of case studies and extrapolate universal generalizations from case-specific circumstances, but to seek to discern challenges confronting fair or alternative trade, or ethno-development projects more broadly, that emerge from these varied cases. One of the difficulties associated with evaluating the impacts of artisan fair trade is the paucity of research conducted at the grassroots level with producers of fair trade handicrafts. As a consequence, it is necessary to expand the scope of analysis to include a range of ethno-development projects that may not be formally regulated under fair trade standards, but that share many of the ideals of fair trade, including higher pay for producers, gender equality, social empowerment, and labour standards. Ethno-development emerged as a subfield in development practice in the 1980s, as NGOs sought models for sustainable development that would achieve the dual goals of promoting environmental sustainability and cultural preservation. NGOs working from an ethno-development perspective seek to base projects on activities that will strengthen cultural traditions, arguing that these kinds of development projects can contribute to processes of cultural revitalization. Here, I will rely on an ethnographic case study of weaving co-operatives in Bolivia conducted by Robyn Eversole (2006) to point to some of the opportunities offered by fair trade, including higher incomes and increased gender equality, as well as some of the challenges facing artisan fair trade, including the limits to social empowerment and the need for more nuanced theorizing about the complex socio-cultural context in which artisan production occurs, with implications for class, gender, and social stratification.

Antropólogos del Surandino (ASUR) is a support organization for women weavers in the region surrounding Sucre, Bolivia. Established in the mid-1980s by Bolivian anthropologists, it was designed to assist Quechua-speaking weavers from the Chuquisaca Valleys to improve weaving practices and gain more equitable access to markets for their products. At this time, tourist trade in handicrafts was having a negative impact on the quality of weaving and the designs employed, as tourists were seeking inexpensive weavings and did not understand and/or were unwilling to pay higher prices to support the intensive labour required for high quality Jalq'a or Tarabuco weavings. As such, women were producing lower quality weavings that they could sell inexpensively to tourists, and many of the more complex patterns that previously typified weavings of the region were being abandoned. ASUR's goal was to revitalize local weaving traditions by developing a higher paying market for quality textiles, and by providing economic incentives and technical support to women weavers to do so. The ATO granted members of weaving co-operatives easy access to high quality wool and dyes, eliminated middlemen in the commodity chain by purchasing the textiles directly at higher prices, and paid the women on delivery rather than upon sale of the goods. In fact, women discussed their motivations for joining one of ASUR's weaving co-operatives both in terms of accessing higher earnings and in revitalizing weaving traditions.

While ASUR is not officially recognized as a fair trade organization, it adheres to many of the principles of fair trade, including paying high prices for the textiles it purchases, providing technical and educational support to producers, including a gender component to the project through its work with women weavers, forging direct relationships with purchasers, and strengthening and validating cultural identity. Additionally, ASUR seeks to educate the consuming public about different forms of textile production, the significance of the textiles produced, and why the textiles produced by the women's co-operatives are more expensive than similar products sold on the streets. Textiles are sold directly from ASUR's store in Sucre, and attached to that store is a textile museum that furthers the goal of educating the public about the history of textile production in the region and the connection between textiles and cultural identity. This matches fair trade goals of narrowing the gap between producers and consumers. Eversole (2006) highlights ASUR's success in providing a secure alternative income for women while revitalizing cultural identities and weaving traditions in the region that hinge, in part, on the ATO's ability to develop strong markets for the weavings, enhancing weaving skills and developing market knowledge among members of the co-operatives, and meshing textile production with other aspects of women's lifestyles, especially the rhythms of agrarian life.

The case study by Eversole also points to some of the possible challenges facing alternative trade in handicrafts. First, it emphasizes the need to develop market knowledge, enhance productive capacities, and orient artisan crafts, at least in part, to harmonize with consumer desires. While the ASUR project achieved this, the process was long and involved a substantial commitment of time and resources by the ATO spanning 20 years of work with the co-operatives. A second challenge of fair trade has been to produce local markets for its goods, which ASUR has achieved through the creation of its own store in Sucre, but which has been slower to develop in other instances where producers remain reliant on international consumption.

Other challenges facing handicraft fair trade are more difficult to quantify or measure. For example, the ASUR project, like many handicraft ethnodevelopment initiatives, targets women as the primary beneficiaries of the project. This resonates with grassroots development approaches since the 1980s and the principles of fair trade that seek gender equality through these economic activities. Yet, simply making women protagonists of development projects does not necessarily ensure their social empowerment or the achievement of gender equality in the communities in which they live and work. As Le Mare (2008) argues, the capacity of fair trade to resolve issues of gender inequality has thus far been limited. While fair trade projects regularly place women at the centre of work, this often translates into additional labour for women—the women's double-burden (Lipman-Blumen and Tickamyer 1975)—by failing to address the root causes and contexts of women's subordination (Le Mare 2008). Furthermore, the approach to including a gendered dimension to fair trade projects may, in some instances, serve to reify a sociological category of 'woman' (Moore 1988) while obscuring women's 'multilayered entanglements' (Henrici 2007: 147) of class, race, and ethnic identity. Fair trade projects must instead situate gender relationships within and emerging from a complex set of socio-cultural forces, meaning that attention to gendered inequality must also consider the historical marginalization of project participants in ethnic, racial or class hierarchies (Henrici 2007; Eversole 2006). Finally, there is no single standard of 'gender equality' that can be measured and applied across varied cultural contexts, meaning that gendered empowerment must be approached in unique ways in different cultural settings.

A second challenge confronting handicraft fair trade relates to the organization of production and fair trade's mandate to ensure just working conditions, democratic co-operative structures and protections against child labour. The co-operative structure that is common in fair and alternative trade does not necessarily readily translate into democratic decision-making processes or the levelling of inequalities among co-operative members. The co-operative model itself is sometimes received as an outside imposition by FTOs or ATOs, contributing at times to a lack of enthusiasm for this form of organizing production (Mayoux 1995). Further, management and leadership positions in a co-operative often come to be occupied by more élite or affluent members, and in some cases women's co-operatives are managed by male staff. This can lead to a reconfiguration of prevailing social hierarchies in the organizational structure of the co-operative. The regulation of labour to ensure just labour practices and protect against child labour also requires a process of translation not unlike that for questions of gendered empowerment, whereby standards governing labour must be flexible enough to adapt to different cultural beliefs and local practices. The WFTO's Sustainable Fair Trade Management System, currently in draft, may represent a step towards providing a set of defined standards governing fair trade practices that are also flexible enough to adapt to the diverse cultural settings and productive practices of handicraft production.

Handicraft fair trade provides the possibility of generating income for marginalized producers by guaranteeing higher prices for their products than they can expect through conventional markets. It is also oriented around promoting the dignity and cultural valorization of artisans by encouraging productive practices that are thought to be tied to local cultural beliefs and traditions. Studies such as that conducted by Eversole illustrate the potential of alternative trade to enhance the livelihoods of local artisans by guaranteeing higher prices, providing technical and educational support to enhance productive practices, and raising the self-esteem of producers who are often socially marginalized. Her study also illustrates the need for fair trade approaches to be attentive to a range of challenges inherent in the organization of fair trade production, to be adaptable to local situations and circumstances, and to seek to address root causes of social inequality in its work.

BIBLIOGRAPHY

Bryant, R. L. and Goodman, M. K., 'Consuming Narratives: The Political Ecology of "Alternative" Consumption', *Transactions of the Institute of British Geographers* 29: 344–66, 2004.

Chibnik, M., 'The Evolution of Market Niches in Oaxacan Woodcarving', *Ethnology* 39(3): 225–42, 2000.
Cohen, Jeffrey H., 'Craft Production and the Challenge of the Global Market: An Artisans', Cooperative in Oaxaca, Mexico, *Human Organization* 57(1): 74–82, 1998.
Eversole, Robyn, 'Crafting Development in Bolivia', *Journal of International Development* 18: 945–55, 2006.
Fridell, Gavin, 'The Fair Trade Network in Historical Perspective', *Canadian Journal of Development Studies* 25(3): 411–28, 2004.
Henrici, Jane, 'Free Trade, Alternative Trade and Women in Peru: A First Look', *Journal of Developing Societies* 23(1–2): 145–57, 2007.
Jaffe, Daniel *et al.*, 'Bringing the "Moral Charge" Home: Fair Trade within the North and within the South', *Rural Sociology* 69(2): 169–96, 2004.
Le Mare, Ann, 'The Impact of Fair Trade on Social and Economic Development: A Review of the Literature', *Geography Compass* 2(6): 1922–42, 2008.
Lipman-Blumen, Jean and Tickamyer, Ann R., 'Sex Roles in Transition: A Ten-Year Perspective', *Annual Review of Sociology* 1: 297–337, 1975.
Littrell, Mary A. and Dickson, Marsha A., 'Alternative Trading Organizations: Shifting Paradigm in a Culture of Social Responsibility', *Human Organization* 56(3): 344–52, 1997.
Low, William and Davenport, Eileen, 'Postcards from the Edge: Maintaining the "Alternative" Character of Fair Trade', *Sustainable Development* 13: 143–53, 2005.
Mayoux, Linda, 'Alternative Vision or Utopian Fantasy?: Cooperation, Empowerment and Women's Cooperative Development in India', *Journal of International Development* 7(2): 211–28, 1995.
Moore, Geoff, 'The Fair Trade Movement: Parameters, Issues and Future Research', *Journal of Business Ethics* 53: 73–86, 2004.
Moore, Henrietta, *Feminism and Anthropology*, Minneapolis, University of Minnesota Press, 1988.
Nash, June, 'Maya Household Production in the World Market: The Potters of Amatenango del Valle, Chiapas' in Nash, J. (ed.) *Crafts in the World Market: The Impact of Global Exchange on Middle American Artisans*, Albany, State University of New York Press, pp. 1–24, 1993.
Raynolds, Laura T. and Long, Michael A., 'Fair/Alternative Trade: Historical and Empirical Dimensions' in Laura T. Raynolds, Douglas Murray and John Wilkinson (eds) *Fair Trade: The Challenges of Transforming Globalization*, New York, Routledge, pp. 15–32, 2007.
Redfern, Andy and Snedker, Paul, *Creating Market Opportunities for Small Enterprises: Experiences of the Fair Trade Movement*, Geneva, International Labour Organization, 2002.
Renard, Marie-Christine, 'Fair Trade: Quality, Market and Conventions', *Journal of Rural Studies* 19: 87–96, 2003.
Scrase, Timothy J., Precarious Production: Globalisation and Artisan Labour in the Third World', *Third World Quarterly* 24(3): 449–61, 2003.
Stephen, Lynn, 'Women's Weaving Cooperatives in Oaxaca: An Indigenous Response to Neoliberalism', *Critique of Anthropology* 25(3): 253–78, 2005.
Tallontire, Anne, 'Partnerships in Fair Trade: Reflections from a Case Study of Cafédirect', *Development in Practice* 10(2): 166–77, 2000.

WFTO, www.wfto.com/index.php?option=com_content&task=view&id=18&Itemid=49 (accessed 18 February 2009), 2009.

Witkowski, Terrence H., 'Fair Trade Marketing: An Alternative System for Globalization and Development', *Journal of Marketing Theory and Practice* 13(4): 22–33, 2005.

Coffee

Peter Luetchford

Coffee can reasonably claim to be the quintessential fair trade product. As the world's most traded commodity after oil, it offers a vital mix of attributes that make it an ideal ethical good. The renowned volatility of coffee markets renders the product synonymous in the minds of many with neoliberal free market speculation, which fair trade seeks to counter and against which it is framed (De Neve, Luetchford and Pratt 2008). The attempt by fair trade to regulate through individual consumption that which is no longer regulated by governments or international agreements has fixed on an economy that encompasses beguiling social and cultural messages and meanings.

Of all the primary agricultural products, it was coffee that led the shift in emphasis in fair trade away from handicrafts. In the 1980s the Nicaragua Solidarity Campaign in Britain and Equal Exchange in the USA promoted Nicaraguan coffee in support of the left-wing Sandinista Government. Other groups, such as Neighbour to Neighbour in San Francisco, organized boycotts of Nestlé, Procter and Gamble and coffee from El Salvador to protest at right-wing dictatorship and genocide (Pendergrast 2001: 287–90). Such politicized initiatives paved the way for a nascent fair trade coffee sector. The establishment in Holland of the Max Havelaar Quality Mark in 1988 opened the door further by providing a key market mechanism to promote the products. When the International Coffee Agreement collapsed in 1989 prices went into freefall, providing the stimulus for the entry of fair trade products into the mainstream economy. In the early 1990s activists and NGOs increasingly promoted fair trade coffees, such as Cafédirect in the UK, as viable and politicized alternatives to the major brands (Barratt-Brown 1990; Coote 1992).

The increasing visibility of fair trade coffee is reflected in reports of impressive growth in sales, though the evidence is inconclusive as much of the data is generated within the industry itself. In many countries fair trade as a market share is understood to be modest (Giovannucci 2001), but there are apparent exceptions. Sales as a percentage of the total coffee market in Germany remained unchanged at 1% between 2004 and 2007; in the UK it grew over the same period from 1.5% to 20% as fair trade coffee entered the major supermarkets (Krier 2008: 46). Perhaps a better indication of commercial success is world trade by weight of coffee, which went from 33,995 metric tons in 2005 to 62,209 metric tons in 2007 (see 'Shaping Global Partnerships: Annual Report 2006/2007', FLO International, p. 15;

'An Inspiration for Change, Annual Report 2007', FLO International, p.11). Two trends are particularly worthy of note in the data. The first is the declining relative importance of coffee as the fair trade sector matures and other products are added to the portfolio. For example, world trade in Fairtrade coffee grew a relatively modest 19% in 2007, while sales of sugar doubled (see 'Global Fairtrade Sales Increase by 47%', www.fairtrade.net/single_view.html, accessed on 28 April 2009). In the same year the value in sales of coffee was superseded in Britain by bananas for the first time (see 'Facts and Figures on Fairtrade: sales of Fairtrade certified products in the UK', www.fairtrade.org.uk/what_is_fairtrade/facts_and_figures.aspx, accessed on 28 April 2009). The second trend is the entry of major players in the industry. The biggest coffee market in the world, the USA, increased its consumption of the fair trade alternative ten-fold between 2000 and 2005 to US $500m. (see 'Facts and Figures: fair trade certified specialty coffee', www.transfairusa.org/pdfs/fastfacts_coffee.pdf, accessed on 29 April 2009, and www.fairtrade.org.uk/what_is_fairtrade/facts_and_figures.aspx, accessed on 29 April 2009).

Meanwhile, in Britain, sales increased less than five-fold in the same period, moving from £15.5m. to £65.8m., prompting fears of future market saturation. The growing importance of the US market is matched by the contribution of major retailers. In 2009 Starbucks doubled its purchase of Fairtrade-certified coffee to US $64m., making it the largest single buyer in the world (Ndzamela 2008).

To what do we owe such astonishing growth? Coffee has key characteristics that put it at the centre of the fair trade imaginary. The first feature is broadly economic, which focuses on the market, and how it operates. The second is more social and concerns the processes, relationships and politics behind production, distribution and consumption. Third, there are distinctive cultural practices and meanings attached to coffee.

Socio-economic discussions on coffee often begin with the volatility of markets and the possibilities this allows for speculation and oligopolistic practices, which is then countered by regulatory regimes. The instability of coffee markets is an outcome of production cycles and uncertainties. Overproduction and underproduction is a symptom of the lag between planting and first harvest (from three to five years, according to variety) which means shortfalls lead to extreme price hikes that encourages the establishment of new plantations. When this new coffee floods into the market there is a crash. Lower prices then lead to cutbacks in production, renewed shortages, and so the cycle recurs (Talbot 2004: 35–36). Market cycles are partly generated by natural and man-made disasters. For example, the Brazilian industry, responsible for around a third of world output, is particularly prone to frost. In 1975 severe cold killed more than half of Brazil's coffee trees and prices soared 100% in a year (Pendergrast 2001: 261). Conflict, too, adds uncertainty; as supply routes from Latin America to European markets were cut in both world wars, so prices dropped. In 1940, for instance, coffee prices fell to an historic low of US $0.0575 per pound (Pendergrast 2001: 177).

Fluctuations in supply and demand and the ongoing rise and fall in value of the crop have long encouraged monopolies, speculation, boycotts, and attempts at regulation as different parties pursue economic interests. The story of the coffee industry is commonly written as a history of such struggles (Dicum and Luttinger 1999; Pendergrast 2001; Talbot 2004). At the beginning of the 19th century, as the modern industry began to take shape, innovations in production, distribution and consumption allowed fortunes to be made (and lost) as companies and entrepreneurs cornered markets and profits. Not for nothing did the magnate John Arbuckle in an 1897 anti-trust case call coffee 'the most speculative business in the world' (cited in Pendergrast 2001: 58). Since the 1980s neoliberal economic policies have allowed transnational corporations (TNCs) to dominate the chain; they have consolidated their interests by working the financial markets using information technology, and they have driven out regional competitors by aggressive cost-cutting. In 2004 four companies (Nestlé, Philip Morris, Sara Lee and Procter and Gamble) controlled 60% of the market in the main consuming nations, while trading was dominated by eight importers (Talbot 2004: 103–7).

Alongside the scope the beverage has allowed for profit are social and political concerns at the cost of such speculation, particularly the effects of unstable prices on economies dependent upon coffee production. This has encouraged various attempts to regulate supply and demand, and hence prices. Until the rise of fair trade, regulation was largely initiated by producing countries through national coffee boards and government institutions, such as Colombia's National Federation of Coffee Farmers (FNC), the Brazilian Coffee Institute (IBC), and the Coffee Board of Kenya. In addition to promoting the qualities of their coffee, these organizations were charged with controlling revenues and supplies. After the 1929 economic crash prices fell from 22.5 cents to 8 cents per pound in two years, prompting Brazil to unilaterally burn 7m. bags. However, it is more common for producer countries to form coalitions to regulate supplies. From 1963 to 1989 the majority of producer nations adhered to a series of International Coffee Agreements. The system, administered through the International Coffee Organization, used quotas with trigger prices to regulate supplies. The USA was crucial to the success of the agreements because of its capacity to break quotas by sourcing from non-signatory nations, but despite its ideological commitment to *laissez-faire* the US was persuaded to back regulation because of concerns at the advances of communist ideology in Latin America (Pendergrast 2001: 228). These agreements faded, along with the communist threat, when producer countries failed to agree quotas in the late 1980s (Talbot 2004: 81–97).

The recent history of the coffee industry has therefore been characterized by the increasing power of TNCs, alongside a decreasing capacity for producer nations to control prices. Two effects of these processes concern fair trade.

The first is the much noted diminishing returns to producers as international coffee agreements failed and big business developed its stranglehold on the industry. The figures show a marked shift towards value added in consumer countries, and by major companies, at the expense of producer countries from the end of the 1980s (Talbot 2004: 166–69, 181). What is more, the percentage of the value paid to producers drops significantly from around 20% to nearer 10% in the same time period. While producers do better when prices are high, consumers tend not to benefit from low prices as companies take the opportunity to increase profits. The 50% drop in green coffee prices at the end of the International Coffee Agreement saw a fall in the retail price of only 1% (Talbot 2004: 115). Fair trade sets out to redress this imbalance.

The second important change in the coffee industry as a whole that has important consequences for fair trade is the rise of specialty coffees as a response to the cuts in costs and quality by the major brands (Pendergrast 2001). Specialty coffees add value by differentiating between qualities of coffee, imparted by such things as altitude, soils and climate, growing and harvesting techniques, processing, roasting, freshness, as well as brewing techniques. In the case of fair trade, qualities intersect explicitly with the social and the cultural as the coffee is linked to small farmers who must engage in sustainable agriculture and be organized into democratic associations to qualify (FLO 2009). These social forms are then advertised to consumers as suitable subjects with whom to establish a relationship. As a primary product, it is easy to imagine a farmer working in the fields to produce the coffee one imbibes (personal communication, James Carrier). Further, because these growers are understood to be small, independent landowners, they resonate with consumers in the West with an image of peasant forms of production (Guthman 2004; Kearney 1996). Such people hold associations with families and communities, and so evoke reciprocal relations that stand in symbolic opposition to the self-interested economy. These social beings, are, however, also politicized. Small family farmers and co-operative forms of organization are understood to be marginalized in mainstream global exchanges, yet to be central to their national economies. As many as 25m. people are estimated to gain livelihoods from coffee production. Their struggles, in which they have long contested the power of élite processors and exporters in national arenas, and their suffering, have become global issues, identified with by concerned citizens and consumers (Gonzalez 2001; The Economist 2006).

Today fair trade coffee is regulated through the labelling system adhered to by the NGOs which spearheaded the social and political consumer movement, and the major companies which have more recently entered fair trade. The main certifying body, Fairtrade Labelling Organizations International (FLO) holds a register of certified producers and traders, and maintains specific standards for coffee certification. The minimum price is the chief mechanism of market regulation. The fair trade minimum price for washed Arabica was set at US $1.21 in 1989, and remained unchanged until 2008, when it was increased to $1.25 (FLO 2007a). It is clear that the 'fair price' has not kept pace with inflation over the years. On the other hand, the premium, paid when the market price rises above the minimum price, has done better. Remaining unchanged for many years, it was doubled from $0.05 to $0.10 per pound in 2007 (FLO 2007b).

The aim of these minimum prices and premiums is to support farmers and farmers groups in times of poor prices, and it is generally agreed that they have had that effect to some degree (Jaffee 2007; Luetchford 2008a; Ronchi 2002). While fair trade has buoyed up producer groups at such times, the benefits are less obvious when prices rise, as co-operative managers may seek to speculate on the open market on behalf of their members (Luetchford 2006). A more serious challenge to the fairness of the system focuses on who benefits. While a large number of producer groups are on the fair trade register, many only sell a small proportion of their output through fair trade deals. Thus, some well-placed groups, such as UCIRI from Mexico, sell up to 100% to fair trade, while other co-operatives have struggled to break into the market (Fridell 2007; Smith 2007). Second, although around 70% of the premiums go directly to the producer, with a small percentage retained by organizations as development capital, larger producers will benefit disproportionately because premiums are indexed against the amount of coffee grown. Whilst much is made of the small coffee farmer in promoting fair trade, the difference between a grower with 1 ha and a farmer with 5 or 10 ha of coffee remains unrecognized. Further, the focus on small farmers obscures relations of production, particularly dependence on wage labour. FLO sidesteps this issue by giving no labour standards for coffee as they only certify associations of small farmers. However, farmers with as little as 2 ha are likely to be dependent on wage labour at harvest time (Luetchford 2008b). Other fair trade initiatives, such as the Rainforest Alliance, do work with big growers and have labour standards. Their certification scheme is, however, primarily environmental and aims to encourage sustainable practices associated with shade grown, organic coffees, and biodiversity in plantations. Because the Rainforest Alliance gives no price guarantees for coffee some consider it a weak version of fair trade (McAllister 2004).

Coffee has a distinct social life in the world of consumption, which lends it power as a medium for conveying a broad raft of messages. It offers, as Schivelbusch tells us, a 'motley catalogue of often mutually contradictory virtues' (1993: 19). While oil powers the machinery of modern life, coffee powers the minds and bodies of modern subjects. The drink enhances individual efficiency in economic activities, but it also holds a key role in mediating all kinds of social relationships, from business to romance. Standing at the interface of economy and society, coffee is an ideal medium for ethical consumption. It offers a prime example of the social consequences on marginalized producers of self-regulating markets, and appends this to a particular kind of social subject, the small family farmer, who merits assistance. Coffee is not only good to drink; it is also good to think and act through.

BIBLIOGRAPHY

Barratt-Brown, M., *Fair Trade: Reform and Realities in the International Trading System*, London and New Jersey, Zed Books, 1990.

Coote, B., *The Trade Trap: Poverty and the Global Commodity Markets*, York, Oxfam Publications, 1992.

De Neve, G. Luetchford, P. and Pratt, J., 'Introduction: Revealing the Hidden Hands of Global Market Exchange' in De Neve, G., Luetchford, P., Pratt, J. and Woods, D (eds), *Hidden Hands in the Market: Ethnographies of Fair Trade, Ethical Consumption, and Corporate Social Responsibility*, Research in Economic Anthropology, Vol. 28, UK, Emerald, 2008.

Dicum, G. and Luttinger, N., *The Coffee Book: Anatomy of an Industry from Crop to the Last Drop*, New York, The New Press, 1999.

The Economist, 'Voting with your Trolley', Special Report: Food Politics, pp. 81–83, 9 December 2006.

FLO, 'FLO International Adjusts Fairtrade Minimum Prices for Arabica Coffee to Cover Costs of Sustainable Production', www.fairtrade.net/single_view1.html?&L=0&cHash=4f7ebb8c10&tx_ttnews[backPid]=614&tx_ttnews[pointer]=3&tx_ttnews[tt_news] = 32 (accessed on 15 December 2008), 2007a.

——, 'FLO Announces Increase in Fairtrade Premium and Organic Differential for Coffee', www.fairtrade.net/single_view1.html?&cHash=d32cc69b2c&scale=1&tx_ttnews[backPid]=614&tx_ttnews[pointer]=5&tx_ttnews[tt_news]=17 (accessed on 15 December 2008), 2007b.

——, 'Fairtrade Standards for Coffee for Small Producers' Organisations', www.fairtrade.net/fileadmin/user_upload/content/02–09_Coffee_SPO_EN.pdf (accessed on 12 May 2009), 2009.

Fridell, G., *Fair Trade Coffee: The Prospects and Pitfalls of Market Driven Social Justice*, Toronto, University of Toronto Press, 2007.

Giovannucci, D., 'Sustainable Coffee Survey of the North American Coffee Industry', report for North American Commission for Environmental Cooperation and The Specialty Coffee Association of America, www.scaa.org/pdfs/2001_Sustainable_Report_NA.pdf (accessed on 12 April 2009), July 2001.

Gonzalez, D., 'A Coffee Crisis' Devastating Domino Effect in Nicaragua', *The New York Times*, 29 August 2001.

Guthman, J., *Agrarian Dreams: The Paradox of Organic Farming in California*, Berkeley, University of California Press, 2004.

Jaffee, D., *Brewing Justice: Fair Trade, Sustainability and Survival*, Berkeley, University of California Press, 2007.

Kearney, M., *Reconceptualizing the Peasantry: Anthropology in Global Perspective*, Boulder, CO, Westview Press, 1996.

Krier, J.-M., *Fair Trade 2007: Facts and Figures from an Ongoing Success Story: A Report on Fair Trade in 33 Consumer Countries*, www.fairtrade-advocacy.org/documents/FairTrade2007_newfactsandfigures.pdf (accessed on 15 May 2009), Netherlands, Dutch Association of World Shops, 2008.

Luetchford, P., 'Brokering Fair Trade: Relations between Coffee Cooperatives and Fair Trade Organisations – A View from Costa Rica', in D. Lewis and D. Mosse (eds), *Development Brokers and Translators: The Ethnography of Aid and Agencies,* Bloomfield, CT, Kumarian Press, 2006.
——, *Fair Trade and a Global Commodity: Coffee in Costa Rica*, London, Pluto Press, 2008a.
——, 'The Hands that Pick Fair Trade Coffee: beyond the charms of the family farm', in G. de Neve, P. Luetchford, J. Pratt, and D. Woods (eds), *Hidden Hands in the Market: Ethnographies of Fair Trade, Ethical Consumption, and Corporate Social Responsibility*, Research in Economic Anthropology, Vol. 28, UK, Emerald, 2008b.
McAllister, S., 'Fairtrade Foundation or Rainforest Alliance: Who is the Fairest?', *The Guardian*, G2 p. 8, 24 November 2004.
Ndzamela, P., 'Fairtrade Coffee Sales Steady in Economic Downturn', *The Guardian*, 30 October 2008.
Pendergrast, M., *Uncommon Grounds: The History of Coffee and How it Transformed Our World*, London, Texere, 2001.
Ronchi, L., 'The Impact of Fair Trade on Producers and their Organisations: A Case Study with Coocafé in Costa Rica', *PRUS Working Paper* No. 11, UK, University of Sussex, 2002.
Schivelbusch, W., *Tastes of Paradise: A Social History of Spices, Stimulants, and Intoxicants*, New York, Vintage Books, 1993.
Smith, J., 'The Search for Sustainable Markets: The Promises and Failures of Fair Trade', *Culture and Agriculture* Vol. 29, Issue 2, pp. 89–99, 2007.
Talbot, J., *Grounds for Agreement: the Political Economy of the Coffee Commodity Chain*, Lanham, MD, Rowman and Littlefield, 2004.

Cocoa

Amanda Berlan

Cocoa is a major agricultural commodity with a rising global consumption. The current global annual consumption represents approximately 3.5m. tons of cocoa and on average it increases by 2% annually. While cocoa is mainly produced in poorer countries, its consumers are largely (though not exclusively) concentrated in the developed world. Europe is the world's largest cocoa consuming area and is estimated to account for up to 40% of global consumption. The second largest cocoa consuming area is North America which also uses very significant tonnages of cocoa. The annual rise in consumption is in part due to new markets such as India and changing consumer preferences in existing markets.

Cocoa is mostly used to make chocolate products although it can also be used (in the form of cocoa butter) in many beauty products such as soaps, moisturisers, lip balms and shampoos. Within Europe, figures vary but it is generally accepted that people in the UK, Germany and the Netherlands are big consumers of chocolate and other cocoa-based products. For example, the total UK confectionery market (of which chocolate products make up the largest segment) is valued at an impressive £4,000m. a year. The US confectionery market is presently estimated to represent US $14,000m. annually and it is predicted that this will rise to $18,000m. by 2011.

As chocolate represents an enormous market both in Europe and globally, cocoa has played a significant role in the development of Fairtrade. Even though cocoa labelled Fairtrade still only accounts for around 1% of the overall global production of cocoa it constitutes a rapidly expanding market. In contrast to the 2%–3% growth in the conventional market, between 1996 and 2006 the annual average growth of fair trade-labelled cocoa products was 23% (Barrientos 2008).

However, cocoa is not only important in the development of Fairtrade because of the size of the market it represents and its rapid growth. In the UK it has also played a special role because a cocoa product, Green and Black's Maya Gold chocolate bar, was the very first product to be awarded the Fairtrade mark in 1994. More broadly, the UK is seen as one of the leading Fairtrade markets globally. The UK Fairtrade Foundation reports that 'the UK market is doubling in value every 2 years, and in 2007 reached an estimated retail value of £493 million' and that it has 'more products and more awareness of Fairtrade than anywhere else' (www.fairtrade.org.uk/what_is_fair trade/faqs.aspx, accessed 7 July 2010).

Until Fairtrade chocolate products started to achieve wider recognition, they were not as widely available as today and their sales channels were limited to alternative food shops and awareness-raising events. Since then, there has been a rapid growth in the market for ethically-sourced chocolate in Europe and North America and in the UK. For example, there are now over 300 cocoa-based products certified Fairtrade. These include chocolate bars, hot drinks, cocoa powder, chocolate-covered nuts and dried fruit, snack bars, biscuits, cakes, buttons, Easter eggs, Valentine's Day gifts, Advent calendars, truffles, boxed assortments and many others. An increasing number of companies are also using Fairtrade cocoa butter in their cosmetics such as body scrubs, soaps and moisturisers.

The enormous growth is further reflected in the fact that big companies are acquiring Fairtrade certification on some of their main brands. For example, some supermarkets now have own-brand Fairtrade chocolate bars and large companies such as Cadbury's, Nestlé, Ben & Jerry's and Green & Black's now have Fairtrade certification on some or all of their products.

Having examined some of the changes in consumption which have taken place, it is necessary to consider how these have impacted on producers. As a crop, cocoa requires heat and humidity, so it can only be grown in a limited number of places. These are mainly in the developing world. Traditionally, West Africa has produced most of the world's cocoa and it still accounts for over 70% of total production. Globally, the largest producer countries are the Ivory Coast, Ghana and Indonesia. The two countries which export most Fairtrade certified cocoa are Ghana and the Dominican Republic. Other countries producing Fairtrade cocoa include Belize, Ecuador, and Peru, among others. However, relative to Ghana and the Dominican Republic, they produce much smaller quantities of Fairtrade cocoa.

The reasons why Fairtrade in cocoa is more developed in some countries than others are varied. In some countries, production is small so there is little scope for producer co-operatives to become major players in the global Fairtrade cocoa market. However, for the most part, such developments have been linked to in-country factors (such as economic liberalization policies, see Ghana case study below) and to more ad-hoc processes whereby socially-minded local entrepreneurs interested in cocoa teamed up with international donor agencies and Alternative Trading Organizations to set up producer co-operatives. For example, it was an international development initiative which paved the way for the creation of the Dominican cocoa co-operative, CONACADO.

This initiative, funded by the German group GTZ, aimed to improve the quality of Dominican cocoa but a local economist adapted the programme to ensure that it also altered existing power structures within the Dominican cocoa industry and enabled the creation of CONACADO. The co-operative was formed in 1988, and included 182 local producer associations organized into eight regional blocks. Prior to this, there was a single block already set up by a group of cocoa producers who had decided to pool their cocoa in order to sell it directly to exporters at a better price. Many of the smaller producer associations also already existed but they were mainly for social purposes before they became a channel for marketing cocoa (Roche 2006) and before CONACADO received Fairtrade certification. Therefore, cocoa did not become a significant Fairtrade commodity as a result of globally co-ordinated efforts but rather following a combination of local factors, existing local networks, international co-operation and the efforts and ideas of key individuals.

Although sale and export arrangements vary to some extent between countries, many issues are common to cocoa producers worldwide. Many consumers in the West think that cocoa is grown on large commercial plantations but 90% of it is grown on small farms. Most cocoa production units are family-run and cover 2–5 ha of land (ICCO 2010), which is also used to produce food crops such as yams and plantain for personal consumption and for sale on local markets. Cocoa is grown in rural areas, which often do not have a good infrastructure and lack schools, medical facilities and reliable roads. As Fairtrade aims to help small disadvantaged producers, it is well-suited to helping cocoa growers. However, it is also important to be realistic about the extent to which Fairtrade can bring about change; Fairtrade alone cannot solve all the problems connected with rural poverty or address these in a short space of time.

Furthermore, one of the major problems of cocoa farming worldwide, and in the agricultural sector more broadly, is that farmer communities are ageing and many young people prefer to migrate to urban areas rather than to become producers. Any initiatives such as Fairtrade, which seeks to enhance the economic and social sustainability of farming and to make rural areas more appealing, are therefore necessary to secure the future of cocoa production. In order to make cocoa farming more sustainable, it is also necessary to ensure that farmers receive education on good farming techniques, have access to seedlings, plant new trees and manage some of the challenges of cocoa production. While some governmental and non-governmental organizations work in individual countries to help farmers to meet these challenges, Fairtrade co-operatives through their grassroots links are highly effective channels for delivering these kinds of services and assistance. However, these factors also illustrate that the needs of farmers extend beyond funding community projects.

More broadly, like any crop, growing cocoa involves dealing with pests, diseases (such as Black Pod Disease and Witches' Broom) and environmental problems which can cause considerable damage. However, if managed properly, these problems can be reduced and instances when they have devastated entire harvests are not very common. Cocoa is more vulnerable to environmental disasters in certain regions and Fairtrade has helped farmers who have suffered as a result of this. Following Hurricane George, the Dominican Republic lost almost two-thirds of its production of cocoa in 1998. After a democratic vote among its members, CONACADO used the Fairtrade premium in 1999 to help clear some of the damaged farms and to create nurseries for new planting material. Although Fairtrade cannot solve all the problems associated with crop failure or environmental damage, this example shows that it can help to mitigate the devastating effects of such events.

In order to be certified by Fairtrade Labelling Organizations International, cocoa producers have to be organized in co-operatives which they have control and ownership of. As previously outlined, the biggest co-operatives currently exporting Fairtrade cocoa started as small initiatives which grew with financial and other support from Alternative Trading Organizations and international development organizations. These co-operatives now include thousands of farmers (see the case study below) who are organized democratically into farmer associations or village 'societies' (which are the sub-groups making up the co-operative). As a result of being in these, producers benefit from increased bargaining power. Producer co-operatives are also able to obtain credit of up to 60% of the purchase price prior to shipment in order to help finance their activities.

Globally, most cocoa producers sell their crop individually to export companies, sometimes via intermediaries. Fairtrade cocoa co-operatives reduce the number of intermediaries wherever possible. They also seek to give greater returns to producers in other ways. For example, CONACADO undertakes some of the processing of beans into cocoa butter, powder and liquor locally in order to add value and therefore to increase revenue for producers.

Following allegations of labour abuses, there have been concerns about the possible use of child and forced labour in cocoa. Since then, programmes involving individual countries' governments, chocolate manufacturers and other key stakeholders have been set up or expanded to promote good practices in cocoa. One of the key principles of Fairtrade is that it works to eliminate any negative labour practices such as forced labour and forms of child labour which contravene ILO Convention 182 on the Worst Forms of Child Labour. In order to make sure that there are no abuses in the supply chain, Fairtrade cocoa co-operatives sensitize farmers on issues such as child labour.

Fairtrade-certified cocoa beans command a minimum price of US $2,200 per metric ton (which includes a $200 premium for social projects), which is paid directly to producer organizations. If the world market price is above this price, the higher of the two is paid. The premium is used to improve local infrastructure in village communities and fund projects such as water wells, school buildings, community toilets, income-generating projects, training in farming techniques and scholarships.

Environmentally, Fairtrade standards restrict the use of agrochemicals and encourage sustainable practices. Approximately 10% of the cocoa which is Fairtrade certified is also certified organic. Organic production can be difficult to achieve but it can also generate significantly higher premiums than conventional cocoa. The Fairtrade minimum price for organic cocoa is US $2,500 per metric ton, which includes a premium of $200. Non-Fairtrade organic cocoa also fetches higher prices, but this is not fixed and varies according to the world market. During 2006–07 the premium for organic cocoa has on occasion gone as high as $1,800 per ton (Barrientos 2008). Overall, organically-produced cocoa accounts for less than 1% of the total world production. The best quality cocoa comes from Ghana, and this secures a premium on the world market of up to $200–$250 per ton over the prevailing international cocoa price. It is currently the only country to achieve a quality-based price premium.

Other forms of ethical or environmentally-friendly certification schemes, such as Rainforest Alliance, are also gaining increasing recognition among consumers. Rainforest Alliance has worked in partnership with other stakeholders to support cocoa farmers in Latin America and West Africa and it is achieving significant growth. It reported that 2009 had seen a 26% increase compared to 2008 in the number of companies buying from Rainforest Alliance-certified farms or forests (www.rainforest-alliance.org/news.cfm?id=annual_growth, accessed 7 July 2010) and that sales of Rainforest Alliance Certified cocoa had grown from US $4.5m. in 2007 to $16.75m. in 2008 (www.rainforest-alliance.org/agriculture.cfm?id=edward_millard, accessed 7 July 2010). However, Rainforest Alliance has been said to have lower standards than Fairtrade. For example, Rainforest Alliance has received criticism for having weaker labour standards or for not offering minimum prices (Jaffee 2007).

Patterns of chocolate consumption have evolved in the developed world in recent years. In addition to the growing demand for ethical and environmentally-sustainable cocoa, chocolate with a higher cocoa content is becoming more popular owing to changing consumer tastes and greater awareness of the potential health benefits of cocoa. Such factors may have a positive influence on the demand for Fairtrade cocoa as consumers increasingly favour a combination of higher cocoa content and fair and environmentally-sustainable practices.

In conclusion, it is clear that considerable successes have been achieved in the quest to secure better returns for cocoa growers and to enhance the social, economic and environmental sustainability of cocoa. Although many challenges such as ageing, rural poverty or tree diseases still remain, Fairtrade has been pivotal in making several positive changes and helping to ensure the long-term sustainability of cocoa.

KUAPA KOKOO: A CASE STUDY

Kuapa Kokoo is a Fairtrade co-operative in Ghana with a strong business model and an impressive track record of helping farmers. It was set up as a local initiative with Western support in 1993 and was certified Fairtrade in 1995.

As previously noted, the Ghanaian cocoa industry has an international reputation for excellent quality. The Ghanaian industry has undergone considerable changes in recent years, the most significant of which was its partial liberalization in 1993. Prior to this, the only institution which was allowed to export cocoa was the government Cocoa Marketing Board (CMB). CMB also took care of a number of other services relating to cocoa, such as quality control, and provided subsidies on agricultural inputs. Following partial liberalization, there are now multiple Licensed Buying Companies which have licences to export cocoa. This has had implications for Fairtrade in Ghana as one of the groups which benefited from this change was Kuapa Kokoo, which was able to set up a company exporting cocoa directly to Fairtrade organizations abroad.

As an organization, Kuapa Kokoo is made up of distinct units: a farmers' co-operative; a commercial company which deals with cocoa sales; a trust fund which manages funds for social development; and a credit union which helps farmers to make savings and to manage their finances. Crucially, Kuapa Kokoo also owns almost half the shares in the UK-based chocolate company Divine Chocolate. This not only enables them to receive a share of profits but also to take part in important decision-making (Kuapa Kokoo has two representatives on the board of Divine). This is a unique and inspiring business model, especially in the chocolate industry which is dominated by big companies. This model enables a producer organization to obtain higher returns by selling chocolate as a manufactured product rather than selling unprocessed cocoa beans, or cocoa butter, powder or liquor. From a modest couple of hundred farmers, Kuapa Kokoo has grown to include over 45,000 farmers in different cocoa-producing regions of Ghana. Prior to such initiatives and to the increased worldwide interest in trade justice which has accompanied the fair trade movement, cocoa producers were virtually invisible players in global markets.

In addition to the returns identified above, Kuapa Kokoo's Fairtrade premium funds many social projects, including water wells, public toilets, mobile health programmes for rural areas, classrooms blocks, storage facilities and even two mobile cinema vans for farmer education programmes.

The 'fairness' of Kuapa Kokoo is also demonstrable in a number of other ways. Union membership is open to all cocoa farmers irrespective of gender, ethnicity, religion or any other factor. All members of the local village societies which make up the Union are eligible to stand for election to any of the positions on the Executive Council. A further distinguishing feature of Kuapa Kokoo's activities has been their promotion of gender equality and their initiatives to help women. These have included training in business management and planning, and income-generating activities such as soap-making using cocoa waste and palm oil extraction. Women are included at every echelon of the co-operative ranging from local Kuapa Kokoo Societies to the National Executive Committee.

While all the achievements detailed here are considerable, it is also important to remember that they are the result of many years of hard work and they have also benefited from the strong support of other organizations (such as Twin in the UK and the Body Shop, which donated its shares of Divine

Chocolate to Kuapa Kokoo in 2006). These are important factors to consider when assessing the lessons which can be drawn from this example. Overall, Kuapa Kokoo provides an excellent example of the practical benefits of Fairtrade and how it works both to provide immediate benefits and long-term solutions to the challenges facing cocoa producers.

BIBLIOGRAPHY

Barrientos, S., Asenso-Okyere, K., Asuming-Brempong, S., Sarpong, D., Anyidoho, N., Kaplinsky, R. and Leavy, J., 'Mapping Sustainable Production in Ghanaian Cocoa: Report to Cadbury', Institute of Development Studies and University of Ghana, Legon, 2008.

Barrientos, S., 'Voluntary Initiatives and Corporate Codes of Labour Practice' in *Development and Change*, Vol. 39(6):1–14, 2008.

ICCO, www.icco.org/economics/promotion.aspx, 2010.

Jaffee, D., *Brewing Justice: Fair Trade Coffee, Sustainability and Surviva*, University of California Press, 2007.

Roche, G., 'Impact du commerce équitable sur les revenus des agriculteurs. Le cas de CONACADO en République Dominicaine' presented at the 2nd International Colloquium on Fairtrade and Sustainable Development. Montreal, June 2006.

A–Z glossary

Meera Warrier

A

Advertising

Advertisements are messages aimed at selling either a product or a service, seeking support and participation, raising awareness, or providing information. Through informing and influencing recipients, advertising is a crucial element of commercial enterprises in a capitalist system. It is through advertising that multinational companies successfully penetrate the daily lives of people across the globe to sell their wares.

Advertising is closely linked to **consumerism** and aims to generate and satisfy material desires. Potential customers are induced by advertisements to purchase commodities and services that may well not be essential. Indeed, advertising works through creating desire, and then performing a sleight of hand to make the desire seem like a basic necessity or need. Design, **branding**, packaging and display have become major preoccupations in contemporary markets, and are as important to the success of commodities as their utility. It is global communication in the form of advertising that has facilitated the spread and intensification of **commodification** and consumerism around the world. And as such, advertising has been crucial for the emergence of international culture.

Global advertising has been the ground for arguments regarding the nature of **capitalism**—as to whether corporations are presenting potential buyers with 'choice', or seducing their customers with tyranny, with advertising deluding the consumer into thinking they are the agent, while masking the source of real agency, the producers or capitalists themselves.

The Fairtrade mark has effectively become the distinguishing advertiser for goods traded following the Fairtrade Foundation's certification criteria. But bigger and more controversial players like Starbucks and Nestlé have jumped on the Fairtrade bandwagon to suggest they are making concessions and being 'fair' to poor producers (consider, for instance, Nestlé's ad campaign, 'coffee with a conscience' or Starbucks' strap line, 'We've always been crazy about coffee. Now we're certified'). However, the smaller, older and more committed players in the field see this as a case of 'fair-washing' as the advertisements belie the fact that these companies use certification on a very small part of their stock, and their business practices, especially in relation to poor producers, remain unchanged.

Advocacy

This refers to the active support of an idea or cause, especially the act of pleading or arguing for something with a view to helping people make informed choices. Advocacy is used to influence public policy and resource allocation decisions, and may be motivated by ethical, faith or moral principles or might simply exist to protect an asset or interest.

Fair trade sits in an unusual position as it can be seen both as an activist-led advocacy campaign and a consumer-driven commercial venture. With growing consumer concern about the injustices of the neoliberal trade agenda, there is lobbying at national and supranational levels for fair trade. At the 2004 Doha round of trade negotiations, developing countries lobbied for a reduction in Northern agricultural subsidies. There is still advocacy work to be done by fair trade lobbyists towards reducing tariffs in relation to processed and commodity products.

Other events that see lobbying by those in favour of fair trade are Euro Co-op, EFTA and NEWS! There was a sponsored fair trade conference (*Fair Trade: A Contribution to Sustainable Development?*) at the European Parliament in 2004, and a symposium on fair trade at the 11th UNCTAD meeting in 2004.

The conflict between the global and local perspectives can threaten advocacy efforts in favour of fair trade. Support for local farmers and local produce being done out by big supermarket chains can often take precedence over supporting those at a distance. It is worth noting, however, that Northern farmers continue to benefit from subsidies and social safety nets that are unavailable to poor Southern farmers. Another threat to fair trade advocacy comes through a questioning of its validity and effectiveness in helping the poor Southern farmer, as most value addition is still done predominantly in the North, and only a very small percentage of the profits accrue to Southern farmers.

African, Caribbean and Pacific (ACP) countries

A group of African, Caribbean and Pacific countries which have received special treatment from the European Union through a series of agreements, including the Lomé Convention and the Cotonou Agreement. The Cotonou Agreement, signed in 2000, provides the general framework for relations between the Union and the 79 ACP countries. The framework is reinforced by regional and national components and supplemented by a financial component represented mainly by the European Development Fund (EDF).

Agreement on Agriculture

This is a **World Trade Organization (WTO)** agreement which focuses on improving market access and reducing trade-distorting domestic support payments and export subsidies in agriculture. It was negotiated in the 1986–94 **Uruguay Round**. The negotiations have resulted in four main portions of the Agreement: the Agreement on Agriculture itself; the concessions and commitments Members are to undertake on market access, domestic support and export subsidies; the Agreement on Sanitary and Phytosanitary Measures; and the Ministerial Decision concerning Least-Developed and Net Food-Importing Developing countries.

The agricultural package also addresses issues of vital economic and political importance to many Members, including provisions encouraging the use of less trade-distorting domestic support policies to maintain the rural economy, allowing actions to be taken to ease any adjustment burden, and also the introduction of tightly prescribed provisions that allow some flexibility in the implementation of commitments. Specific concerns of developing countries have been considered, including the concerns of net-food importing countries and least developed countries, though the effectiveness of these measures remains questionable.

Agribusiness

Agribusiness (often also referred to as corporate farming) is a term used to refer to the various businesses involved in the modern food production chain, and describes the vertical integration of large-scale agriculture and farming. Agribusinesses bring together such diverse agricultural activities as farming, agrochemicals, farm machinery, food processing, distribution, and wholesale and retail sales. The benefits of vertical integration in the agricultural sector include economies of scale, larger market shares, control over the whole production chain, as well as enhanced competitiveness.

Corporate farming has been criticized from several quarters. From a consumer perspective, the concentration of market power is seen to harbour potentially negative outcomes. The absence of competition, for instance, could help monopolists keep prices high. In addition, large-scale farming and vertical integration are said to have caused many undesirable environmental side effects, including the loss of biodiversity and natural habitat, affecting the overall quality of agricultural produce and food products.

AgroFair

This alternative trading organization was founded by a coalition of fruit farmers and farming co-operatives in Ghana, Ecuador and Costa Rica, with investment capital provided by **Solidaridad**. In the early days, an independent Dutch banana ripening company, Ambtman, held one-third ownership, but its shares were later bought out by Solidaridad. The company was also restructured to make producers 50% owners. The board membership is constituted such that producers have a say in the sales and marketing of their product in European markets. And the producers receive 100% of the profits.

The uniqueness of the practices of AgroFair can be appreciated when placed in the context of a North-South trade in bananas dominated by three big multinational companies—Dole, Del Monto and Chiquita. Uniban, the Colombian union of banana growers, and the Noboa family in Ecuador are two other groups who have a direct say in the sales and marketing of bananas in the North.

Since its inception, AgroFair has grown to include other NGO partners such as Twin Trading in the UK and CTM, an Italian Fair Trade importer (which does not use the FLO logo or certification system). The holding company has sales divisions in the UK, the Netherlands and Italy. The Netherlands division maintains all purchasing and logistics centrally. And the AgroFair Foundation provides grants and loans to producer groups for quality improvements. AgroFair works with both co-operatives of small family farmers and plantations that employ farm workers, provided a minimum price is paid for labour and a social premium is made available to spend on development projects benefiting the community.

AgroFair's entry into the European market was not an easy one for two reasons. First, the European Union has a complex system of country import quotas for bananas in order to protect banana imports from former French and British colonies. Second, importers must be licensed, and licences are given on the basis of the previous year's trading volume. Only 3% of licences are granted to new entrants, and these are given to companies that have a track record of importing other fruits into Europe. As such, despite an intensive postcard campaign, 'Give Fair Trade bananas a fair chance' and much lobbying, AgroFair's only route into Europe was through buying licences from existing licence-holders, increasing the cost on the product which already required a high export price.

AgroFair's first bananas appeared in the Dutch market in 1996 and were subsequently adopted in 70% of the supermarkets there. But supply problems developed due to both the small volumes involved and the life of the product, particularly as the group had difficulties accessing space on ships controlled by the large MNC importers. The company, however, did turn profitable by 2000, and has since diversified its basket to include pineapples and mangoes (2002). It now sells to a number of major supermarkets in Europe. It received another big boost in 2004 when the Co-op supermarket chain in Switzerland announced that all of its bananas would be Fairtrade certified, with AgroFair as its primary supplier, giving AgroFair a 50% market share in that country.

AgroFair also sells non-fair trade fruits for logistical reasons, such as filling a container load, or to provide a market to farmers, or simply to test out supply chains for the future. But it is its entry into the fair trade market in Europe that has had a transformative impact on the global banana industry. It forced banana MNCs to consider offering fair trade or some other form of socially responsible product. Subsequently, Fyffes (the fifth largest banana importer) and Dole looked to register with FLO to offer Fairtrade bananas. Dole and Del Monte are also pursuing **Social Accountability International** certification for their company-owned farms in response to growing pressure from consumers and retailers. See www.agrofair.com.

Ahold

Ahold is the main retail group in the Netherlands, which founded the **Utz Kapeh** label in 1997 as a product safety traceability system. It stocks a range of fairly traded goods. Under its Albert Heijn fascia it also offers own label coffee (CaféHonesta). Albert Heijn has recently launched its new 'pure and honest' corporate brand, which is comprised of five different categories 'to give customers a broad selection of choices in responsible products' (see www.ahold.com/node/3260). These categories are AH pure & honest organic, fair trade, sustainable catch (fish), free-range meat and ecological cleaning products. Max Havelaar's inspection label is to be found on all of the AH pure & honest fair trade products, guaranteeing that the products have been sourced and produced according to international fair trade conditions. See www.ahold.com.

Aid

Foreign aid and development assistance describe financial and other forms of support (including the provision of goods and services), made available by one international actor in order to help another. This can also include loans and grants from public and private sources. Depending on its purpose, aid aims either at political and economic development or at humanitarian assistance.

Financial aid is given by national governments, private donors, international aid agencies, multilateral institutions such as the **World Bank**, or by development NGOs (such as Oxfam). International aid provided by national governments is often explicitly or implicitly linked with foreign policy aims. The promise and granting of aid, or its obverse, the threat to withhold or cut aid, are important instruments in the foreign policy mix of a nation state. A classic example of financial aid as a foreign policy instrument was the Marshall Plan, the economic face of the Cold War strategy under the Truman Administration. It was aimed at strengthening Western Europe as a potential ally against the Soviet Union.

An oft-quoted critique of financial aid as a foreign policy instrument is the potential establishment of a donor-recipient relationship, ultimately empowering the donor, and creating a dependency culture. This becomes particularly salient when one considers that financial aid often comes with a range of political and economic conditionalities.

Aid also includes offers of humanitarian assistance by individuals, international institutions, national governments, relief organizations and private actors in order to respond on a temporary basis to natural disasters or emergency conflict situations. Humanitarian assistance is not so much a duty under current international law as a moral obligation. There are moves to make humanitarian assistance a legal requirement rather than a form of voluntary assistance. Those in a crisis, natural or man-made, could, therefore, demand humanitarian assistance from the international community, at least in the form of the provision of a minimum level of subsistence (see also **Trade-not-Aid**).

Aid for Trade

The **World Trade Organization (WTO)** co-ordinates the international Aid for Trade programme, in which developing countries are helped to build trade capacity and infrastructure by ensuring that their trade projects are part of their aid and economic strategies. The Doha Ministerial Declaration made technical assistance and capacity building a key component of the development dimension, and in December 2005, the Sixth Ministerial Conference in Hong Kong created a new WTO work programme on Aid for Trade, with the broad aims of providing additional assistance to countries to ease adjustment to trade liberalization and to increase their capacity to take advantage of more open markets. Subsequently, in July 2005 Heads of State at the G8 Summit at Gleneagles agreed to increase help to developing countries to build their physical, human and institutional capacity to trade. A Task Force came up with a set of recommendations, endorsed in 2006, giving a monitoring role to the WTO. This monitoring and evaluation role consists of an annual global review to be held in the Committee on Trade and Development followed by a debate on Aid for Trade in the General Council (see also **Trade-Not-Aid**).

Alter Eco *see* **France Alter Eco.**

Alternative trade movement

The alternative trade movement grew out of efforts by charities in Europe and the USA to create markets for the produce of impoverished and displaced people. The activist campaigners leading the earliest **ATOs** were driven by a sense of the injustice of the unequal trading conditions between North and South. The origin of the movement is traced back to the Mennonite Central Committee when it established trade links with poor communities in southern parts of the USA in the late 1940s to generate employment and income. Other efforts included networks of church-based sales and stores, like Ten Thousand Villages, which grew out of the Mennonite effort, or SERVV, an initiative of the Church of the Brethren. There were also large developmental and religious agencies working in the Global South like Oxfam, Caritas and Bread for the World that were helping organize disadvantaged groups into partner associations and co-operatives to export their products, primarily handicrafts. Such efforts began to gather momentum and grow in the 1960s and 1970s. It was the European organizations which began to frame their work as 'alternative trade', and established a network of 'world shops' to sell craft products and some coffee and tea. While the volume of traded goods was still negligible, sales grew quite rapidly, and the profile of alternative trade began to take on the status of a 'movement'.

There is a strong solidarity and developmental strain characterizing this movement. Consider, for instance, the efforts of Twin Trading to provide socialist countries' access to Western markets. 'Cafe Nica' was sold in violation of an official embargo on products from Nicaragua in the 1980s to protest against the Government's policies in Central America. The developmental strain is visible in slogans such as 'trade, not aid' in the context of the sale of bananas, stressing instead local development and empowerment. The movement saw itself providing a critique of **capitalism** and the global economic system, and positioned itself as distinct from both charitable giving and the inefficiency and corruption of big industry.

In 1988, when the **UCIRI** co-operative demanded that it be allowed to join larger mainstream sales prompting the creation of the Max Havelaar label (a label which could be placed on coffee sold under any brand so long as coffee farmers had received a premium price that constituted a 'fair' return), the term 'alternative trade' was replaced by 'fair trade'.

Alternative Trading Organizations (ATOs)

The umbrella term 'ATO' covers a range of possibilities, including privately held companies, worker-owned co-operatives, companies limited by shares, partly producer-owned companies and not-for-profits. The thread uniting all ATOs is a commitment to reducing poverty through improving the terms of trade for the world's poorest producers, even though each organization might have a different way of achieving this objective.

The first Alternative Trading Organizations (ATOs) were set up to promote imports from small producers in developing countries, acting as import agents, and selling the produce on to retail outlets. These organizations, like Oxfam, Traidcraft and Twin Trading, were attempting to provide an alternative to conventional international trade—cutting out middlemen, trading directly and providing alternative distribution channels. Run largely by Northern volunteers, they were trying to support small producers marginalized by mainstream trading arrangements, or who had had no opportunity to trade with the developed world. They encouraged producers to collaborate as trading groups and helped **non-governmental organizations (NGOs)** that had grown up in local markets to help impoverished artisans and craftsmen bring their goods to market. Often these ATOs also had their basis in religious or other community-based organizations, working as social entrepreneurs, using a business mindset to address social problems. Their products, largely handicrafts and textiles until the 1990s, were sold mostly through catalogues and world shops (see also **Alternative trade movement**).

The ATO structures and mission are unique in the business world and whilst this does not necessarily mean they are small scale (Gepa in Germany, for instance, had a turnover of €54m. in 2008/09), it does make it difficult for ATOs to access working capital or investment for expansion. ATOs are generally reluctant to incorporate venture capital or public shareholders into their structure for fear of diluting the social mission or producer ownership components of the company structure. On the other hand, traditional lending companies are not often equipped to assess risk for a company that is, for instance, a third owned by coffee farmers in Ghana, with higher cost goods than its competitors, and with slim profit margins to show.

Even as fair trade has got mainstreamed, and high street supermarkets have started selling fair trade products, the term ATO is still used to distinguish between companies that were set up with the explicit purpose of delivering fair trade benefits to producers, and second-mover companies that have adopted the Fairtrade label to meet a market opportunity. While nearly all ATOs have adopted the **Fairtrade Labelling Organizations International (FLO)** certification, some of the features distinguishing ATOs from more mainstream players are, first, that all or nearly all their products are traded according to Fairtrade principles which include pricing, direct trade, long-term relationships and credit provision for producer groups. Second, ATOs are typically structured to return the maximum amount of income to farmers, even above the Fairtrade minimum, and in that sense they are still 'alternative' in that profit is not their key interest.

Altro Mercato

The CTM Altro Mercato consortium was founded in 1988 in Bolzano, Italy, with the goal of offering solutions to address inequalities between North and South. In 1998 the original co-operative CTM (Cooperativa Terzo Mondo or Third World Co-operative) became a consortium, focusing its actions on developing the network of Fair Trade Organizations, and supporting activities for a fairer economy in the South. Today, CTM Altro Mercato is the largest Fair Trade Organization in Italy comprising 130 organizations (associations and co-operative societies) that manage 350 world shops (Botteghe del Mondo) throughout Italy and outside. These organizations, while acting as alternative traders, also inform and educate their local public about trade issues. The group has the goal of promoting a solidarity economy that generates initiatives aimed at the self-development of marginalized producers at both the international and local levels. The consortium offers a wide range of goods made by small producers in the South that are marketed by a network of not-for-profit organizations.

CTM Altro Mercato imports over 200 food and 3,000 handicraft products directly from 150 producer partner organizations worldwide. The consortium also offers social audit research and training for key partners. The strength of the brand in Italy is such that the consortium has made a strategic decision not to carry the **FLO** label on any of its products, including those for which it is eligible. CTM Altro Mercato is a member of **IFAT** and through IFAT became a registered Fair Trade Organization in 2004. See www.altromercato.it/en.

Anti-dumping duties

Goods are said to have been 'dumped' when they are exported to a country at a price below the cost of manufacturing it in the exporting country. Anti-dumping duties are specific import duties imposed by importing countries on goods which are dumped by foreign exporters, especially when those imported goods are found to cause or to threaten material injury to the industry of the importing country.

Anti-globalization movement

This might be described as a loose agglomeration of efforts to construct an alternative economic and social reality to counter the neoliberal vision. The movement is credited with having forced the failures of globalization onto the political agenda, raising important questions around social justice. Some of the clarion calls uniting this movement have been, 'Another world is possible' and 'Fair trade, not free trade'.

Opposition, or resistance, to globalization has taken various forms. It has been highly fragmented, and has included such different groups as the Zapatistas in Mexico, American militias, Aum Shinrikyo in Japan, environmental NGOs, the women's movement, New Ageists, and religious fundamentalists. Uniting the many different hues and views of the anti-globalization movement is its opposition to neoliberal or corporate globalization. It claims to fight for equity, social justice, democracy and security for everyone. Although trade does figure in the agenda, and the movement has gained visibility in the context of various rounds of WTO meetings (e.g. Seattle, Cancun, Doha), the vision is much broader and seeks global social and economic justice.

Opposition to the neoliberal vision has come from the left and the right of the political spectrum. On the right are those motivated by a fear of reduced living standards, a loss of national identity and culture by the diffusion of powerful foreign influences, particularly through the media, and the loss of national sovereignty. This anti-globalist rhetoric denounces free trade agendas, the power of multinational companies and international institutions, the perceived threat posed by transnational migration and imported labour, and the perceived Americanization of national cultures and the general permeability of national borders to transnational influences. In the Global South, this has taken the form of rising nationalist populism and religious fundamentalism, such as the Hindu nationalist parties in India or Osama bin Laden's al-Qa'ida. On the left of the political spectrum are those claiming to be guided by the ideals of equality and social justice for all people in the world, not just for the citizens of their own countries. One of the main arguments of this group is that globalization is widening the gap between the haves and the have-nots, benefiting the rich (and the richer nations) disproportionately. They seek to construct a new international economic and political order based on a global redistribution of wealth and power and include activists, political parties, NGOs and campaigners concerned with the environment, fair trade, labour standards, exploitation and human rights issues, all aiming to achieve a level playing ground and more equitable relations between the Global North and the Global South.

Apparel industry

The apparel industry is often cited as a precedent for the current conflicts and contradictions in relation to fair trade. Several manufacturers of clothing and shoes gained positive media coverage in the 1990s after they signed up to corporate codes of conduct. This was an industry that had come under immense criticism for labour abuses in 'sweatshops', largely based overseas in the East and Far East. However, many of the corporate codes have proved to be too weak to afford workers meaningful protection. But embracing these codes in the 1990s has helped these companies in the public's eye as these brand names are now seen as being socially responsible.

In *No Logo*, Naomi Klein argues that although apparel corporations were initially resistant even to voluntary codes of conduct, they eventually came to see these, even when monitored and enforced by non-governmental and labour organizations, as preferable to regulation enshrined in law or in trade agreements.

Asia Fair Trade Centre of Excellence

This centre was founded to act as a resource to help craft producers to improve the quality of the information flows between themselves and their consumers in order to be able to target new product development more efficiently. It draws on consultancy expertise from successful Fair Trade Organizations, and attempts to spread best practice amongst smaller groups. One of its most notable successes has been its support of a fair trade craft presence at the Bangkok International Gift Fair, a major international industry event, which it uses to connect small-scale producers and large Northern buyers. With a view to selling to the 'premium' gifts market, the centre seeks to understand the needs of that market, and then fit the design and quality control process to target this by simultaneously and systematically raising skill levels amongst fair trade producers to bring handicrafts into the key position occupied by fair trade food products.

Asia Fair Trade Forum

This is a regional partnership supporting a dual track approach to market development that both engages with the **Fairtrade Labelling Organizations**

International (FLO) registration, and seeks to grow demand closer to home. Forums such as this are part of a strategy to examine the potential for developing demand within the South rather than continuing reliance exclusively on Northern markets, particularly targeting the growing middle classes in Southern countries.

B

Bananas

Bananas constitute the fourth most consumed product in the world, grown almost exclusively in the South. As consumer demand for this fruit has grown, the pursuit of increased yields and profit has gone hand in hand with stories of abuses of land and people, especially in Latin America.

The global banana export industry is concentrated in the hands of five large companies that control almost the entire consumer market from farm to distribution. Dole, Del Monte and Chiquita together account for 55%–60% of world trade. Fyffes in Europe and Noboa in the USA control another 25%. It is a highly vertically integrated industry with a very tight time frame to market due to the product's very short shelf life.

On account of their perishable nature and sensitive supply chain logistics, export bananas are grown mostly on large monocrop plantations that employ hundreds of farm workers. Small farmers grow less than 10% of export bananas, and they are largely concentrated in the Caribbean. Fair trade thus has to address the development needs of both small producers and farm workers and operates two models—one specifically aimed at co-operatives and the other for organizations of farm workers. Certification includes payment of a living wage, provision of decent working conditions, and the presence of independent unions or worker associations.

The banana industry has had a bad press, particularly with the dropping real wages of workers as MNC margins are squeezed by retailers trying to get a better deal, or the associated health hazards of using insecticides and pesticides on a large scale in plantations that are very vulnerable to crop destruction. For example, there were media reports on a lawsuit brought by ex-workers against Chiquita, Del Monte and Dole for health problems allegedly developed from their exposure to dangerous pesticides whilst working on banana farms owned by these MNCs.

The Dutch NGO, **Solidaridad**, founded **AgroFair** in the mid-1990s to improve the prices received by banana farmers in developing countries. It has since become a model through its innovative producer ownership structure. It also introduced a minimum fair trade pricing in the banana industry. Since FLO had not yet begun certifying bananas, AgroFair devised its own environmental and social standards and calculated the minimum cost of sustainable production, taking into account the lower yields incurred by the prohibition of dangerous pesticides. That initial work by AgroFair laid the foundation for the fair trade banana standards adopted by FLO in 1997 for international certification.

Since then, fair trade bananas, together with chocolate and coffee, have captured an important share of the market in several Western European nations, especially where their debut has been accompanied by a strong promotional campaign (in Switzerland, for instance, fair trade bananas have captured half the market).

The politics around certification are well demonstrated in the case of bananas. The world's second largest banana corporation, Chiquita, negotiated with Transfair to receive certification. While there are those that support Chiquita's move on the grounds of perceived benefits including distribution, market access, visibility, and volume, Chiquita also has a history of working with the USA to suppress democratic movements in South America since the 1950s. As such, questions are raised about its credentials to be a partner in a movement for a fairer society.

The Body Shop

The Body Shop International plc is the second largest cosmetic franchise in the world, following O Boticario, a Brazilian company. The company, founded by Dame Anita Roddick, is now part of the L'Oréal corporate group. The Body Shop launched Community Trade in 1987, signalling their commitment to trading fairly and responsibly with suppliers. They source directly from farmers and offer suppliers a stable, long-term income. Operating with this fair trade model, they currently work with over 25,000 farmers and producers worldwide who supply them with 20 of their naturally derived ingredients and over 60 different gifts and accessories. See www.thebodyshop.co.uk.

Branding

Brands are augmented products that are differentiated and well positioned versus other goods in that product category. In order to dominate, a global brand must be a leading brand in all the important markets in the world. A brand is usually marked by a logo, symbol, trademark, brand name, colour, or shape, and is distinguishable by its positioning, its marketing mix, distribution, strategic principles and **advertising**. Often price, rather than appearance or functionality, can constitute the key differentiator, marking a branded product as a status symbol (e.g. Nike shoes).

Global brands, while global in reach, originate in particular countries. The majority of global brands today are based out of the USA. In non-Western societies, consumption of the brand may help make aspirational American/Western lifestyles feel more accessible. No global brand, however, is fully globally standardized in terms of brand name, packaging and advertising throughout the world. They simply share the same strategic principles, positioning and marketing, and comparable brand loyalty in every market throughout the world.

Branding is considered a symptom of an advanced or postmodern consumer culture, where minute differences between products, or minute improvements in them can determine variations in demand. Consumption thus becomes differentiated on the basis of signifiers—their 'brand names'. Here consumption, or the capacity to consume, is also reflexively consumed, captured in terms such as 'taste', 'fashion' and 'lifestyle', which become critical sources of social differentiation, displacing class and political affiliation (see also **Commodities** and **Consumerism**).

It is argued that the key criteria for successful brands have changed significantly over the past 30 years—from pragmatic, price- and value-driven imperatives towards a bundle of meanings that suggest a brand is adopting a definable position in a given moral or ethical framework. Driving this shift has been the increasing volume of accessible information on social issues globally, and the use of the internet to disseminate information widely on, for instance, unethical corporate behaviour. As a consequence, the 'concerned' consumer now focuses on production and supply chain issues as well as the intrinsic properties of a product and the service package surrounding it. Consumer focus has moved down the supply chain. The result of this increased consumer interest has been a dramatic rise in demand for, for instance, fairly traded products.

Fair trade itself has become a brand (Fairtrade) that consumers associate with social justice. However, the fair trade movement has not been particularly strategic about pushing their 'brand', particularly since it is offered in the market by a range of players, including national labelling initiatives. In addition, a number of fair trade businesses like Equal Exchange and Cafédirect have been creating their own brand values and the Fairtrade mark is only part of that message. Then there are supermarkets' own-label fair trade products. To date there has been no attempt to co-ordinate the range of brand meanings associated with fair trade.

Consumers benefit from having only one phrase and one logo to understand when searching for socially responsible products. However, with a mushrooming in labels, with 'sustainable', 'organic', 'kosher', 'shade grown', 'locally grown', etc., brand meanings become confused and consumers experience what has been termed 'label fatigue'.

The Fairtrade mark signifies buying into a fairer contribution to the producer's life and environment, acting as a signifier between consumer, producer and the attached values. That signification is triggered by independent accreditation or certification. The Fairtrade Foundation's certification mark is aimed to reassure the consumer by representing proof of a defined social audit of all accredited Fairtrade products. It acts as a brand encompassing the range of ethical meanings incorporated in the Fairtrade supply chain process.

'Ethical' branding has begun to play an even more strategic role as its role in encouraging repurchase is recognized. Companies now try and combine ethical values with statements of unique and premium quality. It is third party certification that gives credence to these corporations, and companies choose to open their financial accounts, submit to an audit of their supply chain, and even pay for this process, because there is branded value in this certification. Indeed, companies are finding that any fair trade marketing undertaken by a competitor increases brand equity behind the fair trade label and benefits all products carrying that label. And this works for non-competitor products as well—someone buying fair trade bananas might recognize the fair trade logo on the coffee shelves as well, and decide to buy that. Competitors have also been joining forces to promote logos together. For instance, in April 2004 TransFair USA announced the creation of a joint marketing fund to which licensed companies could contribute for the generic marketing of TransFair USA's 'Fair Trade Certified' seal. This seal is tied to a product category rather than a brand and companies could request specific geographic regions for promoting the label.

There are, however, significant differences even within fair trade products. For example, coffee offers more opportunities for product differentiation through different flavours, origins, growing regions, and brands. Bananas, on the other hand, are more commoditized. However, since supermarkets tend to carry only one brand of banana (unlike coffee), any company that can undercut a competitor and provide lower-cost bananas can capture large volumes of business because whilst consumers may be brand aware, they are not necessarily brand loyal. Thus, it is a highly competitive buyers market in which supermarkets can exercise power over MNCs to extract margin, often passed on by the MNCs to the weakest link in the chain, the producers themselves.

Bretton Woods system/institutions

In July 1944 delegates from 44 countries met in Bretton Woods in the USA and managed to reach a series of multilateral agreements on the post-Second World War international economic order. The new framework was based on a stable, co-operative international monetary system, which would prevent financial crises. Exchange rates were fixed against the US dollar and the US dollar was fixed to gold at a rate of $35 per ounce. The strength of the US economy, the fixed relationship of the dollar to gold, and the commitment of the US Government to convert dollars into gold at that price implied that the US dollar was as good as gold. Thus, the Bretton Woods system managed to secure the advantages of the gold standard without its disadvantages. Countries were committed to ensure the convertibility of their currencies into foreign currencies and to **free trade**.

These agreements were the outcome of lengthy negotiations between the USA and the UK. There were considerable differences between both positions. The US proposal was drafted by Harry Dexter White and the British plan by economist John Maynard Keynes. Keynes envisioned the establishment of a world reserve currency administered by a central bank with the authority to issue money and to take large-scale action. In case of imbalances in the balance of payments, creditors and debtors could change their policies. Countries with payment surplus would increase their imports from deficit countries and, thus, facilitate the creation of a trade equilibrium. However, the overwhelming political, military and economic power of the USA ensured that White's plan was implemented at Bretton Woods. Consequently, Bretton Woods institutions were shaped by neoliberal ideas (see **Neoliberalism**), which stressed controlling inflation and budgetary austerity rather than actively eradicating poverty.

While a number of Bretton Woods institutions are still in existence, they have changed substantially since their inception. The fixed exchange rate system collapsed in the 1960s, due to recovery in Western Europe and Japan and the unwillingness of those countries to revalue their currencies against the US dollar. The link of the US dollar with gold was finally severed by US President Richard Nixon in 1971.

The Bretton Woods agreement created several multilateral institutions to manage the new international economic system: the **International Monetary Fund (IMF)** and the International Bank for Reconstruction and Development (IBRD) (see **World Bank**). The World Bank and the IMF have come under severe criticism for the neoliberal underpinnings in their policies. The IMF, rather than being a lender of last resort, is viewed as an institution of neocolonial governance on behalf of its Organisation for Economic Co-operation and Development (OECD) shareholders, ensuring that policies agreed by industrialized countries are carried out by the South. Its economic bail-outs in the form of **structural adjustment** programmes have at best had mixed results, with several instances of no effects or negative fall-outs. The World Bank has been criticized for commanding large resources and exercising immense control over other financial institutions, while having no accountability and a near monopoly on research.

C

Cafédirect

This fairly traded brand of coffee was the very first of its kind. It was set up in the early 1990s, with its first product launch in the UK in 1991 (roast and ground coffee). Today this is the fourth largest coffee brand in the UK market and is worth £8.4m. It is managed by Penny Newman, and was founded jointly by Equal Exchange UK, Traidcraft, Oxfam and Twin Trading. The company states that its mission is to be the 'leading brand which strengthens the influence, income and security of producer partners in the south and links them directly to the consumer'. See www.cafedirect.co.uk.

The company had to be financially supported by its founders for over 12 years as it found it difficult to negotiate outside sources of investment. It went through a major reorganization in 2003, which gave producers a more active role and influence in the company's affairs through ownership of shares and representation on the company's board. In 2004 Cafédirect offered a share issue to raise capital and make its ownership structure more inclusive. However, to ensure that the company's fair trade purpose remained sacrosanct, public shareholders have limited voting rights and its founders retain guardian shares of the company.

Cafédirect always intended to be in the mainstream and compete directly with other mainstream coffee suppliers. It was set up as a for-profit business, and was the first fair trade company to engage in some major marketing campaigns. Cafédirect used individual suppliers' stories to highlight the key differences in coffee coming through the fair trade process vis-à-vis other mainstream coffee supply chains. It repositioned its strategy from 2000 to stress the quality, range and differentiation of its products.

Though the company started with one product, it is today selling about 41 products, including drinking chocolate, gourmet and speciality coffees and teas. The company's turnover for the 15 months ending 31 December 2009 was £24.3m. The company pays fair trade prices and premiums, and reinvests a proportion of its profits in producer capacity building. In 2009 Cafédirect paid Fairtrade premiums of £917,000 (up from £886,000 in 2008). The company works with 33 producer organizations in 11 countries involving over one-quarter of a million producers, partnerships which have enabled independent social development projects in local infrastructure, schools and health care facilities in the communities with which they work.

CAFOD

CAFOD was born out of a Family Fast Day organized by the National Board of Catholic Women in response to a request from the people of the Caribbean Island of Dominica for help with a mother-and-baby healthcare programme in 1961. The following year the Catholic Bishops of England and Wales officially set up CAFOD (then known as the Catholic Fund for Overseas Development). Today it is called the Catholic Agency for Overseas Development and works in over 40 countries worldwide. The aim of this organization was to provide a focus for all the small-scale charitable efforts which were already taking place.

CAFOD was one of the group that established the Fairtrade Foundation, the UK's third party auditor of fair trade practices for selected goods. It is an anti-poverty, faith-based organization. It works with poor and disadvantaged communities in the Global South to overcome poverty and bring about sustainable development and well-being; protects lives and relieves suffering during emergencies, and reduces the risks to vulnerable communities as a result of conflict and natural disasters; raises awareness and understanding of the causes of poverty and injustice to inspire a commitment to lasting change; and challenges those with power to adopt appropriate policies. See www.cafod.org.uk.

Capital flows

As economies have become more open and integrated with the rest of the world with globalization, countries have received high levels of capital flows. During the 1970s and 1980s capital flows were mainly directed to governments or to the private sector through the banking system. There has been a dramatic rise in capital flows in the 1990s, taking the form of **foreign direct investment** and, increasingly, portfolio flows, including both bond and equity flows, as developing countries liberalized their domestic financial markets and opened them up to foreign investors. In 1997 the World Bank stated that the proportion of emerging stock markets allowing free entry to foreign investors roughly doubled to nearly 60% between 1991 and 1994. This period also saw developing countries privatizing public sector or government enterprises, and developing deeper and more liquid financial markets.

A critical reason for the growth in capital flows has been advances in information and communications technologies, making it much easier to evaluate and monitor investments around the globe. The management of risk has also been rendered easier with technological advances and with the development of new financial instruments and financial products.

Standard models of capital asset pricing suggest that investors seeking to diversify their portfolios should hold equities in different markets roughly in proportion to the share of these markets in total market capitalization. However, even though the 1990s saw a significant increase in capital flows, international portfolio diversification is far from complete, with shares of foreign assets still lower than those in domestic assets, creating what is called a 'home bias'. Part of the reason for this is that capital flows to developing countries tend to still be concentrated around a few 'emerging' markets. Between 1990 and 1997, for instance, about 75% of private capital flows went to a dozen countries, of which 60% went to six countries: the People's Republic of China, Brazil, Mexico, Thailand, Indonesia, and the Republic of Korea.

Capital flows are influenced by both global and domestic factors but their relative importance tends to vary over time. While capital flows provide significant benefits to investors and recipients, their sensitivity to economic conditions makes recipient countries vulnerable to sudden reversals, as evidenced in recent 'boom and bust' cycles. The challenge for developing countries is to design economic policies that secure the most benefits from capital inflows while reducing their vulnerability to sudden reversals. Adopting more flexible exchange rates and strengthening domestic financial systems have been some of the ways countries have sought to reduce their vulnerability.

Capitalism

Capitalism might be described as an economic system, or mode of production, in which the means of production are privately owned and controlled. Grounded in a belief in the sanctity of private property rights and the efficacy of the free market, advocates of the capitalist system see 'capital' as a 'factor of production' along with land (earning rent) and labour (earning wages). Each combine through the process of production, distribution and exchange via the market, and in the process generate wealth. Profit maximization is regarded as the primary motivation for economic activity and the economy is organized according to the market, i.e. the forces of demand and supply.

The drive to maximize profits leads capitalism to go 'global' as it expands to exploit new markets with new products. From the appropriation of the surplus value by an owner from a worker, capitalism expands to an appropriation of the surplus value of the whole world by some core areas. As such, capitalism is seen as producing a truly global system. Globalization is variously seen as an outcome of capitalism in the modern period, or the product of the 'disorganized capital' of post-industrialism or post-modernity.

Capitalism emerged in the 17th century in Europe. The growth of capitalist market economies aided the breakdown of feudalism and the rise of liberalism. With its emphasis on individualism and the role of property, capitalism is sometimes regarded as the economic side of liberalism. The classical theoretical model of capitalism sees rational individuals, with perfect information, pursuing their interests, free of governmental or geographic obstacles. Freedom and liberty are central values for liberalism and capitalism. Both seek to limit the power of the state and maximize the choice of the individual. Capitalism, therefore, was and still is seen as a condition for liberal democracy.

There are many different forms of capitalism. The two best known are laissez-faire or free market capitalism, and Keynesianism. In its most extreme version, free market capitalism advocates market liberalization and the retreat of the state from the economic sector. The market is perceived as a self-regulating mechanism that should not be encumbered by external forces. These ideas find their expression in the works of Adam Smith (1723–90), as well as in contemporary economic **neoliberalism**. A second perspective, generally attributed to John Maynard Keynes (1883–1946), accepts capitalism as the most reliable mechanism for the generation of wealth. However, far from being self-regulating, Keynes views unregulated capitalism as chronically unstable. Market adjustments can take a long time, labour is not as flexible as demanded by market forces, and economic crisis and market failure can cause social unrest and instability. Hence, he argues, the state ought actively to intervene and regulate the market. This system of capitalism laid the foundation of the welfare state and dominated economic policies in the developed world from the end of the Second World War until the 1970s.

With the collapse of the Communist states in Eastern Europe, capitalism and liberalism are seen to have emerged as global systems without any credible ideological challenge. An economic system operating along capitalist lines now encompasses most of the world, and economic motives constitute an important (though by no means the only) reason for creating global linkages. The capitalist logic dictates that surplus is accumulated, which is reinvested in further production for profit. The contexts for accumulation have slowly spread to all aspects of life, with society getting thoroughly monetized and the new communications and financial flows enhancing possibilities for accumulation. Complex networks of international finance exist, and **multinational companies (MNCs)** constitute the significant organizers of capitalism worldwide. Raw materials, capital and labour are now sourced globally.

Since all parties in a capitalist order seek to accumulate, there are perpetual and pervasive contests over the distribution of surplus, between firms, classes, races, sexes, countries, etc. It has been argued that capitalism has led to combined and uneven development, with more and more areas in the periphery lured into dependency in an ever-expanding, world-wide consumer society.

Today the globalization discourse has become polarized through the ideological debate between the right and the left, often depicted as a clash between capitalism and anti-capitalism, framed in the language of anti-globalization (see **Anti-globalization movement**).

Caritas International

Caritas is a global movement working in solidarity for a fairer world, inspired by the example of Christian faith and Catholic Social Teaching. The 165 national Caritas members make the biggest network of Catholic charities in the world devoted to reducing poverty and campaigning for social justice.

Caritas' work is about ensuring that the poorest and most marginalized are the driving force in emergency response, sustainable development and peace building. To achieve this, it focuses on six key areas: peace and reconciliation; emergencies; economic justice; climate change; HIV and Aids; and women and migration. See www.caritas.org.

Centre-periphery *see* **Dependency theory.**

Certification in Fairtrade

The first fair trade products gained credibility with customers by being located in world or charity shops such as Oxfam in the UK or Ten Thousand Villages in the USA. However, as fair trade groups ventured into new products and began to expand their outlets, it became evident that consumers would benefit from a certification label that identified an independent fair trade audit process for the product in question. The certification process began with the Max Havelaar Foundation in the Netherlands, and a number of national initiatives co-existed in Europe, the USA, Canada and Japan between 1989 and 1995. Realizing that economies of scale could be reached by jointly monitoring producer groups and co-ordinating standard setting, discussions began with the aim of forming an internationally co-ordinated inspection and labelling system, and in 1997 the 17 existing national initiatives joined together to form **Fairtrade Labelling Organizations International (FLO)**, which rapidly became the largest social certification system in the world, covering the most products in the most countries. Today there are around 19 international fair trade labelling organizations, and FLO's membership is also still growing.

Fair trade product certification principles include direct purchasing from democratically organized producers; transparent and long-term trading relationships; agreed minimum prices, a social premium for investing in capacity building, technical assistance and social development projects. The principles have been set out to shorten the supply chain to relink producers and consumers, and maximize producers' returns.

But the process of acquiring certification can be quite complex and expensive. Few new products are certified each year, and in fair trade, these are still largely confined to agricultural products. Textiles or handicrafts are more diverse in terms of production techniques and specifications, and it is nearly impossible to devise and audit certification standards that can broadly be applied to them all.

FLO and its member National Initiatives certify products, not companies. But consumers often associate the certification seal with the entire company's dealings so that it creates a halo effect. As such, companies manage to attain a 'socially responsible' veneer with their consumers without having to alter their business practices with the vast majority of their products. Furthermore, companies that have only a few lines that are fairly traded could use the profits from non-fair trade sales to promote their fair trade lines, a route not open to companies only dealing in fair trade products, thus disadvantaging the latter.

FLO's certification process involves more than 60 local inspectors doing the groundwork. Once a producer group has registered for an inspection, an FLO inspector spends a period of time onsite commensurate with the size of the co-operative or plantation involved (e.g. one or two weeks). Following the inspection, the FLO inspector writes a compliance-assessment report on the group's adherence to the relevant product standards, which the Certification Committee reviews to determine a group's compliance. Once the standard-setting, producer inspections and Certification Committee approvals are finalized, traders can apply to the Labelling Initiative (LI) in their country to participate in FLO's system. Approved traders are audited on their Fairtrade transactions, submitting to FLO and/or the LI transparent reports of all sales and purchases of Fairtrade produce to the point of labelling the final product. Existing FLO-certified producer groups are reinspected annually, and in addition, there are further random inspection visits by FLO inspectors.

Overseen by the Certification and Appeals Committee, FLO conducts trade audits of producers, exporters and importers. When an importer buys the product from a Fairtrade co-operative, the LI in the country in which that product is intended for sale tracks the supply chain. The companies that buy the Fairtrade-labelled product from FLO-registered traders require a licence from the LI in order to sell that product. Thus, FLO ensures that producers and traders comply with the standards and that producers invest the benefits received through Fairtrade into development projects.

Other social certification systems and labels include business-facing ones such as the **Social Accountability International** and **International Standards Organization**, and consumer-facing ones such as **Utz Kapeh** and the **Rainforest Alliance**. There is also now a registration model, promoted by **IFAT**, which has created the Fair Trade Organization (FTO) Mark as a company label to be used largely by producers and importers of handicrafts.

Child labour

The use of children on plantations, despite laws existing to protect children, has resulted in bad press, particularly for the banana industry. Governments, like that of Ecuador, have in the past relied on lack of enforcement to be able to increase its supply of bananas to an international market trying to squeeze prices down. The cheaper prices for consumers meant that workers did not get minimum wages, and often children were employed to cut costs.

FLO fair trade standards require farms and co-operatives to abide by International Labour Organization standards and domestic laws regarding, for instance, the use of child labour. A dilemma is often perceived in this situation—it is argued that banning child labour shows a lack of sensitivity to cultures where it might be commonplace for children to help the economy of their families through labouring, and local laws permit this. However, in Ecuador there was evidence of children working in hazardous conditions, exposed to pesticides, heavy labour and even sexual harassment. Several recent initiatives to stop using child labour (e.g. the 2004 Common Code for the Coffee Community that Nestlé, Sara Lee, Kraft and Tchibo have signed up to) forbids the use of child labour on coffee farms.

Chiquita

This is one of the three biggest **banana** companies in the world, together with Dole and Del Monte. Following media reports in the 1990s regarding a lawsuit brought against Chiquita, Dole and Del Monte for health problems, the company began working with the New York-based NGO, **Rainforest Alliance**, to improve environmental and working conditions on company-owned banana farms. However, it still does not guarantee a minimum price to banana farmers.

In 2000 the company adopted the core values and updated the code of conduct to include **Social Accountability International's** SA8000 labour standards. The same year the Rainforest Alliance certified 100% of Chiquita's farms in Latin America to strict environmental and social standards of the Better Banana Project, and in 2003 the company received the 'Corporate Conscience Award' from Social Accountability International.

However, Chiquita has not quite managed to rid itself of its murky history, with past tales of abuses of plantation workers in Colombia and a case against the company for financially supporting paramilitary groups in that country.

Chocolate

Whilst the fine processing of chocolate is done in the North (consider Swiss or Belgian chocolates, for instance), the cocoa beans that are the key ingredients in the product are grown in developing countries. And it is the link with the cocoa bean producer that fair trade companies have sought to make in the minds of the consumer through brands like Day Chocolate, a Fairtrade firm operating in the UK. And whilst mainstream coffee and chocolate brands have been slow to adopt fair trade practices, supermarkets have increased their own fair trade offer through the development of own-label Fairtrade products. For example, when the UK-based supermarket chain, the Co-operative Group, converted its own-label chocolate bars to Fairtrade, year-on-year sales increased 25%, despite a small price rise. If the fair trade chocolate market continues to grow, the big chocolate brands will have to take notice of these trends (see also **Divine Chocolate**).

Christian Aid

Christian Aid is a Christian organization that works towards a world free from poverty. It works to eradicate the causes of poverty, and is part of a wider movement for social justice. Christian Aid work on climate change, conflict, HIV and malaria, rights and justice, and trade.

Christian Aid was one of the partners in setting up the Fairtrade Foundation, the UK's third party auditor of Fair Trade practices for selected goods, in 1994. Their trade agenda seeks to make trade bring about positive changes rather than deepening and prolonging poverty, and to achieve this, they are trying to ensure that the European Union does not coerce its former colonies to open up their markets through economic partnership agreements; remove all IMF and World Bank conditionalities attached to loans and debt-cancellation agreements; and ensure that WTO agreements support development rather than free trade for its own sake. See www.christianaid.org.uk.

Citizens' movements for corporate accountability

People in many parts of the world have been fighting corporate abuses against communities, workers and the environment. Unions, for instance, have been forming innovative alliances across borders. Many citizens' fights have been at the level of survival—communities or workers clashing with corporations over the pollution of water or the air, or corporate decisions to shut down plants or abuses of workers' rights. Two arenas of citizen influence have been attempts to amend trade agreements, including fighting for a 'social clause' in GATT which defines violations of workers' rights as an unfair trade practice inviting sanctions (and more recently, environmental rights and standards), and second, corporate codes and related initiatives by corporations themselves, governments and citizen groups.

Clean Clothes Campaign (CCC)

The Clean Clothes Campaign (CCC), a civil society campaign, is dedicated to improving working conditions and supporting the empowerment of workers in the global garment and sportswear industries. Since its inception in the Netherlands in 1989, the CCC has worked to help ensure that the fundamental rights of workers are respected. The CCC educates and mobilizes consumers, lobbies companies and governments, and offers direct solidarity support to workers as they fight for their rights and demand better working conditions.

The Clean Clothes Campaign is an alliance of organizations in 13 European countries, and membership includes trade unions and NGOs covering a broad spectrum of perspectives and interests, such as women's rights, consumer advocacy and poverty reduction. The CCC relies on a partner network of more than 200 organizations and unions in garment-producing countries to identify local problems and objectives, and to help them develop campaign strategies to support workers in achieving their goals. The CCC co-operates extensively with similar labour rights campaigns in the USA, Canada, and Australia.

The CCC has developed a 'Code of Labour Practices for the Apparel Industry Including Sportswear' based upon the conventions of the International Labour Organization, the principles of which include a minimum employment wage, safe working conditions, set working hours and a right to a living wage. The CCC pressures retailers and manufacturers to adopt the Code of Labour Practices and ensure that these principles are upheld. Successful campaigning by the CCC has led many businesses to adopt a list of standards for suppliers. The CCC also presses companies to ensure that their buying practices, such as pricing and delivery schedules, do not make it unfeasible for factories to provide decent work. See www.cleanclothes.org.

Cocoa

According to the World Cocoa Foundation, about 45m. people over the world depend on cocoa for their livelihood. About half of the world's cocoa comes from Côte d'Ivoire and Ghana in West Africa, with Indonesia being another major producer. As for other commodity crops, like coffee, prices for cocoa beans are set by international commodity traders in the London and New York stock exchanges, artificially causing large fluctuations in its price, the brunt of which is faced by small farmers who, after harvesting the pods, may find that the income they earn does not cover production costs. Between 2000 and 2003, prices went from a 27-year low to a 16-year high! It is this instability in price and uncertainty about the market that fair trade tries to assuage by establishing a long-term relationship with producers, paying a fair minimum price, and a further premium to invest in community projects. The cocoa so produced is mostly used in chocolates, a higher end and more value-added activity that takes place in the North, and still largely a preserve of MNCs (see also **Divine Chocolate**).

Code of practice

Codes of practice (or codes of conduct) are at best a compromise between a low-bar and high-bar approach to business ethics. Most industry codes of conduct focus on the performance of the supplier, and do not touch upon the trading relationship between supplier and buyer.

FLO fair trade standards, for instance, require farms and co-operatives that employ significant numbers of workers to abide by International Labour Organization standards and domestic laws regarding the use of child labour, the right to organize, the use of dangerous chemicals and machinery, working hours, and other fundamental labour rights. FLO inspections verify that workers receive, at the very least, the country's legal minimum wage, or the local wage, whichever is higher. The fair trade process thus independently verifies wage and **labour standards** that may exist but which may not be enforced in producing countries. Similarly, the **IFAT** Code of Practice specifies that fair trade working conditions should conform to 'local statutory regulations' and further stipulates that equal employment opportunities must be in evidence.

For commodity farmer members of co-operatives, the fair trade floor price is the equivalent of a minimum wage, and is intended to provide farmers with sufficient income to cover their costs of production and provide for their families. For estate owners who hire labour to work on their farms, the fair trade floor price is considered enough to pay workers the minimum wage or the local wage (whichever is higher) and provide decent working conditions. The fair trade standards for hired labour require that International Labour Organization minimum labour standards are met regarding pay, worker safety and so on, and the standards ensure that this is possible through a guaranteed minimum price. However, when it comes to long-term contracts, FLO standards do not codify what a long-term relationship must be beyond the signing of the contract. Nor does IFAT include any explicit statement of the duration of trading relationships in its Fair Trade Code of Practice.

While the IFAT Code of Practice simply states that trading relationships should be characterized by 'equitable commercial terms, fair wages and fair prices', for nearly all fair trade products certified by FLO, there is a requirement that all producers be paid a minimum price for their product, regardless of how low the market price goes. Requiring fair trade importers to pay the social premium even when the market is high represents an attempt to offer farmers incentives to sell to the fair trade market even when prices are high in the non-fair trade market, thus ensuring the sustainability of the market. The IFAT Code of Practice effectively sidesteps the issue by not including any statements about social premia. (See also **Ethical Trading Initiative** and **Corporate social responsibility**.)

Many fashion houses are increasingly trying to co-opt the emotional value of ethical behaviour into their brand meanings via explicit codes of conduct or public statements on issues such as banning sweatshop labour from their supply chain. However, consumers remain cynical, as many so-called 'ethical' brands have been caught out in breach of their own codes (Nike is one example).

Coffee

This is one of the most valuable **primary commodities** in global trade. Second only to oil, coffee is a significant source of foreign exchange and a vital commodity for national economies. From the early 1960s until 1989 the coffee market was managed under the **International Coffee Agreement (ICA)**, designed to maintain relative market stability and high prices. Aside from a few price spikes due to Brazilian frosts, the world price for coffee fluctuated between US $1 and $1.50, and producer and consumer nations together set quotas for producing countries to maintain stable supply levels. Unless the price of coffee rose above this range, producing countries kept within their fair share of production levels.

When the ICA collapsed in 1989 coffee prices plummeted to US $0.49 per pound, well below producers' costs, and remained there for five years. Subsequent price increases in 1994/05 and 1997 resulting from frosts in Brazil only brought more coffee into the market as Viet Nam had begun to emerge as a major exporter. The glut devalued the premium robusta and Arabica coffee beans, causing high quality coffee typically sold at $1.60 per pound to drop to 48 cents. By 2002 coffee was trading at its lowest levels in three decades.

Coffee was the first labelled Fairtrade product sold in the North, and continues to be the highest volume and highest value product for most national fair trade markets. In developing the fair trade model, ATOs identified the points in the coffee export chain where poor farmers could capture more value and reconfigured trade and power relationships to ensure higher returns to primary producers. Fair trade works with small coffee producers, organized into co-operatives, which represent 50% of the world's production, and probably an even larger percentage of 'speciality' coffee production, grown on small shaded plots in regions that produce their own distinct flavours. The small farmer's isolation translates into a lack of access to markets, price information, futures exchanges and technical assistance, all of which the fair trade movement tries to address.

The global coffee roasting industry is dominated by five companies—Kraft, Nestlé, Sara Lee, Procter and Gable and Tchibo—which buy almost half of the global supply of green coffee beans. Eight MNCs control the export of more than half of the world's coffee production. Some 70% of the world's coffee is grown on plantations of less than 25 ha, and estimates of the world's production grown by very small family farmers owning less than 5 ha average at around 50%. Brazil, Viet Nam, Colombia and Indonesia account for over 60% of the production, and almost all coffee is produced in the developing world. But the supply chain is largely controlled by transnational coffee exporters and roasters.

Commodification

In its most basic sense, commodification means to turn into or treat as a **commodity** or make commercial. Karl Marx used the term to define the transformation of social relations, formerly untainted by commerce, or those to which no monetary value could be attached, into commercial relations, or relations that involved buying and selling. As such, commodification expresses a concept fundamental to Marx's understanding of the way **capitalism** develops. It is through the production of commodities that exchange surplus is created, extracted and amassed. A resource becomes commodified when it is incorporated into capitalist accumulation processes.

A key feature of capitalism relates to the kinds of objects that function as commodities. For instance, Marx was critically concerned with the commodification of the labour process, in which an individual worker's real, material activity, his labour, is transformed into a substitutable, abstract activity that could be measured in units of time. Labour, so abstracted, becomes another cost to the process of production.

The character of commodification has not remained unchanged over the history of capitalism. In the early capitalist period, under commercial capitalism, profit was acquired through trade in agricultural and mining outputs, and sale of luxury items. From the 1960s, commodification is seen to be intensifying in three areas. First is the increasing consumption, at a personal level, of global or branded products (see **Advertising** and **Branding**). Second is the increased volume and variety of financial instruments that have become channels for accumulation in their own right, rather than simply furthering capitalist production in agriculture or manufacturing. And finally, the last few years have seen new forms of commodification, as the content that passes through electronic processing systems, whether data, ideas, messages or images, are also getting commodified. Indeed, in the 21st century, information and communication technologies (ICTs) are moving to the core of capitalism, as accumulation processes spread to intangibles such as finance, communications and information, rather than tangible merchandise.

Commodities

The term commodity encompasses any object that has a value in relation to other goods, and can therefore be the object of economic exchange. In its original and simplified sense, commodities are things of value, of uniform quality, produced in large quantities by several different producers such that items from different producers might be considered equivalent and comparable. Commodities are given a non-standard form when they are branded, when they become unique in some sense, and distinguishable from other similar commodities. Branded products also tend to be priced differently, usually higher than similar but non-branded commodities (see **Advertising** and **Branding**).

In business parlance, a commodity is an undifferentiated product whose market value resides not so much in something inherent in it or its use, but in the owner's right to sell it. Thus, for instance, any product traded on a commodity exchange is a commodity. Examples include agricultural products, foreign currencies, metals, oil and financial instruments.

In Marxist political economy, a commodity is simply any good or service offered as a product for sale on the market. This also includes items treated like commodities, such as human labour, or even works of art or natural resources, that might be traded in the market (see **Commodification**). The production and distribution of commodities is the central defining feature of **capitalism**, structuring the entire society. Under capitalism, everything becomes a commodity in that everything can be bought or sold.

Commodity chains

Commodity chains might be considered a tool that helps analyse the hierarchies of production in the global economy by reconnecting production, distribution and consumption. The concept of a global commodity chain helps understand how marketing and consumption patterns in core areas (largely Northern countries) shape production patterns in peripheral and semi-peripheral regions (largely Southern countries) (see **Comparative advantage** and **World systems theory**).

Commodity chains link, at the global level, networks of labour and commodity production processes. The production and distribution of goods today take place in complex global networks that tie together groups, organizations and regions, with backward and forward linkages. Design, distribution and marketing constitute important nodes from where innovative strategies are developed that allow enterprises to capture a greater share of wealth within a chain. Indeed, a firm's growth and success is often based on its ability to capture a succession of nodes along the commodity chain, increasing its expertise and control over the critical areas of design, distribution, marketing and **advertising**, often leading to a complete reshaping of both production and consumption. This is, however, not to say that all production is governed by large transnational enterprises determining where to locate production. Nation states still exercise some control in determining the kind of production undertaken within its boundaries.

The outsourced or transnational linkages are critical. There exists a division of labour between the core or post-industrial societies specializing in certain services, and managing the command and control operations, and the non-core societies at various levels of industrialization (largely agriculture- or manufacturing-based). The chains formed between these sites may be producer- or buyer-driven. Producer-driven commodity chains operate in high-tech and specialized industries, able to exercise control over both raw materials and components, as well as retailing. As such, core firms control these commodity chains at the point of production, and they operate from within established areas of accumulation. Buyer-driven commodity chains, on the other hand, are controlled at the point of consumption. They tend to be more mobile and most of the labour intensive production is likely to take place in cheaper, developing country locations.

Economic globalization does not imply that the costs and benefits of economic activity are globalized or more equally distributed. Instead, the extension of the value-creation chain to different locations around the world has also brought about a new allocation of advantages and disadvantages. The unequal nature of the different points in the chain becomes evident, for instance, when examining the ecological division of labour between countries of the South (or East) and the North. As supply chains lengthen, there is a tendency to separate costs and benefits by redistributing them up and down the chain, with the environmental repercussions and other competitive pressures being shifted to the majority world, while profits and control are concentrated in the minority world. From a fair trade perspective, the global commodity chain approach highlights the primary marketing message that neoliberal economic structures have left many producers in the developing world disenfranchised within the supply chain.

Common Agricultural Policy

This is a set of agricultural subsidies offered by the European Union which acts as a trade barrier and grossly distorts trade relations with that region to the disadvantage of producers in the South. The subsidies are said to amount to as much as the entire gross domestic product of sub-Saharan Africa.

Comparative advantage

David Ricardo's theory of comparative advantage describes the benefits of the international division of labour. Ricardo was seeking to establish the case for removing all barriers to trade, and this theory was considered revolutionary at a time when trade was seen as a zero-sum game. Using a model with two countries and two products, Ricardo displayed how under given costs of production, international trade would be beneficial for both countries. If each country specialized in the production of the goods and services in which it was most efficient, both countries would eventually benefit from international trade since it would enable them to consume more than they would have been able to otherwise.

The theory of comparative advantage laid the foundation of modern neoliberal economic theory (see **Neoliberalism**). It suggests that the economy will prosper and economic growth and living standards will improve if a **free trade** system is adopted, with countries trading to their comparative advantage. The **structural adjustment** programmes prescribed by the **International Monetary Fund (IMF)**, for instance, urge developing countries to open their economies and to drop any protectionist barriers inhibiting the free movement of international trade (see **Protectionism**) and to follow export-oriented industrialization strategies. The **World Trade Organization (WTO)** also encourages states to remove tariff and non-tariff barriers and facilitate the functioning of the specialized international division of labour.

Ricardo's theory concentrated on differences in labour productivity as the sole reason for the existence of a comparative advantage, and this was perceived as quite narrow in scope. Modern trade theory in the form of the Hekscher-Ohlin model takes the notion of comparative advantage a step further. It focuses on factor endowments (capital and labour) and argues that a comparative advantage arises from the relative differences in factor endowments between countries.

Consumerism

Consumerism is most commonly used in a rather pejorative sense, suggesting the attainment of pleasure through identification with, or the purchase of, material objects or services. It is seen as being oriented to 'experiencing', placing greater value on sensation than on science, and the gratification of desires as more important than solving problems.

Consumerism is seen to include both the generation of desire and its gratification. It describes people frenetically acquiring, and usually just as quickly discarding, a variety of goods that provide the user with some kind of instant but fleeting gratification. It is essentially ephemeral in nature—it centres on the satisfaction of passing desires, especially cravings for novelty, fashion, entertainment and fantasy. It rejoices in excess while at the same time it is unable to see that the excess exists.

While an interest in consumption might be said to be historically universal across societies, in a consumer culture, or under consumerism, the items consumed take on a symbolic as opposed to a merely material value. A discourse about lifestyle choices is created, shaping desires, and marketing dreams as needs, thereby opening up new spaces for capital accumulation. Consumption begins to appear as the main form of self-expression and the chief source of identity. Need creation is effectively managed through design, packaging, **advertising**, and **branding** of products.

Consumerism is seen as an outcome of late capitalist restructuring. It has been expanding since the 1950s, with food and beverages, designer clothing, health and fitness aids, recreational drugs, sports and tourism, all being channelled to the creation and gratification of desires parading as needs. The core ritual of consumerism is shopping. Its largest consumers are urban, middle-class youth, proportionately greater in the North, though the South and East are quickly being sucked into consumerism through globalization. Marked-up prices and short product lives feed the growth of capitalism.

Three waves of consumerism are identified. The first focused on value for money, basic product information and reliable labelling; the second concentrated on consumer safety and manufacturer accountability. The third and most recent introduced environmental and ethical issues linked to notions of corporate citizenship and social responsibility, and is characterized by consumer awareness of issues like animal welfare, **environmental degradation**, human working conditions and trade justice.

Fair trade is seen as both an activist and a consumerist movement. As an activist movement it has been driven by campaigners who frame the perceived inequality in trading relations between developing and developed worlds as an ethical issue. As a consumerist movement it is driven by individuals' desire to know more about the actions of corporations and the nature of the products they buy, both of which can be perceived as a broader reaction against their historically passive role in the marketing relationship. Companies are seen to be accountable for their actions and interactions within their own supply chain, particularly as it is an integral part of their operations and a defining feature of their character as companies.

Coocafé

Cooperativa de Café, known as Coocafé, was founded in 1988. It is a secondary level service co-operative, and originally comprised five primary level co-operatives (which has now increased to nine). Coocafé is said to represent 3,500 farmers, including 256 women, and indirectly benefits 15,000 people. A major impact of the Coocafé/Fairtrade partnership has been to strengthen the operation of farmers' organizations at local, national and international levels. Coocafé members produce around 4,140 tons of arabica coffee beans each year, 80% of which is exported. Most of the co-operatives produce shade grown coffee, and are in transition to organic production.

Coocafé began working with European Fair Trade Organizations in 1989 and registered with **Fairtrade Labelling Organizations International (FLO)** in 1995. Just about half of its production is sold to the Fairtrade market. Of the remainder, a small amount is sold for national consumption, and the rest is sold to the conventional export market, frequently at higher than normal prices because of Coocafé's increased knowledge of the market and awareness of trading procedures. Coocafé established its own export department in 1997 with technical and marketing assistance from FLO, and in April 2002 Coocafé purchased its own warehouse and processing plant. The group of co-ops is now integrated from seed purchase to the export of bagged coffee.

Coffee produced by Coocafé is imported to the UK by Van Weely, Twin Trading, Equal Exchange and Wakefield and is marketed by 11 companies, including Cafédirect and Matthew Algie. Coocafé has also diversified into the export of yucca and plantain chips. See www.coocafe.com.

Co-operatives

Co-operatives emerged out of the need for an approach to business exchange that was not driven solely by the demands of capital but also by human rights and social justice. It is now the most widely distributed business structure in the world, ranging from retail giants like the John Lewis Partnership, to tiny producer groups in developing countries. Some of the drawbacks involved in isolated deals with middlemen in a buyer's market are overcome through organization into co-operatives as membership in a co-operative allows small farmers to benefit from group selling and buying, even with large traders in the North, thus at least partially addressing information imbalances in the trading system. It also helps small farmers reap benefits from financial markets while reducing their exposure to risk from price fluctuations. Larger co-operatives are also able to access competitive bids for formal loans and spread the benefits to their farmer members.

Under a co-operative structure, farmer members own shares in an umbrella business organization, with equity ownership usually proportional to the amount of product they sell through the co-operative. As the co-operative is owned by the farmers themselves and all co-operative profits are shared democratically according to the wishes of the farmer members, the market access component does not become exploitative.

The **Fairtrade standards** demand that small farmers be organized into co-operatives to distribute the Fairtrade premia. This also guarantees that farmers become engaged in the development of their businesses or communities. The co-operative structure allows small farmers to voice their opinions collectively, giving them more leverage at the national level. Furthermore, FLO Fairtrade standards require farms and co-operatives that employ significant numbers of workers to abide by International Labour Organization standards and domestic laws regarding the use of child labour, the right to organize, the use of dangerous chemicals and machinery, working hours and other fundamental labour rights. However, whilst FLO inspects co-operative management for adherence to the co-operatives' election policies and democratic structure, it cannot force management to devolve more power to the electorate, or even ensure management turnover.

Core-periphery *see* **Dependency theory.**

Corporate accountability

Traditionally, corporations professed accountability only to their shareholders. The notion of corporate accountability, however, stretches beyond shareholders to all those affected by a corporation, and includes, for instance, legal rights for local communities to seek compensation when they have suffered as a result of the corporation failing to uphold the environmental and social duties placed on them. Rather than allow corporations to take charge of improving their social and environmental performance voluntarily, human rights, development and environmental groups are lobbying to make it enforceable so that corporations can be held to account. It is argued that whilst ethical consumerism and voluntary corporate social responsibility (CSR) placed a focus on the consumer and on the individual company (all too often located in the Global North), it ignored the real issues of social and environmental justice for communities affected by the corporation but based in the Global South. Newer corporate accountability initiatives seek to promote complaints procedures, independent monitoring, compliance with national and international law and other agreed standards, mandatory reporting and redress for malpractice.

Corporate social responsibility (CSR)

The relationship between private profitability and public responsibility lies at the heart of the corporate social responsibility (CSR) agenda. Public opinion, particularly from public interest **non-governmental organizations (NGOs)**, is largely believed to have shaped the drive to ensure that privately-owned businesses, particularly **multinational corporations (MNCs)**, embrace the idea of corporate citizenship and are made responsible for achieving shared public policy objectives. In pursuit of the goal of **sustainable development**, they are to run their businesses in close conjunction with different stakeholders, with particular focus on the economic, environmental and social repercussions of their businesses, rather than a limited focus on profitability and shareholder value. Performance of companies is to be measured on these three effects, with independent audits to measure performance. With reputation becoming a key factor in firm success, it is believed that firms would try and act in socially responsible ways to ensure a good name. Corporate responses have included increasing attempts to offer greater transparency in their activities, principally in the form of self-policing codes of conduct for suppliers/producers and more values-driven mission statements that strive towards an 'ethical' approach to operations.

The concept and practice of CSR has been endorsed by a growing number of business ventures, particularly the larger MNCs that have been taken to task by hostile public campaigns for not showing socially responsible behaviour. Evidence of CSR's increasing take-up is in the growing membership of business organizations committed to it, e.g. the World Business Council for Sustainable Development, the Prince of Wales Business Forum and CSR Europe. A number of governments and regional bodies are also wedded to the idea, including the European Commission, which has responded to pressure from member governments to establish a full-fledged CSR policy. The CSR framework has been applauded for forcing a number of MNCs to provide better conditions—environmentally, socially and economically—particularly in developing countries, a classic recent instance of which has been the case of Shell in Nigeria.

Critics see the concept of CSR as oversimplifying the issues involved, particularly with respect to the meaning of sustainable development, and how it might be achieved. Offering fairly traded products, for instance, might be a way for a corporation to demonstrate social responsibility in a broad sense. However, MNCs are known to have a few product lines embrace fair trade principles through product certification, whilst the overall principles and prerogatives that inform their operating policies, goals, benchmarks and decision-making criteria, and their business model remain unchanged. Such MNCs are seen to ride the Fairtrade wave, building up their brand on the back of Fairtrade, but not really embracing the philosophy or adopting a new business model.

Cotton

Cotton is vital to the global textile industry and to the social and economic development of developing countries. Two-thirds of all cotton is produced in the developing world. For most cotton farmers in cotton-producing communities it is their only means of income and their only cash crop. In West Africa, for example, cotton makes up to 40% of export income. Many cotton farmers live in poverty, trying to survive on less than US $2 a day. World prices in cotton have been unstable for a long time and farmers have been severely affected by falling prices.

Cotton farmers in the USA, the European Union and the People's Republic of China are highly subsidized, and the large volumes they produce are dumped in markets worldwide, driving prices down and leaving small-scale cotton farmers in poorer countries in no position to compete. These farmers also find themselves under further pressure from the rising input costs of fuel, pesticides and insecticides.

Fairtrade works in 59 countries, with 650 cotton-producer groups touching the lives of approximately 7.5m. farmers, workers and their families. There are 33 cotton-producer groups in India, Burkina Faso, Cameroon, Mali, Senegal, Brazil, Egypt, Peru and Kyrgyzstan. West Africa and India are the biggest cotton-producing areas.

Ethical trading companies such as People Tree, Gossypium and Bishopston work very closely with their supply chains and guarantee that their products are sourced ethically. The certification of cotton addresses the injustices affecting cotton farmers, but the manufacturing process is not yet guaranteed in the same way. **Fairtrade standards** require that all companies involved in the manufacturing of a Fairtrade-certified cotton product must submit documentation of decent working conditions. The monitoring of labour conditions, however, is complex and ultimately the responsibility of the retailer. Organizations such as the **Ethical Trading Initiative**, the **Fair Wear Foundation** and **Social Accountability International** have made efforts to improve working conditions in the garment industry, and Fairtrade sees itself as complementing this work and raising the bar by encouraging more responsible sourcing practices amongst brands and retailers.

Coyotes

This is the term used for middlemen who buy goods off farmers and often it is this link in the supply chain that is the most exploitative. (This word is also used to designate middlemen who arrange transport for illegal labourers from South America into the USA.) Such middlemen (also referred to as 'piranhas' or 'sharks') are part and parcel of the supply chains of a number of commodities particularly, for instance, coffee, where the coyote buys from the small farmer and sells either directly to transnational-owned mills or independent mills which would then process the coffee cherries, and sell on to transnational brokers or exporters. The middleman's price offer is often well below what the farmer might get in an open market. Once farmers are organized into co-operatives, this exploitative link is cut, and farmers are able to capture much more of the value chain, as they, rather than the middlemen, can access the profits.

There is an argument that the coyote method of product consolidation and commercialization is more efficient than a co-operative model. However, this efficiency would only translate into higher prices for farmers if there was competition at the level of buying. As coyotes form cartels and effectively isolate suppliers from buyers, there is no competition the farmers can benefit from.

To skew the system further in the coyotes' favour, many small farmers also rely on coyotes for financing, thus contracting out their crop for the next season at a reduced rate against any credit extended. In many Southern countries, rural financial infrastructure is virtually non-existent, again giving ample scope to coyotes to charge financing rates as high as 100% per annum.

Coyotes thus play many roles—trader, money-lender, transporter, packer and distributor. They are a risk when they can take advantage of the producers they buy from, especially if the producers are in a weak bargaining position and are not organized.

Credit

Provision of credit is critical to the fair trade paradigm. Access to credit is a key issue for farmers as rural banks are either non-existent or do not lend in the small amounts that family farmers might require. Thus, credit for farm machines and fertilizers is often available only through exploitative **coyotes** at extremely high rates of interest. By providing access to credit and information, fair trade seeks to correct market imperfections, particularly for farmers with seasonal crops who could benefit from loans out of the harvest season. As importers generally have much easier access to credit than developing country producers, importers are required to pre-finance up to 60% of the total purchase of seasonal crops, enabling farmers to receive an advance for their crop even before it is exported, smoothing their income streams.

Whilst availability of pre-finance credit is generally good for stronger co-operatives/exporters, few have access to term finance. Medium-term loans are necessary for investment in warehouses, transport and processing equipment. For most co-operatives their relationship with fair trade buyers has been instrumental in getting them access to medium-term finance. Some organizations such as Oikocredit (an ecumenical development co-operative society), Creditosud (an Italian social bank) and Shared Interest try to fill the gap, either through direct lending or the provision of guarantees to local banks. However, lending and borrowing in a foreign currency are not ideal and there is still a gap when it comes to provision of local lending.

CTM Altro Mercato *see* **Altro Mercato.**

D

Day Chocolate Company

This is a Fairtrade organization that has been instrumental in bringing producers from the South onto a more equal footing with Northern businesses and markets. It was conceived when, in 1997, the Ghanaian cocoa co-operative, **Kuapa Kokoo**, voted at its annual general meeting to invest in a chocolate bar to be sold in the UK market. Together with Twin Trading, Kuapa Kokoo set up the Day Chocolate Company in 1998, with support from The Body Shop, Christian Aid and Comic Relief. The company was named in memory of Richard Day, a key member of the team at Twin Trading that had helped Kuapa Kokoo develop its organization. The Department for International Development guaranteed Day's business loan, and NatWest offered banking facilities.

The company is 30% owned by Kuapa Kokoo, and two members of the co-operative sit on the 11-member board of Day Chocolate. The company includes in its mission statement not only the mandate for fairly traded chocolate, but also to act as a model for other businesses to change their trading practices. Day is part of the Biscuit, Cocoa, Chocolate and Confectionery Alliance, a UK trade industry group, through which it hopes to increase its power and voice within the confectionery industry.

Day's main consumer-facing brand, Divine chocolate, was launched in the UK in 1998. Two years later, in October 2000, it launched Dubble chocolate bar, which is co-branded with Comic Relief. Day Chocolate has achieved impressive distribution of Dubble and in the process has taken Fairtrade into new arenas such as the Blockbuster video chain, all major supermarkets, regional confectionery distributors and independent shops. Two other successes followed, with the Co-op chain of supermarkets launching a co-branded Co-op/Divine private label in 2000 and then converting its entire range of own-brand chocolate to Fairtrade two years later. That same year (2002), Starbucks too converted all of its own-brand chocolate to certified Fair Trade, co-branded with Divine.

Divine's trading arm, located in the UK and the USA, invests increasing amounts in technical assistance, using the business process as a vehicle for development and a market demonstration of how 'fair' business can be. Divine operates in a broader context in which 14m. small cocoa producers compete in a global cocoa industry that is seeing declining prices from a handful of global brand multinationals including Nestlé, M&M/Mars and Cadbury.

Day Chocolate have used innovative means to educate their consumer base about cocoa farming, providing schools educational packs and setting up pen friend programmes between British school children and their Ghanaian counterparts in cocoa-growing regions.

Debt crisis

Debt has been a serious problem for developing countries, including the newly industrializing countries (NICs), particularly since the late 1970s, as overseas borrowing has financed much of the industrial growth of the NICs. Following the Iranian Revolution of 1979 and the resulting second oil shock (after the first in 1973), the US Federal Reserve adopted a tough anti-inflationary monetary policy by raising interest rates. That move was to push the international economy into recession, with serious consequences for the developing world. The resulting debt crisis of the 1980s is still considered something of a landmark for developing countries.

Several factors were to play a part in moving countries to the brink of financial disaster. First, the worldwide recession in the late 1970s resulted in plummeting demand for manufactured goods and materials in the older industrialized countries. Protective barriers, largely in the form of non-tariff barriers, were erected, thus slackening developing countries' exports, with devastating consequences for these countries. Second, the governments of industrialized countries began to pursue very tight financial and fiscal policies that, while reducing price inflation in their economies, jacked up interest rates. As a consequence, the floating interest rate debts that the NICs had incurred began to cost far more to service than when they were initially incurred. For instance, the value of the US dollar appreciated vis-à-vis other currencies, so that interest rates of loans denominated in US dollars experienced a sharp rise. Since most loans were denominated in US dollars, the debt of many developing countries increased in real terms.

Crisis point was reached when Mexico spectacularly collapsed in August 1982 after the Mexican Government announced that the country was no longer able to service its interest payments, let alone hope to repay its foreign debt. Mexico's announcement ushered in the debt crisis of the Third World. Before long other countries in Latin America (for instance, Brazil, Venezuela and Argentina) and Africa found themselves in equally difficult financial quandaries. It became clear then that a number of developing countries, particularly the middle-income group, were in financial difficulty. These were the countries that had come to depend most heavily on commercial lending. The very poor countries were less affected as commercial banks had generally been unwilling to lend to these countries, so that their borrowing was mostly in the form of public sector aid.

The debt crisis wiped out decades of progress in the affected countries. The 1980s subsequently came to be known as the 'lost decade' for the developing world. There was little money to be spent on social programmes and development as servicing interest payments of foreign loans alone accounted for a substantial chunk of government expenditure. By the early 1990s many developing countries had emerged poorer and with smaller economies compared to the beginning of the 1980s, severely undermining poverty alleviation measures in these countries.

Debtor nations had to turn to international financial institutions like the **International Monetary Fund (IMF)** to reschedule their debts. But while total breakdown was averted, the severe conditions placed by these institutions created huge social and political problems for the countries involved. Indeed, the debt crisis enhanced the power of the IMF and the **World Bank**. It was, in many ways, to contribute to the triumph of **neoliberalism**.

Such financial crises have hardly been limited to the 1980s. The threat of catastrophe still looms, as the collapse of the Mexican peso in December 1994, the repercussions following the fall of the Thai baht in 1997, the economic crisis in Russia in 1998, and the Argentinian crisis in the early part of this century, illustrate. (See also **Debt trap** and **Capital flows**.)

Debt trap

As a result of the **debt crisis** of the 1980s many developing countries are caught in a debt trap where they are committed to spend a large proportion of their gross domestic product (GDP) on servicing external debts rather than on domestic economic and social development. Indeed, between 1980 and 1994, most of the US $1,300,000m. in developing country debts consisted of an accumulation of unpaid interest rates rather than new credit. Notwithstanding various initiatives to reduce the debt burden of developing nations, the net South-North transfers of official and commercial global loans has exceeded previous flows, including those in colonial times.

While the debt crisis was managed, it was never resolved. Indeed, the gap between the industrialized North and the underdeveloped South has sharply increased over the last two decades. According to the **World Bank**, developing countries are forced to pay more to creditors in debt payments than they receive in loans and grants. The Jubilee 2000 campaign highlighted that the developing world is spending US $13 on debt repayment for every $1 it receives in grants. Some countries are forced to dedicate 20%–25% of their export earnings towards debt repayment.

The burden of debt repayment commitments severely limits the capacity of the developing world to tackle issues such as poverty reduction. In fact, the ongoing debt crisis has resulted in a humanitarian disaster. Over the last 20 years Africa, for instance, has experienced falling incomes, falling investment rates, a rise in poverty, disease and infant mortality and a decrease in life expectancy. Relatively poor countries are forced to accept rising poverty levels while, at the same time, exporting scarce resources abroad. Rising poverty and unemployment only further increase the pressure on the environment and social stability, resulting in political unrest.

While the arguments in favour of debt relief are overwhelming, some commentators argue that debt relief would create a moral hazard. Countries would fail to adhere to the stringent budgetary constraints imposed by, for instance, the **International Monetary Fund (IMF),** and continue to borrow in the expectation that they would not have to repay their debt. It might also stifle much needed inward investment, as investors become increasingly wary of investing in these countries. However, over-borrowing is only one side of the coin. On the other side is over-lending. Consequently, it might be argued that creditors ought to share responsibility and write at least part of the unsustainably high debt levels off. Debt traps are the result not only of local failures; creditors and the workings of the global financial system in general also bear responsibility (see also **Capital flows**). However, hardly any supraterritorial democratic frameworks have been available to the affected countries (see **Democracy**).

Since the 1990s there have been several initiatives to bring the pressing issues of debt traps to the attention of the international community. Some governments concluded so-called Brady Deals to convert part of their bank debts into bonds at lower interest rates. Similarly, the Paris Club of official creditors developed a series of measures to help low-income countries. In 1996 the IMF and the **World Bank** formulated a Highly Indebted Poor Countries Initiative (HIPC) offering relief from unsustainable debt. The HIPC was extended in 1999 with larger funds, less stringent eligibility criteria and faster delivery of relief. **Non-governmental organizations (NGOs)** and direct action campaigns have also helped to publicize the issue of debt traps and debt relief. Examples are the World Social Forum, the Live Aid campaign and grassroots action, such as that under the aegis of the Jubilee 2000 Coalition spanning over 60 countries that helped generate increased debt relief for the South.

Del Monte

This is one of the three major worldwide exporters of bananas. Together with Dole and Chiquita, it accounts for almost two-thirds of world trade in bananas. Del Monte is pursuing **Social Accountability International** certification for their company-owned farms in response to growing pressure from educated consumers and retailers.

All three banana MNCs have recently been diversifying out of plantation ownership to reduce their exposure to weather and political risk. They still, however, sign long-term contracts with independent growers and thus in effect control the entire supply chain. They are thus isolated from labour disputes on individual farms, yet control the quality and supply logistics whilst still exerting pressure on independent suppliers to lower prices (see also **AgroFair**, **bananas**, and **Chiquita**).

Dependency theory

This arose in the 1960s and 1970s as a direct critique of modernization theories, which focused on factors internal to countries in the **Third World** to account for their low levels of **development**. Dependency theory analysed underdevelopment as integral to the power asymmetries or the broader relations of domination and dependency between the First World and the Third World, the former colonizers and colonized, or core and peripheral countries.

Underdevelopment, they argued, was the result of structural inequalities operating at the level of world capitalism. Thus, underdevelopment and poverty are not so much the result of a lack of modern values and the absence of modern economic and social structures in developing countries, but are directly related to the organization of the international political economy.

There was increasing acknowledgement of the issues of underdevelopment and global inequality with the institutionalization of economic aid programmes set up individually by most capitalist rich societies through the 1950s and 1960s. Aid began to form part of a spectrum of relationships (including trade and debt) between rich and poor states which appeared to reinforce global **inequality** rather than leading to development and 'catching up'.

Dependency theory focused on the allocation of capital, and argued that international capitalists deliberately use capital allocation to control the pattern of development in developing countries. In fact, capitalism could not flourish even in middle-income countries unless there was a deliberate suppression of indigenous development. Amongst the foremost proponents of dependency theory were Andre Gunder Frank, Fernando Cardozo and Theotonio Do Santos.

Today, it is often argued that developed and industrialized countries actively secure dependent relations through various policies at the national and international levels, effected through, for instance, the control of international organizations such as the **International Monetary Fund (IMF)**, and by setting the rules for international governance, international trade and international finance. However, unlike modernization theorists, dependency theorists are less optimistic regarding the successful transition of developing countries through the adaptation of certain practices and norms, so long as they are working within the confines of the current structure of the international political economy. They would go so far as to argue that developing countries have no meaningful choices.

In course of time, the rise of the newly industrializing countries seemed to discredit dependency theorists. Critics pointed out that dependency theorists were not only overly pessimistic regarding the prospects of development in the Third World but also tended to overlook the impact of domestic forces within developing countries, or the way external influences are always mediated through internal structures.

Developing countries

This term is often used interchangeably with the Global South, or **Third World**. The term developing countries encompasses a range of different levels of **development**, with some countries, or regions within countries mired in poverty. Thus, the countries of sub-Saharan Africa are amongst the worst off even amongst developing countries, and rural areas tend to perform much worse than urban areas, with limited amenities and access to basic services. The majority of the world's population, at over 80%, live in developing countries, which together have a share of less than 22% of global wealth. Globalization is said to be skewing this balance even further, with the wealthier countries and richer people able to capitalize on opportunities presented by globalization, while over three-quarters of the world remain on the peripheries of the world economy.

The weighted averages of three development indicators, per capita income, life expectancy and infant mortality, are often used to measure levels of development. Poverty, together with a lack of employment opportunities (both unemployment and underemployment), are considered key features of countries designated as developing countries. A large proportion of the workforce in these countries is still to be found in the agricultural sector. And where some form of employment is available, it is largely confined to the disorganized informal sector.

The three key concerns for developing countries today seem to be to build and sustain economic growth, ensure that such growth is equitable, and ensure that all foreign debts are paid off. Their relative marginality in terms of investment and trade, except for a small minority of newly industrializing countries, means that they have remained largely receivers of globalizing processes with limited or no positive fall-outs.

Virtually all developing countries have over the last couple of decades embraced the doctrine of the market and liberalized their economies. Indeed, the **Uruguay Round** is often viewed as having effected the restructuring of the international economic system, rolling back the state and opening up the Third World for the transnationalization of their economies, though it was done in the guise of bringing certain sectors of trade and economic activity, such as agriculture, textiles and clothing, and services, within the purview of multilateral rules and discipline. **TRIPS**, for instance, while overtly presented as a mechanism to prevent criminal activity, is seen by its critics as a means for ensuring rentier incomes for **multinational companies (MNCs)** through global monopoly rights.

Development

From the mid-20th century, the term has referred to an economic process, generally understood to involve the expansion of production and consumption and/or rising standards of living, especially in the poor countries of the **Third World**. In the period immediately following **decolonization**, 'development' emerged as the new universal prescription for poverty and inequalities, with its promises of economic growth and socio-cultural modernization. It is associated with the international projects of planned social change set in motion in the years after the Second World War that gave birth to development agencies and development projects.

The development narrative was framed in terms of moving along a predetermined track, out of backwardness and into modernity. The mid-20th century thus saw a revival of a 'stage' theory of development. The world was divided into the developed and the underdeveloped, suggesting a continuum, movement along which brought one to the pinnacle of 'development', which most Western societies were seen to be at.

The first challenge to the idea that individual societies moved along different routes/stages into modernization came from neo-Marxists, particularly in the form of **dependency theory**, neo-Marxist modes of production theory, and **world systems theory**, all of which insisted that differences between societies had to be related to a common history of conquest, imperialism and economic exploitation that systematically linked them. The proponent of world systems theory, Immanuel **Wallerstein**, for instance, argued that underdevelopment did not denote an earlier stage in the transition to industrialization; rather, it was the result of countries, largely those that had been colonized, being involved in the world economy as peripheral, raw material-producing areas. Thus, instead of being undeveloped (with its suggestion that poverty was an original condition, and which sought non-systemic explanations such as the nature of the state or culture), the Third World now appeared as actively 'underdeveloped' by a First World that had 'underdeveloped' it. Thus, in various ways, the promise of development was critiqued for having been no more than a set of conceptual and organizational tools for managing, legitimizing, and sometimes contesting and negotiating over what was a pre-existing set of geopolitical inequalities.

By the 1970s the wider institutional context for development began changing quite dramatically as mainstream development agencies began to place a new emphasis on the basic needs of the poor, and on the distinction between mere economic growth and 'real' development, understood in terms of human welfare measures such as infant mortality rates, nutrition and literacy.

Today there is increasing acknowledgement that the development project was built on faulty foundations. Given that the path of production and consumption followed by industrialized countries has been fraught with disastrous consequences on, for instance, the environment and the ecological system, the notion of developing countries following the same path came to be questioned. The need for models of **sustainable development** was now put forward. Furthermore, the picture of social and cultural modernization sold as part of the development package was now criticized for being replete with Eurocentric values and ideals.

More recently, a number of critical analysts have heralded the end of 'the age of development'. This comes in a context where the state, in its redistributive role, is in retreat, the goal of industrialization has been abandoned, and there is a commitment to market forces and private enterprise, creating greater inequalities and greater deprivation for larger numbers, particularly in large parts of Africa. There is, however, a grave danger in being too hasty to hail the end of development as, with it, the project for equity and justice for the world's less well-off is also likely to be abandoned.

Divine Chocolate Ltd *see* **Day Chocolate Company.**

Dole

This is one of the three largest MNCs in the banana trade which is now entering the fair trade market in Europe in the wake of the success of Fairtrade bananas. They are well-positioned to do so as a number of mainstream retailers in Europe prefer to work with established international logistics experts such as Dole to deal with the complexities of the supply chain.

The entry of these MNCs into fair trade, however, has not been without controversy given a past that has seen mistreatment of workers, low prices to producers and unfair trading practices with competitors (see also **AgroFair**, **bananas**, **Chiquita** and **Del Monte**).

Drop the debt

Most **developing countries** use a significant proportion of their foreign exchange earnings to service their debts, rather than invest the money in developmental activity. Debts are owed to both countries of the North, as well as multilateral institutions such as the IMF and the World Bank. There is also the view that a number of these loans were made by creditors to serve their own interests, funding corrupt regimes or failed projects, and the poor are being made to pay the price for their creditors' mistakes. There have been several campaigns launched to underwrite or cancel these debts, noticeably the Jubilee Debt Campaign. As a result of public campaigning, in 2005 the G8 cancelled all of the debts (worth about US $40,000m.) owed by 18 poor countries to the World Bank, IMF and African Development Bank. So far some $88,000m. of debt has been cancelled through international schemes, following pressure from debt campaigners. Many more poor countries, such as Kenya and Ecuador are still waiting for their debts to be cancelled and meanwhile, continue to pay more in debt repayment than on health or education.

However, most rich countries, including the UK, count this debt cancellation as part of their aid budgets, meaning that ultimately it is poor countries who pay—through reduced aid. More than US $400,000m. of unpayable debt must still be cancelled for all governments to be able to meet their people's basic needs, with at least some cancellation for around 100 countries.

E

Environmental degradation

Global environmental degradation encompasses a wide range of issues and problems. They include, for instance, physical changes of the environment (air pollution, acid rain, ozone depletion), development activities (including growth in energy production and use, growth in waste, tourism, and intensified agriculture) and changes in the human condition (population growth and an increasing strain on natural resources). Environmental degradation can be the direct result of human activity (deforestation, desertification, etc.) or an indirect consequence (waste-related issues). It is today presented as a global concern requiring collective solutions at the international level. A number of reasons are cited for this. First, a number of environmental problems have global consequences, regardless of the actual location of the cause of the problem. Carbon dioxide emissions, for instance, contribute to global climate change irrespective of where the emissions are coming from. Second, there is a marked increase in the exploitation of what might be called the global commons, or resources shared by the world community. Examples include the depletion of the oceans due to over-fishing and pollution. Then there are a number of environmental issues that may not be global in reach but whose fall-outs nevertheless might be across boundaries (such as acid rain, for instance).

There is no denying that the processes leading to the over-exploitation of natural resources and environmental degradation are intrinsically linked to wider socio-economic processes and, ultimately, form part of the contemporary global political economy. Environmental degradation is linked to the generation and distribution of wealth. As such, it cannot be addressed without taking into account **inequality** and the factors underlying world poverty. Indeed, there are those who argue that globalization is restructuring the control over resources such that the natural resources of the poor are systematically being taken over by the rich, while the costs of their economic success, the pollution and the environmental degradation, are being passed on to the poor. Several examples are cited to support this argument. For instance, in the run-up to the Rio conference, the Global North was identified as contributing to the destruction of the environment disproportionately, generating 90% of the historic carbon emissions, and most of the waste. Large **multinational corporations (MNCs)** have exploited Third World resources to sustain and multiply their global activities. And resource- and pollution-intensive industries are simply being relocated to the Global South through the economics of **free trade**.

The late 1960s is identified as the period when there began to be increasing awareness of environmental risks the world over. Since the 1972 UN Conference on the Human Environment in Stockholm, the United Nations has been at the forefront in dealing with issues concerning co-operation over environmental issues. The conference institutionalized the importance of environmental concerns by establishing a number of principles, institutions and programmes to offer a framework for international co-operation. The 1970s and 1980s saw the emergence of many environmental interest groups, non-governmental organizations, green movements and international institutions as international actors alongside governmental agencies.

An important milestone in environmental consciousness at a global level was the publication of the Brundtland Report in 1987, training the spotlight on the concept of **sustainable development**, which has gained discursive ground, but remains an aspiration in so far as economic growth remains the primary goal of national economies. The 1992 Rio Conference agreed on three conventions to limit climate change, preserve biodiversity and combat desertification. However, international co-operation necessary to make these conventions effective has not always been easy to achieve.

The Fair Trade agenda has developed in parallel with the 'green' tradition of sustainability and environmental awareness. However, there has been a shift in consumer attitudes to environmentalism over the last couple of decades. The focus on green environmentalism has broadened from a product focus into a more general concern over the entire production process, particularly highlighting the human/social element. Together with this has been increased awareness over other environmental issues including, for instance, packaging and waste, organics, genetically modified produce, and animal testing.

Equal Exchange

This company was co-founded in 1986 in the USA by Jonathan Rosenthal, Rink Dickinson and Michael Rozyne. Inspired by liberation struggles in Latin America and Africa, the founders set up the USA's first commercial Fair Trade Organization that would 'be a support mechanism for … countries once they achieved national liberation and had set up an economy'. The founders were front runners with fair trade in the commercial US market—until their arrival all alternative traders in the US fair trade movement were explicitly not for profit, often religious organizations, dealing with textiles and handicrafts.

Equal Exchange has been a 100% fair trade coffee importer and roaster since its inception and adopted the international fair trade certification model and 'Fair Trade certified' logo for its coffees in 1999. The company has a strong commitment to fair trade partnerships with producer co-operatives, not only paying fair trade prices, but also providing pre-financing and trading directly with farmer co-operatives to link them directly with consumers.

The company is set up as a worker-owned co-operative to prove that alternative business structures can be successful. All employees are offered membership, and all employees own a share and receive the same share of the company's profits. Employees nominate and elect the company's board candidates and themselves hold six of the nine director positions. Furthermore, the top executive can earn no more than three times the salary of the lowest-paid employee.

The company diversified its basket to fair trade teas in 1998, cocoa in 2002, chocolate bars in 2004 and sugar in 2005. It has been profitable for just over 20 years and has won numerous awards for making a commercial success of an unorthodox and ethical business, including the Natural Product Expo's Socially Responsible Business Award in 1999 and the 2000 Business Ethics Magazine Award for Stakeholder Relations. See www.equalexchange.co.uk.

Ethical sourcing

Fair trade is perceived as having made a significant contribution towards influencing the behaviour of mainstream companies when sourcing their products, representing as it does a new partnership approach to the buyer-supplier transaction which aims at equality of exchange, underpinned by a developmental rather than confrontational agenda. Fair trade recognizes the power discrepancy between the developing and developed worlds and focuses firmly on the producer rather than the consumer. The aim is to maximize returns to suppliers rather than buyer margins, within an agreed developmental structure. It aims to treat the producer with more fairness than conventional trade. By requiring companies to conform to minimum guidelines to lay claim to independent certification of fair trade standards, competitors must play on a more level and ethical playing field.

Supply chain information is increasingly embedded in modern products, often through provenance. Fair trade has focused much of its marketing effort on promoting the specifics of product origin and the nature of production. With modern management information systems firmly in place in multinationals, most supply chains are closely monitored to establish efficiency. In such conditions, responsibility for the nature of the supply chain may be fully allocated to the corporation since there can be no recourse to a defence based on ignorance of working or environmental practices. However, the increasing trend for conventional companies to espouse ethical principles—from ethical sourcing of supermarkets to cause-related marketing whereby companies donate a percentage of the consumer price to a charity or environmental group—has also created increased competition for fair trade products.

Ethical Trading Initiative (ETI)

This is an informal agreement between civil society (including NGOs and trade unions) and business, sponsored in the UK by the Government's Department for International Development, and set up to improve trading conditions for all stakeholders. The rationale for its development was a widespread perception of abuses of the labour force in global supply chains, particularly via subcontracting that hides the real conditions workers operate in, often in a context of weak government and ineffective labour laws. The ETI aims to develop and encourage the use of a widely endorsed set of standards, embodied in codes of conduct, and monitoring and auditing methods which would enable companies to work together with other organizations outside the corporate sector to improve labour conditions around the world. ETI, however, is not an auditing organization. Rather, it shares learning that can improve international labour standards. With a combined turnover of over £107,000m., ETI's company members include supermarkets, fashion retailers, department stores and stone sourcing companies, as well as major suppliers to retailers of food and drink, flowers, clothing, shoes, homewear, promotional and other products. A criticism levelled against it is that it has not been able to address the inequalities and power imbalances that exist in the buyer-seller relationship. See www.ethicaltrade.org.

EurepGAP

This is a private sector body that sets voluntary standards for the certification of agricultural products around the globe. It covers the certified product from before the seed is planted to the point it leaves the farm. It is an equal partnership of agricultural producers and retailers that want to establish certification standards and procedures for Good Agricultural Practices (GAP). It is a business-to-business label, and therefore not directly visible to consumers. The standard is designed to maintain consumer confidence in food quality and food safety. Other important goals are to minimize detrimental environmental impacts of farming operations, to optimize the use of inputs and to ensure a responsible approach to worker health and safety.

EurepGAP started in 1997 as an initiative by retailers belonging to the Euro-Retailer Produce Working Group (EUREP). They were reacting to growing concerns of consumers with regard to product safety, environmental and labour standards and decided to take more responsibility for what happened in the supply chain. The development of common certification standards was also in the interest of many producers as those in contractual relations to several retailers complained that they had to undergo multiple audits against different criteria every year. It is in this context that EUREP started to work on harmonized standards and procedures for the development of Good Agricultural Practices (GAP) in conventional agriculture. See www.eurepgap.org.

European Fair Trade Association (EFTA)

EFTA was a strategic institutional arrangement to address issues of networking and information exchange to link producers and traders, and also macro-issues of fair trade market governance and development. Together with its US counterpart, the Fair Trade Federation (FTF) and the Network of European Worldshops (NEWS!), EFTA was part of the 1990s Northern-centred institutional development of **IFAT**. EFTA was established in 1990 as an association of 11 importing organizations located in nine countries across Europe (Austria, Belgium, France, Germany, Italy, the Netherlands, Spain, Switzerland and the UK). Together they import from over 400 marginalized producer groups across Africa, Asia and Latin America. EFTA aims to support the work of its member organizations and to foster greater co-operation and co-ordination among them. It circulates information and organizes member meetings in order to facilitate information exchanges and networking, dividing overlapping functions between members for greater efficiency, and identifying and pursuing joint initiatives.

The seven largest EFTA members (fair trade importers) have seen their sales figures increase by 80% in five years, and altogether the 11 EFTA members sold more than US $250m. worth of labelled and non-labelled fair trade goods in 2004. EFTA publishes fair trade figures and analysis for Europe and a twice-yearly newsletter. It also publishes the EFTA Yearbook, a research and advocacy document, once a year. See www.european-fair-trade-association.org.

Exploitation

To exploit generally implies to take unfair advantage of. The definition of what 'unfair' conditions entail might be specific to the context. The concept of exploitation is applied to social, political or economic relationships of uneven power. Exploitation is often used in connection with the structure of the global political economy, **neoliberalism**, free market policies, the division of the world into a developed global North taking advantage of an underdeveloped South, and **capitalism** in general.

Marxism advances a specific theory of exploitation that is intrinsic to capitalism. All societies are class societies and are prone to class conflict, and in capitalist societies this struggle is between the capitalist class (bourgeoisie) and the working class (proletariat). Class struggle arises through one group in society gaining a monopoly over the economy via the ownership of the means of production, providing this group the ability to control surplus produce. In capitalist society the capitalist class owns and controls the means of production while the working class owns nothing but its labour, which it has to sell for a wage. Based on technological innovation, capitalist societies are able to produce a surplus over and above the immediate physical needs of the workers. However, according to Marxism, a particular group or class appropriates this surplus. Thus, in a class society, one class through the exploitation of another appropriates the social surplus. And hence, according to Marxist theory, capitalist relations are built on systematic exploitation. Workers are denied a fair remuneration, and are paid less than their labour is worth.

These power dynamics characterized by dominance and exploitation happens both within and between societies. Marxism maintains that free market relations are structurally exploitative. Firms and corporations are the main instruments of exploitation. Many commentators argue that the current structure of the global economy systematically exploits the developing world for the benefit of developed countries, leading to uneven development, poverty and the North-South divide. **Dependency theories**, **world systems theory** and modern Marxist thought analyse in great detail the exploitative relations inherent in the world economy and such theories are at the forefront of the **anti-globalization movement**.

Exploitation is not limited to the structural level; it is also inherent at the micro level. The exploitative behaviour of **multinational companies** is cited as an example. Due to their disproportionate size and power, and their transnational nature, they are able to take advantage of less regulated markets in the developing world, where they have to pay only subsistence wages and can avoid adhering to environmental and labour standards. The most notorious examples in this context are the use of **child labour** and **sweatshops,** characterized by long hours, low wages and unsafe or harsh conditions. Nike and Gap Inc. are two prominent multinational companies that use **developing countries** for their supply of cheap labour and sell their produce to the developed world.

F

Factor endowment

This relates to the amount of land, labour, capital and entrepreneurship that a country possesses and can exploit for manufacturing. A country also needs robust institutions to access and distribute these resources equitably, and to obtain the greatest benefit from its factor endowment.

Fair Trade Advocacy Office (FTAO)

The Fair Trade Advocacy Office (FTAO) lobbies for fair trade and trade justice with the aim of improving the livelihoods of marginalized producers and workers, particularly in the South. Based in Brussels, the office is a joint initiative of **Fairtrade Labelling Organizations International (FLO)**, the **World Fair Trade Organization (WFTO)** and the **European Fair Trade Association (EFTA)**. The office monitors European and international trade and development policies, ensures a constant dialogue between the fair trade movement and political decision-makers, develops political positions in the area of trade justice and publicizes information through newsletters and brochures.

The office carries out advocacy through: (i) following policy developments on a number of issues that could affect fair trade; (ii) liaising with European Commission officials, Members of the European Parliament, other EU officials and African, Caribbean and Pacific Group of States (ACP Group) officials in Brussels; (iii) presenting the fair trade movement and its positions on different policy areas to international organizations, EU institutions, and civil society; and (iv) writing position papers, briefing documents and press releases (www.fairtrade-advocacy.org).

Fair Trade Federation (FTF)

This is an organization in the USA bringing together a number of wholesalers, retailers and producers whose members are committed to providing fair wages and good employment opportunities to economically disadvantaged artisans and farmers worldwide. The FTF acts as a trade association helping smaller fair trade groups network in order to leverage shared skills and knowledge, and addressing key strategic issues for the fair trade movement as a whole.

There is a membership fee scaled according to turnover. The FTF offers its members access to its trade network and members directory, as well as an in-house journal and links to fair trade events (www.fairtradefederation.com).

Fairtrade Foundation

This was established by Oxfam, Traidcraft, Christian Aid, New Consumer, the World Development Movement and CAFOD as the UK's third-party auditor of fair trade practices for selected goods. In 1994 the group launched the Fairtrade audit mark in the UK, which signalled to the consumer that a social audit of the product had been carried out guaranteeing that it was genuinely fair trade.

The Fairtrade Foundation identifies four levels of target consumers—core Fairtrade supporters; partial adopters; occasional conscience buyers; and well-wishing bystanders. The Foundation has focused its efforts on raising awareness through a variety of marketing channels, including the annual Fair Trade Fortnight (www.fairtrade.org.uk).

FLO—Fairtrade Labelling Organizations International

FLO was established in 1997 and is the worldwide fair trade standard setting and certification organization that audits products throughout the supply chain. It is a non-profit, multi-stakeholder organization, with its headquarters in Bonn, Germany. FLO's mission is to 'improve the position of the poor and disadvantaged producers in the developing world, by setting the Fairtrade standards and by creating a framework that enables trade to take place at conditions respecting their interest'.

FLO consists of 24 organizations, including 19 Labelling Initiatives (covering 23 countries), three Producer Networks and two Associate Members. They own the Fairtrade Mark, the product label that certifies that international **Fairtrade standards** have been met. The label is now available on thousands of products in around 50 countries. FLO currently sets standards for bananas, cocoa, coffee, fresh fruit, honey, juices, rice, sugar, tea, spices and herbs, flowers, sports balls, and wine. It has generic and product-specific standards. The generic standards govern the terms of trade for all Fairtrade products. FLO's Fairtrade mark signifies that for a given product the fair trade standards, including minimum pricing, credit provision, and long-term relationships, have been met. They must be met by all Fairtrade producers and traders. Product-specific standards apply to particular products like cotton or bananas. One set of standards here relate to small farmers, including smallholders organized in co-operatives or other organizations with a democratic, participative structure, and the other to workers in plantations and factories.

FLO sees its role as four-fold: (i) setting international Fairtrade standards; (ii) organizing support for producers around the world; (iii) developing global Fairtrade strategy; and (iv) promoting trade justice internationally. The standards apply to all Fairtrade producers, as well as the companies who market Fairtrade products, such as importers, exporters and licensees. FLO internationally and the local Fair Trade Organizations in each member country have a responsibility to increase the levels of consumer understanding of fair trade and generate publicity to make the market grow.

FLO consists of two organizations, FLO e.V. and FLO-CERT. The former is a multi-stakeholder association involving FLO's 20 member organizations (Labelling Initiatives), producer organizations, traders and external experts, and it develops and reviews standards and assists producers in gaining and maintaining certification in order to capitalize on market opportunities. Fairtrade standard development involves developing producer organizational requirements (including generic product group standards—one for smallholder co-operatives and one for plantations), sustainable production requirements, and trade standards for requirements between producer, exporter and importer relations. Once product standards have been developed and approved, producers are inspected for their compliance with the standards. And FLO-CERT works with more than 60 local inspectors to carry out this work.

In early 2004 FLO-CERT was legally separated from Flo e.V. as a subsidiary of FLO. This separation between standard-setting and standard inspection/certification functions was aimed at reducing the potential for conflict of interest and is in accordance with ISO Standards for certification bodies. It is also designed to help FLO cover the cost of inspection and trade-auditing functions for both producers and traders.

The Fairtrade Labelling Initiatives (see **National Initiatives**) and the Producer Networks are full members of FLO and have the right to vote at the annual General Assembly. There are also two associate members, Fairtrade Label South Africa and Comercio Justo México. All members and certified producer organizations participate in FLO's decision-making through the General Assembly and their respective Assemblies: the Labelling Initiatives' Assembly or relevant Producer Network Assemblies.

FLO's Board of Directors consists of six National Initiative representatives, four producer representatives (African, Asian, Latin American—coffee, and Latin American—non-coffee), one ATO representative and one commercial trader representative, representing more mainstream business. Each group elects its representatives at its membership meetings and via email nominations and voting. The board meets quarterly to review financial statements and decide on major policy initiatives and strategic direction for Fairtrade labelling worldwide. Three committees report to the Board: Standards and Policy, Certification, and Appeals (which handles certification appeals). The board nominates a director who hires staff to carry out FLO's day-to-day activities. These fall into three categories: (i) inspecting producers' compliance with fair trade standards and auditing fair trade transactions, carried out by FLO-CERT; (ii) organizing business facilitation by co-ordinating producers and traders to match supply and demand, carried out by FLO's product managers; and (iii) supporting FLO producers by providing market information and connections to NGOs that help with producer quality improvements, and organizational capacity building, carried out by the FLO Producer Support Network.

Critics have argued that FLO's institutional structure has come to reflect prevailing market discourse at the expense of the broader collective of fair trade producers and traders using the Fairtrade certification system. The Meeting of Members (MoM), the ultimate decision making forum, is made up of LIs which are market-oriented, and hold a majority over producers and traders in the FLO Board's decision making. According to FLO's Constitution, the Board's President is elected by (and from among) the LIs and holds a casting vote on decisions. The six LI board directors are also chosen by the LIs themselves and not the wider stakeholder group. Through the MoM LIs have pursued their interests unimpeded on controversial issues, sometimes in contradiction to decisions made by the Board. Thus, whilst there is participation by producers, critical decision making excludes them, and this came to the fore when, for instance, Nestlé became a member of FLO, making a small proportion of the coffee they sold come under the Fairtrade umbrella, whilst continuing to pay very low prices to the majority of the coffee producers they bought coffee from. There has also been resistance to FLO having begun the practice of certifying plantations—LIs view this as necessary to grow Fairtrade products in the mainstream market, whilst producers see this as compromising the very terms of fair trade, taking the focus away from empowering producers. Critics see the LIs' stance as an acquiescent response to market pressures to conform, blurring the focus on marginalized small-scale producers who are often displaced by just these large-scale plantations and commercial farm operations.

The FLO model of product certification is expensive for companies to adopt because of both minimum price requirements and certification fees. The FLO system is also limited in that it certifies products rather than trading practices. Some companies have adopted other methods of verifying or supporting their claims to social responsibility, including promoting their own company programmes, adopting other third-party systems, or implementing industry codes of conduct (www.fairtrade.net).

Fairtrade minimum price

This is the price set by **FLO** through its Standards Unit and covers all the costs of growing and producing a product efficiently. The price is decided on the basis of discussions with people involved in different ways in the production and trading of the product. It is set when the Fairtrade product is first launched and there is room for updating as required. The trader buying the product must pay at least this minimum price. This price may, however, vary between different countries for the same product, as costs for production vary too.

Fairtrade premium

This is the amount of money paid on top of the agreed Fairtrade price, to be used by producers, in consultation with each other, for an activity beneficial for the whole community, which might include education, healthcare, farm improvements or processing facilities to improve income. It is meant to support producers to improve their business or their community or environment. The premium is set by **FLO** and is usually between 5% and 30% of the farm gate price. The Hired Labour Standard states that the premium is not to be given out directly to individual workers in cash or in kind. The use of the Fairtrade premium is decided by the General Assembly of Members in the case of small farmer organizations and by a Joint Body in the case of plantations.

Fairtrade standards

FLO's Standards and Policy Committee is responsible for setting producer and trade standards for fair trade products. The Committee meets five to six times a year and consists of two FLO staff as well as representatives from three National Initiatives, one commercial trader, one ATO, one producer group and one independent body (historically an NGO or alternative financer involved with producer issues).

Fairtrade standards can be divided into three parts: (i) producer organizational requirements which include two sets of generic product group standards, one for co-operatives of small-scale family farmers and one for plantations; (ii) sustainable production requirements, which consist mostly of environmental standards regarding sustainable production and vary by product; and (iii) trade standards, which are regulations governing relations amongst fair trade producers, exporters and importers, and include the fair trade minimum price, plus the requirement for credit provision and long-term relationships between producers and importers. The Standards and Policy Committee must approve producer and trade standards for new products, as well as changes to existing standards.

According to FLO, Fairtrade standards are designed to support the sustainable development of small-scale producers and agricultural workers in the poorest countries in the world. The key objectives of the standards are to: ensure that producers receive at least prices that cover their costs of sustainable production; provide an additional **Fairtrade premium** which can be invested in projects that enhance social, economic and environmental development; enable pre-financing for producers who require it; facilitate long-term trading partnerships and enable greater producer control over the trading process; and set clear minimum and progressive criteria to ensure that the conditions of production and trade of all Fairtrade-certified products are socially and economically fair and environmentally responsible.

Fairtrade standards are set in accordance with the requirements of the ISEAL Code of Good Practice for Setting Social and Environmental

Standards (see **ISEAL Alliance**). The standards distinguish between minimum requirements, which producers must meet to be certified, and progress requirements that encourage producers continuously to improve and to invest in the development of their organizations and their workers.

When new Fairtrade standards are proposed or existing Fairtrade standards are reviewed, there is a process of consultation with the relevant stakeholders. Stakeholders can comment at each stage of the process, which include: (i) project description; (ii) standard drafts; and finally, (iii) comment period, which is a given time frame in which stakeholders may provide formal feedback.

FLO's hired labour standards (in relation, for instance, to plantations) have been criticized for failing to adequately support labour unions. The standards do not, for instance, specify the certification implications if workers do not unionize despite the presence of independent trade unions in the region. Plantations with large social premium income (e.g. Fairtrade banana plantations in Ecuador) have well-funded Joint Bodies and farm workers may not find it necessary to join a union as their wages and benefits are guaranteed by the FLO inspection, and their income and well-being are improved by the social premium.

Critics say there is a tendency for FLO to take the assumed advantages of co-operatives for granted. Whilst FLO inspects co-operative management for adherence to the co-operative's election policies and democratic structure, it cannot force management to devolve more power to the electorate, or even ensure management turnover.

There are also issues around price-standardization. The costs of complying with Fairtrade standards include, for instance, those of belonging to a co-operative, organizing a workers' assembly, paperwork associated with inspections and reporting to FLO, attending world and regional Fairtrade assembly meetings and so on. Whilst some attempt is made to accommodate regional differences in costs of living and production, averages tend to be taken, which entails that while a product might have the same price in two different countries, this may not reflect differences in cost of living and purchasing power in each of those countries.

Fairwashing

This is the term which connotes misinformation disseminated by a corporation in order to present an environmentally friendly public image. In the case of fair trade, a number of alternative trading organizations, wholly committed to fairly traded goods, find themselves sitting alongside established brand leaders that certify only a certain percentage of their lines as Fairtrade but use the Fairtrade image generated from that small proportion to prop up their image as a whole (also described as the 'halo' effect).

In some instances this has led to companies dropping third-party certification altogether. For example, in 2004 Dean's Beans Massachusetts, Larry's Beans in North Carolina, Just Coffee in Wisconsin and Café Campesino in Georgia all pulled out of the Transfair USA certification system, whilst not abandoning their commitment to fairly traded products.

Fair Wear Foundation (FWF)

This is an international verification initiative dedicated to enhancing labour conditions for workers in the garment industry across the world. It works closely with a growing number of companies that produce clothing and other sewn products and that take responsibility for their supply chain. FWF keeps track of the improvements made by the companies it works with and, through sharing expertise, social dialogue and strengthening industrial relations, increases the effectiveness of the efforts made by companies. See also **Apparel industry**.

Flo-CERT

This is an independent certification company owned by **FLO** that inspects producers and traders to ensure they comply with **Fairtrade standards** (see www.flo-cert.net).

Foreign direct investment (FDI)

Foreign direct investment refers to transboundary **capital flows**, where control over the resources transferred and the production process remains with the investor. It is long term, and entails investments in fixed facilities and assets as also intermediate goods including capital, technology, management skills, access to markets and entrepreneurship.

FDI is contrasted with portfolio investments, which refer to the transfers of specific assets and intermediate products between two agents through the market, but where control over the resources is given up by the seller in favour of the buyer.

For many poor and transitional states desperately in need of capital to stimulate growth, encouraging FDI is seen as the answer (see also **Developing countries).** Governments actively try to lure businesses by lowering corporate tax rates, reducing restrictions on the repatriation of profits, relaxing labour and environmental standards and so on. Some of the countries that had been recipients of FDI in the 1960s and 1970s have now become generators of FDI (e.g. the newly industrializing countries of East Asia). However, the European Union, the USA and Japan together dominate flows of FDI. Firms engaging in transnational production, and thereby making foreign direct investments, are variously referred to as **multinational companies (MNCs)**, or transnational or global corporations.

France Alter Eco

Founded in 1999, France Alter Eco initially used profits generated through fair trade stores to support other development projects. It was founded with the support of 15 independent investors, each investing between €2,970 and €74,700 in ordinary share capital, so that the company had €100,000 in equity. After being turned down by about 10 banks, it finally got a line of credit from Credit Cooperatif, a co-operative bank specializing in supporting charities, social enterprise and co-operatives.

Initially the retail outlet bought all of its goods through established Fairtrade importers like Oxfam Belgium and Solidar'Monde in France, but later started to build direct links with producers for around 20% of its products, which in due course grew to about 70% directly sourced from producer groups.

However, sales in the first year were deemed too low for the store concept to be franchised and in May 2001 the Alter Eco team closed the store, focusing their efforts on mainstreaming Fairtrade products in supermarket chains instead, starting with Monoprix. A year later, Alter Eco launched 13 products in Monoprix stores nationwide, and introduced 10 more in 2003. Alter Eco's products are now listed nationwide in Leclerc, System U, Cora and Match supermarkets, and they also have some regional/local referencing in Carrefour, Intermarché, Champion and ATAC.

Alter Eco has increased its capital base since its founding. The original 15 investors hold 69% of the issued share capital. ESFIN Participations, a fund dedicated to investing in socially-driven ventures holds 8.8%. The remainder is held by six individuals. Alter Eco has also raised additional capital from institutional investors like co-operative banks and social funds. Tristan Lecomte, Alter Eco's President and founder, hopes Alter Eco will be producer-owned at up to at least 40% in the long term. See www.altereco.com.

Free trade

The essence of free trade is the absence of any tariff and non-tariff barriers inhibiting the flow of goods and products between countries (see **Protectionism**). The theoretical school that has most invested in propagating the virtues of a free trade system is the liberal/neoliberal tradition (see **Neoliberalism**). According to the liberal international political economy perspective, free trade has the capacity to enhance overall efficiency and productivity and, potentially, benefits everyone.

Free trade's origins can be traced to the 19th century and the theory of **comparative advantage**. Until then, mercantilist theories dominated, according to which trade was a zero sum game. It was the Scottish political economist, Adam Smith, who developed the concept of absolute advantage: all countries could benefit from trade if they specialized in and traded goods they produced best. David Ricardo built upon Smith's postulate and established that trade was an absolute sum game. His theory of comparative advantage demonstrated that countries that specialized in the production of goods and services in which they were relatively efficient would ultimately be better off in free trade relations. This theory, later further developed by Eli Hekscher and Bertil Ohlin (the Hekscher-Ohlin theorem), forms the basis of much neoliberal trade theory.

The record of the free trade system, however, is one of mixed success. Some states, most notably Germany and the USA, preferred protectionist policies to catch up and surpass Britain's economic power (see **Protectionism**). The First World War all but destroyed the international free trade system. The final blow was delivered by the economic upheaval of the 1920s, which led many states to abandon free trade liberalism (see **Liberalism**) for more isolationist policies.

Free trade has been promoted as a means of spurring growth and increasing wealth. For liberals, protectionism diminishes competition and increases monopoly power. It also limits consumer choice and inhibits general development. However, some of the advocates of free trade theory have also been the worst offenders against it. For instance, the protectionist agricultural subsidies in the European Union and in the USA adversely affect agricultural sectors in **developing countries** as well as consumers in developed countries, who are forced to pay premium prices for agricultural products to finance protectionist policies.

Immanuel Kant and Richard Cobden added another dimension to free trade arguing that a free trade system would create a more peaceful world order. This idea informs US President Woodrow Wilson's famous Fourteen Points that outlined a liberal 'reform programme'. Although post-1945 theorists are far more pragmatic, commercial liberalism still propagates the spread of a free trade system as a necessary precondition for a more stable international order. It is part of the foreign policy portfolio of all G8 countries.

Free trade theory has been consistently attacked from various sides. Mercantilists and neomercantilists, for instance, continue to emphasize the centrality of relative gains in an anarchical international system of sovereign nation states. They support protectionist measures to stabilize national economies by shielding infant industries from international competition (the infant industry argument). Mercantilism also argues that states ought to be self-sufficient in certain sectors for security reasons (national security argument). Other points of critique come from the Marxist tradition, from environmentalists, trade unionists and feminist writers. Marxist theorists often put forward a social justice critique of free trade principles, while environmentalists argue that free trade contributes to **environmental degradation** by lowering national and international standards.

Globalization has contributed to a significant increase in **international trade** flows. Free trade systems are being increasingly promoted as part of a wider neoliberal agenda. At the same time, however, resistance against the negative implications of neoliberal globalization and free trade has grown (see **Anti-globalization movement**).

FTO Mark

In 2004 the **International Fair Trade Association (IFAT)** sought to strengthen the credibility and value of fair trade with the outside world by launching the

IFAT FTO Mark. The FTO Mark acknowledges the desire and need among FTOs to differentiate the unique value of their business models from more mainstream traders selling Fairtrade-certified products, and to gain international recognition of their value. The FTO Monitoring System provides a certification mark for 100% FTOs (i.e. organizations whose core function is fair trade). The Mark is a symbol of FTOs' collective knowledge of a way of doing business and trade that produces developmental outcomes.

An important aspect of the FTO business model, symbolized by the FTO Mark, is its participatory nature (in contrast to the FLO certification system). It involves a three-tiered process for guaranteeing quality based on self-assessment, peer review (second-party conformity assessment) and a sample external verification. The Self-Assessment Report requires consultation with stakeholders, setting improvement targets and feeding this information to IFAT. In a Peer Review the FTO shares its Self-Assessment Report with its trading partners, providing an opportunity for trading partners to corroborate and comment on the self-evaluation in the Self-Assessment Report. The third step, external verification, is based on a random selection of a percentage of IFAT members. An independent external inspector assesses and verifies the FTO's self-assessment procedure to ensure the credibility and reliability of its self-assessment report, and this involves interviewing trading partners, cross-checking documents and conducting on-site procedures. The IFAT Registration Sub-Committee oversees the FTO monitoring process and puts forward recommendations for registrations to the Board.

Organizations carrying the FTO Mark include Cafédirect, CTM Altro Mercato and Divine Chocolate Ltd. As both producers and traders have created the FTO standards, they assess each other's performance and progress and in so doing are involved in the allocation of the Mark. Research on IFAT's Monitoring System suggests that this participatory model more easily targets producers in greatest need, is more responsive to mutually identified issues and needs, and maximizes the value returned to producers by removing the expense of independent labelling organizations' monitoring and certification costs.

G

General Agreement on Tariffs and Trade (GATT) *see* **World Trade Organization(WTO)**

Global Compact

The Global Compact is seen as both a policy platform and a practical framework for companies that are committed to sustainability and responsible business practices. The UN built on its own earlier initiative, the Universal Declaration of Human Rights (1948), with the launch of the Global Compact in 2000. It is an initiative in 'voluntary corporate citizenship'. Businesses around the world were challenged to join together with UN agencies and labour and civil rights groups to support 10 principles of human rights, labour, the environment and anti-corruption. With no regulatory powers, it relies on public accountability, transparency and disclosure to complement regulation and to provide a space for innovation. Since its inception, the initiative has grown to more than 7,700 participants, including over 5,300 businesses in 130 countries around the world.

Global Justice Movement

The Global Justice Movement constitutes an umbrella movement for protests against supra national institutions and the neoliberal project, which took concrete and a somewhat concerted shape with the protests against the world trade meeting in Seattle in 1999 when a powerful alliance of consumer protection groups, trade unions, labour activists, environmentalists, debt relief campaigners, human rights proponents, **Third World** farmer associations, animal rights activists and feminists protested against **World Trade Organization (WTO)** policies. Some 40,000–50,000 people are thought to have taken part in the demonstrations in Seattle, which became known as the 'Battle for Seattle'. The protests saw an eclectic alliance where right-wing protectionists concerned about the decline of living standards in the Global North marched side by side with left-wing groups from the Global South. Despite their differences, they were united in their criticism of free-market capitalism and the policies of the WTO.

The Seattle protests brought together several angles and lines of critique against globalization, largely in opposition to neoliberal globalization, **free trade** and laissez-faire **capitalism**. Neoliberal globalization, instead of fostering economic and social development in the Global South, has increased both poverty and **inequality** in the developing world. In addition, the unrestrained and unsupervised market has wrought negative effects on the environment and society at large. Unrestricted free trade is benefiting countries with more financial capacity and leverage at the expense of poor, developing countries. Further, laissez-faire capitalism has entailed the accumulation of power in the hands of a few very large **multinational corporations**, which have the strength directly and indirectly to influence national and international agenda setting. Finally, the lack of transparency and accountability of international multilateral organizations such as the WTO and the **World Bank** means there are no counterpoints or checks on unbridled capitalism.

The movement propagates a form of bottom-up globalization where democratic norms, labour rights and environmental standards are emphasized and promoted on a global scale. It aims to regulate capital, while being respectful of local cultures and building on a shared vision of how best to meet global societal needs. It addresses transnational problems, particularly the global imbalance of power, and envisions a new role for civil society.

While the term '**anti-globalization movement**' is used interchangeably with the Global Justice Movement, the term 'anti-globalization' is misleading inasmuch as the movement represents the globalization of protest. Activists associated with the movement over the last 30 years have employed the same technologies of globalization, such as innovations in information and communication technology, to organize protests and to associate with each other. Mobile phones, laptop computers, the internet and fax machines have allowed activists to create international networks, maintain close contacts, and arrange and co-ordinate activities without the need of a clear organizational structure.

Today, the Global Justice Movement brings together a very broad coalition of church groups, national liberation factions, left-wing parties, environmentalists, unionists and others from different national backgrounds, guided by the ideals of equality and social justice for all people in the world.

H

Harmonization

This is the term used to describe the processes by which regulatory requirements or governmental policies of different states are made identical, or at least similar. It takes several forms, including regulations of the outcome, characteristics or preferences of economic goods, actors, transactions, institutions or production facilities; more general governmental policy objectives; adoption of certain agreed principles intended to influence or constrain the factors taken into account in making policies and rules; and harmonization of institutional structures and procedures. However, even uniform laws, if not accompanied by harmonization of institutions, could lead to differences in implementation and effects. Largely, the only requirement under harmonization is that all countries accept certain minimum standards.

More recently, claims for harmonization of national laws and policies have been closely linked to claims for 'fair trade', with harmonization seen as the mechanism by which unfair differences in legal and other regimes are eliminated to create a level playing field. This is countered by the arguments for **comparative advantage**, and is seen as potentially damaging for the cause of **free trade**, and the interests of competitors from developing countries. Harmonization has, however, been incorporated in GATT agreements as a norm of international economic relations.

Human rights

Human rights are conceived as universal rights that people possess simply by being human regardless of their association with particular political, social or cultural communities. A number of global and regional treaties and declarations concerning human rights have emerged since 1945, particularly following the Nuremberg trials. Amongst the most important ones is the Universal Declaration of Human Rights (1948), which does not have the force of international law, but sets forth international norms regarding the behaviour of governments in relation to both citizens and aliens, and is based on the principle that all human beings are born free and equal, and violations of human rights upset international order. More recently, human rights have begun to incorporate distributional concerns and a right to democratic process.

Apart from being universal, human rights are absolute (in that they cannot be qualified) and they are fundamental (in that they are inalienable). Generally, human rights fall into three categories, succeeding each other historically and each new generation representing a further broadening of human rights. First generation rights concentrate on political rights such as freedom of speech, freedom of assembly, and the right to take part in government. Second generation rights focus on rights in relation to the economy, society and culture. Both first and second generation rights are essentially individual rights. Third generation rights, however, concern community rights such as expressed in the Banjul Charter, with its emphasis on the rights of 'peoples'.

The inclusion of human rights in international law places certain restrictions and responsibilities on state behaviour, and this has not remained uncontested. One critique focuses on the historical origins of contemporary international human rights, and it is argued that the rights enshrined in international law grew in a primarily Western context. By extension, attempts at their universal application represent a form of cultural imperialism that ignores different conceptions of cultural, social and political rights and duties. A second critique highlights that the relationship between sovereignty and human rights remains controversial. Both are fundamental norms of international relations. Problems can occur when the principle of sovereignty clashes with human rights norms. Whether sovereignty prevails under such circumstances or whether states lose their right to non-intervention in domestic affairs has been a difficult question to answer when it comes, for instance, to humanitarian interventions.

International trade law treats some human rights questions such as slave labour as legitimate subjects of enquiry in the context of trade relations, while others like workers' rights, fair minimum wage, or basic rights of bargaining are not treated as such. There has also been a long-standing concern about the absence or relatively weak acknowledgement and enforcement of labour standards in developing countries. The jury is still out on the matter. While there is an ethical assumption that labour standards are basic human rights and therefore absolute and universal, it is less clear whether the choice of labour standards may depend on a country's stage of development and per capita income, and therefore that rights attached to standards in a nation's social welfare may differ. The related economic argument is that countries that do not guarantee and enforce these standards domestically may have an undue cost advantage in their export trade insofar as private costs do not fully reflect the social costs of incorporating these standards.

There is no real evidence to either support or disprove a link between human rights objectives and trade. However, when human rights are violated, policymakers, under pressure to do something, often respond by cutting off trade either to protest human rights abroad or to protect their citizens from harm. And the notions are often linked in international trade practices. For example, US policymakers have used trade sanctions to punish Cuba for its violations of political, civil, and religious rights. However, the US and other governments took a different approach to China when it sought to join the **World Trade Organization**. It was argued that more trade would encourage policymakers to do more to advance human rights.

I

Import substitution

This was a route to industrialization popular in the 1950s and 1960s right up until the 1980s as a strategy to promote economic independence and development. It emphasized replacement of some agricultural or industrial imports with a view to encouraging local production for local consumption, and in the hope that it would generate employment, reduce foreign exchange outflows, stimulate innovation and make the country self-reliant. The real objective of import substitution is not to eliminate trade, but to lift it to a higher stage—that of exporting value-added products, which are not as susceptible to economic fluctuations as raw materials. It reared its head in the USA in the 1970s, when it was used as a means to promote national (Buy American campaigns) and regional development. The approach is deemed to have failed in developing countries, in large part due to the relative inefficiency of Third World production facilities and as a result of their inability to compete in a globalizing marketplace.

Inequality

The issue of the distribution of economic gains and losses from globalization has been central to discussions of this phenomenon. There is extensive evidence that globalization has brought prosperity to many parts of the world in stark contrast to the pervasive poverty that characterized the world a few centuries ago, with poverty defined here not just in terms of income, but also health, life expectancy, nourishment and education. However, the absolute and proportionate gaps in living standards between the world's richest and poorest countries are rising. Indeed, the starkest divergence has been within **developing countries** with, for example, growing inequalities between the coastal regions and hinterlands of China. There are also growing income differentials within developed countries, due to rising inequality in labour earnings, crystallizing in global cities, where the world's highest earners are serviced by janitors, cleaners and cooks on minimum wages or less. Globalization is seen to have given disproportionate opportunities to the already wealthy to increase their wealth, utilizing, for instance, the latest technologies to move money around the world efficiently, while there is little or no impact on two-thirds of the global population. The principal issue thus is one of distributive justice in a landscape ridden with inequalities, including not only disparities in wealth, but also gross asymmetries in access to political, social and economic opportunities and power.

International Coffee Agreement (ICA)

From the early 1960s until 1989 the coffee market was managed effectively through the International Coffee Agreement (ICA). It was designed to maintain relative market stability and high prices: aside from a few price spikes due to Brazilian forest fires, the world price for coffee fluctuated between US $1 and $1.50, and producer and consumer nations together set quotas for producing countries to maintain stable supply levels. Only if the price of coffee rose above this range were producing countries permitted to increase their supply levels. It was an amicable arrangement enabling producer countries to organize collectively at the international level, thus securing higher export incomes from coffee. It also facilitated consumer countries to provide economic assistance (albeit disguised as the agreement) to strategic developing country allies, and it stabilized both supplies and prices of coffee and enabled healthy profits for multinational coffee companies. (For further details on international commodity agreements and the reasons for the collapse of the ICA see **International commodity agreements.**)

Following the collapse of the ICA, coffee prices plummeted to US $0.49 per pound and remained there for five years, which was their lowest in history and well below producers' production costs. Later in the 1990s the massive glut of coffee from Viet Nam devalued Robusta and Arabica, causing high-quality coffee to be sold at $0.48 (against the typical price of about $1.60 per pound), and by 2002 coffee was trading at its lowest levels in three decades. This was particularly significant in light of the fact that coffee is second only to oil as the most valuable primary commodity in global trade, and is produced almost exclusively in the South with a number of national economies depending on it.

International commodity agreements (ICAs)

In 1964, at the first United Nations Conference on Trade and Development (UNCTAD), industrialized countries acknowledged, for the first time, that the development needs of Third World countries had to be addressed through a coherent programme of action on **primary commodities**. The Integrated Programme for Commodities (IPC) was launched under UNCTAD auspices in 1976. It sought to create market structures that achieved remunerative and stable prices, while taking into account the interests of consuming countries. A Common Fund was established to maintain buffer stocks that would be increased (through purchasing operations) when prices were low, and reduced (through sales) when prices went up. But the resulting international commodity agreements (ICAs) did not live long. At the end of the 1970s they covered a wide range of commodities, including tin, sugar, rubber, coffee, cocoa and jute. But by the end of the 1980s the price-stabilizing functions for all of them, with the exception of rubber, had either collapsed or been abandoned. Today the agreements on coffee and cocoa are little more than forums for sharing information and managing administrative matters.

A wide range of reasons can be attributed for the collapse of the ICAs. But some of the common elements were: first, the hostility of Northern governments to market interventions they saw as inherently inflationary; second, the attempt to defend reference prices that were far removed from underlying realities. Buffer stock operations were simply too small to absorb the huge increase in supplies of commodities such as coffee, cocoa and sugar on world markets, which in turn drove down prices. Third, there were also failures in South-South co-operation—new low-cost suppliers of coffee and cocoa in East Asia, which had little interest in restricting their output, were well placed to benefit from the higher prices generated by African and Latin American governments which were restricting supplies.

In 1980, in the midst of another commodity crisis, there were calls for stabilizing commodity prices but richer countries were beginning to see these efforts as inherently inflationary. The ICAs, however, did recognize that supply management was key for achieving more remunerative prices.

International Fairtrade Certification Mark

The International Fairtrade Certification Mark is a registered trademark of **Fairtrade Labelling Organizations International (FLO)**. It certifies that products meet the social, economic and environmental standards set by Fairtrade. The Mark certifies products, but it does not cover the companies or organizations selling these products. It is used in over 50 countries and is a signifier that disadvantaged producers in the developing world are getting a better deal.

The International Fairtrade Certification Mark is owned and protected by FLO International on behalf of its 24 member and associate member Fairtrade producer networks and labelling initiatives. It is now the most widely recognized social and development label in the world.

The Fairtrade Labelling Initiatives that founded FLO originally had different labels. In 2002 the International Fairtrade Certification Mark was created and since then it has gradually replaced the different national labels. Two of FLO's members are still using their own original labels. In Canada and the USA the Fair Trade Certified (trade) labels indicate that **Fairtrade standards** have been met. (See also **Certification in Fairtrade**.)

International Federation for Alternative Trade (IFAT)

Established in 1989, IFAT is a global network of trading organizations bringing together producers and buyers from around the world. It consists of approximately 110 producer organizations and 50 buyer organizations, and its membership is still expanding. IFAT's mission is to 'improve the livelihoods and well-being of disadvantaged producers by linking and promoting Fair Trade Organizations (FTOs), and speaking out for greater justice in world trade'. It was set up with the aim of bringing together existing fair trade networks and FTOs around the world, and for fostering stronger representation and leadership from Southern producer organizations in this global network. IFAT's three main areas of work include developing the market for fair trade, building trust in fair trade (through the FTO Monitoring System) and advocacy. IFAT has played a crucial role in nurturing the development of, and connections between, FTOs that do not have FLO certification. It has helped organize small-scale producers into co-operatives, and supported the development and capacity building of Southern regional and national producer groups.

IFAT's institutional governance structure reflects its South-centric outlook and, as such, is seen as a contrast to **FLO**, which is seen as maintaining a Northern perspective. IFAT's structure reflects the networked nature of the fair trade movement. It operates with a small Secretariat and a number of sub-Committees and international working groups. IFAT's General Assembly comprises of five regions (Asia, Latin America, Africa, Europe and CAJUNs—Canada, Australia, Japan, the USA and New Zealand). Two-thirds of IFAT's membership comes from Asia, the Middle East, Africa and South America and members from Asia, Africa and Latin America have established regional platforms (e.g. **Asia Fair Trade Forum**, the Cooperative for Fair Trade in Africa, and the Associacion Latino Americana de Commercio Justo). Regional networks are autonomous bodies with full decision-making powers with respect to regional activities including networking, market access, promotion of trade between IFAT members, fund-raising, capacity building and promotion of membership.

The Board is the second key group in IFAT, and Southern region members (each of whom are members of their regional Boards or Councils) make up the majority of the Board. The Board consists of five regional Board Directors, three independent Directors, and one (independent) President, all of whom are chosen at the Annual General Meeting by and from IFAT's General Assembly which includes members, provisional members and individual and organizational associates. The Board convenes twice or thrice a year to develop and implement the directives agreed by the IFAT membership, makes policy, and decides on membership applications.

The Secretariat is the third group in IFAT, which acts as the contact point for members worldwide, facilitating and co-ordinating members' initiatives and activities, and using its position at the centre of a global network to make links between, and disseminate information to, individuals, groups and networks. (See also **FTO Mark.)**

IFAT is committed to decentralizing its institutional structure in order to strengthen regional platforms, and is seeking to support this organic development in the hope that the development of the regions will strengthen IFAT globally and make it more effective in pursuing its goals.

International Monetary Fund (IMF)

The IMF is an international organization overseeing the global financial system. The IMF, together with the Bank for International Settlements (BIS) and its sister organization, the **World Bank,** were created as **Bretton Woods institutions**, to manage the post-Second World War international economic order. While the World Bank provided long-term loans and technical assistance to help with development projects, the IMF was founded to oversee the international currency exchange market. In addition, it was to promote currency convertibility and, thus, encourage international trade to supply liquidity to IMF member states in balance-of-payment difficulty. It was not a bank, and as such it provided no loans. Instead it offered rescue packages from a pool of money from which member countries could borrow on a short-term basis if they were in a crisis or needed extra money to stabilize their currencies.

In the 1970s and 1980s the role of the IMF gradually changed. Important factors contributing to the transformation of the IMF included the end of the Bretton Woods system of fixed exchange rates in 1971 and the subsequent move to floating exchange rates, the replacement of Keynesian ideology by a more neoliberal outlook in the USA and the UK, and the **debt crisis** of the 1980s.

Thereafter, the IMF became part of the increasingly neoliberal adjunct of the international political economy, assisting debtor nations meet their balance-of-payments deficits on condition that they implemented a series of economic and institutional reforms. These stipulations have become part of IMF lending practices and its rescue packages. Loan recipients are also expected to undertake structural adjustments of their economies. Raising rates and cutting public expenditure have become typical IMF policies, all of which are seen to be in contravention of the sovereignty of concerned states.

The IMF has helped to facilitate the spread of neoliberal globalization. It is part of the multilayered structure of global governance, actively setting framework conditions for the international economy and intervening in issues of governance in **developing countries**. It has come under scathing criticism for its policies. Integration into the global economy on the back of IMF conditionalities, including demands for the immediate removal of regulations and the liberalization of financial and capital markets, have had devastating consequences for a number of countries. Critics from the **anti-globalization movement** argue that the IMF's policies in the **Third World** have aggravated **poverty** and debt and undermined social stability.

There is an increasing tendency to view the IMF as a tool of Western hegemony through which the West promotes its own economic interests. Such a view is able to gain ground because the IMF largely lacks democratic credentials such as accountability or transparency.

International Standards Organization (ISO)

In 1946 delegates from 25 countries met in London and decided to create a new international organization, of which the object would be 'to facilitate the international coordination and unification of industrial standards'. The new organization, ISO, officially began operations on 23 February 1947, in Geneva, Switzerland. Today, it is the world's largest developer and publisher of international standards and consists of a network of national standards institutes in163 countries, one member per country, with a Central Secretariat in Geneva, Switzerland, that co-ordinates the system.

ISO is a non-governmental organization. It forms a bridge between the public and private sectors. Many of its member institutes are part of the governmental structure of their countries, or are mandated by their government. Other members have their roots in the private sector, having been set up by national partnerships of industry associations. This allows ISO to arrive at a consensus on solutions that meet both the requirements of business and the broader needs of society. Standards ensure desirable characteristics of products and services such as quality, environmental friendliness, safety, reliability, efficiency and interchangeability, all at an economical cost.

ISO makes the development, manufacturing and supply of products and services more efficient, safer and cleaner; facilitates trade between countries and makes it fairer; provides governments with a technical base for health, safety and environmental legislation, and conformity assessment; shares technological advances and good management practice; disseminates innovation; and safeguards consumers, and users in general, of products and services.

ISO has more than 18,000 international standards and other types of normative documents in its current portfolio. ISO's work programme ranges from standards for traditional activities, such as agriculture and construction, through mechanical engineering, manufacturing and distribution, to transport, medical devices, information and communication technologies, and to standards for good management practice and for services. See www.iso.org.

International trade

International trade refers to the age-old exchange of commodities such as goods and services across national boundaries. However, until the industrial revolution, forms of mercantilism limiting international exchange were the rule rather than the exception in Western Europe. Vast empires had been created for the purpose of trade within, while trade between territories belonging to different states was actively discouraged. This philosophy was driven by the idea of relative gain—that there was only a limited amount of wealth in the world and that trade would create winners and losers. The Scottish political economist, Adam Smith, challenged this idea in 1776 with his theory of absolute gains. David Ricardo (1817) took this forward, using the concept of **comparative advantage** to demonstrate how international trade could benefit all parties.

The impact of Smith and Ricardo's views has been substantial. The principle of **free trade** has become a cornerstone of liberal economic thought ever since. **Protectionism** is seen to be ineffective as it limits competition, enhances the monopoly power of some domestic industries and reduces the variety of goods available. Free international trade, on the other hand, contributes positively to economic growth and **development**. Furthermore, since international trade creates economic interdependencies between different countries, it helps to reduce the risk of insecurity and the use of military force in international affairs.

In a globalizing world, there is a proliferation of economic transactions in which territorial distance or borders present little or no constraint. Indeed, the issue is not so much the amount of trade between countries as the fact that much of this commerce forms part of transborder production processes and global marketing networks. Through global sourcing, firms draw materials, components, finances and services from different parts of the world. And with the globalization of production, a large proportion of international transfers of goods and services take the form of intra-firm trade, the share of which is calculated at over 40% in international trade.

Critics of liberal free trade arguments have pointed to the obfuscation of power politics in these arguments. The trade liberalization agenda is seen as having been set by special interests in the North. While trade negotiations, for instance, open up markets in the developing world for manufactured exports from the North, the latter keeps its doors closed to agricultural goods from poor countries over which these countries might have a comparative advantage. Agricultural subsidies to farmers in the North further exacerbate the problem. Thus, trade discussions start from an uneven playing field. It is against these unfair arrangements that the Seattle protestors pointed, when they demanded new rules of trade of the **World Trade Organization (WTO)**.

ISEAL Alliance

The ISEAL Alliance is the global hub for social and environmental standards systems. Working with established and emerging voluntary standards initiatives, ISEAL develops guidance and facilitates co-ordinated efforts to ensure their effectiveness and credibility and scale up their impacts. Its mission is to create a world where ecological sustainability and social justice are the normal conditions of business. ISEAL members are leaders in the field, committed to creating solid and credible standards systems.

ISEAL was originally founded as the International Social and Environmental Accreditation and Labelling Alliance. Its first three-year business plan was developed in 2001 to guide the formal development of the ISEAL Alliance, during which time ISEAL was registered in the UK as a not-for-profit 'Company Limited by Guarantee'. Many of the foundational documents and operational procedures were developed then. These included ISEAL membership criteria and procedures for peer review, and analysis of existing normative documents in standard-setting and accreditation.

One of the outcomes of this first phase was the decision to facilitate the development of a Code of Good Practice for Setting Social and Environmental Standards. The Code of Good Practice was formally approved by the ISEAL Board of Directors in January 2004. It formed an integral part of the ISEAL Alliance Strategic Plan 2005–07 to support credible voluntary standard-setting and conformity assessment practices and to advocate for the recognition of credible voluntary instruments as legitimate market and policy instruments.

Founding members of the ISEAL Alliance include **Fairtrade Labelling Organizations International (FLO)**, the Forest Stewardship Council (FSC), the International Federation of Organic Agriculture Movements (IFOAM), the International Organic Accreditation Service (IOAS), the Marine Aquarium Council (MAC), the Marine Stewardship Council (MSC), the **Rainforest Alliance**, and **Social Accountability International**. See www.isealalliance.org.

K

Kuapa Kokoo

This cocoa co-operative based in Kumasi in the heart of Ghana's cocoa belt is considered one of the most high-profile challenges to current commodity trading practices. Established by Nana Frimpong Abebrese in 1993, with the assistance of the UK-based Third World Information Network Ltd (TWIN Ltd), the co-operative boasts over 40,000 members, and operates 160 local organizations. It combines the roles of a cocoa purchasing agency, a trust fund operating on behalf of its members, and a marketing organization. It provides a link between Ghana's cocoa farmers and consumers in rich countries, partly mediated through the UK-based **Twin Trading** organization. The premium it has secured through fair trade sales has helped it to open new higher value-added markets, like cocoa butter sold to the Body Shop. It has also entered into a joint venture with the **Day Chocolate Company**.

Its fair trade partnership in Divine Chocolate Ltd has ensured that the cocoa farmers have consistently received a better deal, and it has provided training and access to market information. Between 1995 and 2005, 100 projects were financed by a Trust set up to oversee the use of premiums earned. These included the drilling of boreholes, income diversification and generation projects, a credit union, sanitary facilities, schools and education, and the purchase of three vehicles (see also **Divine Chocolate Ltd**). However, there have been limits to what fair trade could achieve—the co-operative sells less than 5% of its members' output through fair trade channels.

Kuyichi

This is Max Havelaar's third significant fair trade initiative after coffee and Oke bananas, and aims to deliver fashion produced in a sustainable manner. It is positioned as a fair trade jeans fashion brand for the young, urban consumer, and sells in several countries across Europe. Set up by **Solidaridad** and cotton producers in 2000, Kuyichi's mission is to make organic cotton production and fair trade manufacturing processes the norm in the fashion industry. Kuyichi promotes itself as being first for organic cotton, and is a strong advocate of producer share-ownership. According to the company's website: 'Fair Trade is about commercial relationships between people. We don't buy "things", we buy from "someone" … Kuyichi is a fair price, fair say and fair share'.

The company is co-owned by the Peruvian cotton farmer co-operative, Oro Blanco, which produces high-quality biological cotton. Unique to Kuyichi is the way it offers consumers a system for tracing their purchase to the multiple producers of the good. Termed 'Track&Trace', Kuyichi garments carry a code that consumers can enter into the MADE-BY system, which then retrieves information correlating to that garment (including, for instance, the co-operative that picked the cotton, the workers who sewed the garment and who designed the item). Kuyichi is co-owned by Oro Blanco, the UK's social investment bank, Triodos, Netherlands-based NGO Stichting Stimulans, and a private investor. The company promoted 'Dance4Life', an international project set up in order to encourage young people to engage in the fight against HIV/AIDS. See www.kuyichi.com.

L

Labelling

Fair trade labelling has moved from being a radical solidarity movement to a mainstream trend in retail, with consumers being offered a tool to reveal their preferences in the market in a way that delivers tangible impact (see also **Branding**, **Certification in Fairtrade, FTO Mark** and **International Fairtrade Certification Mark**).

Labour behind the Label

This is a campaign that supports garment workers' efforts worldwide to improve their working conditions, through awareness raising, information provision and encouraging international solidarity between workers and consumers. Its members include trade unions and their local branches, consumer organizations, campaign groups, and charities. They work together with similar campaigns across Europe and with partners in producer countries and the **Clean Clothes Campaign**, of which they are the UK platform. See www.labourbehindthelabel.org.

Labour standards

The call for international legislation dealing with labour standards dates from the first half of the 19th century in Europe. It was motivated in large measure by ethical considerations and was designed to improve working conditions in relation to hours of work, women's and children's labour, the use of hazardous materials, etc. Even at the time, there were unmistakable links to trade. Early reformers took **free trade** as a given and desirable objective and sought to use moral and international arguments to deal with differences in labour standards. Various international meetings convened in the latter half of the 19th and early 20th centuries dealt with international labour standards on both ethical and competitiveness grounds, though the results obtained were quite modest.

Following the First World War, as part of the Treaty of Versailles in 1919, the International Labour Organization (ILO) was founded, with methods and principles in its constitution to deal with all conceivable aspects of labour standards. However, it did not include any explicit trade sanctions. As per

ILO 1988: 4, action is designed to promote and safeguard **human rights** in three main forms: first, through a definition of rights, especially through national adoption of ILO conventions and recommendations; second, measures to secure the realization of rights, especially by means of international monitoring and supervision but not the imposition of trade sanctions; and third, assistance to nations in implementing measures, particularly through technical co-operation and advisory services. The role and influence of the ILO regarding labour standards has been central to the efforts of the UN and associated regional organizations designed to protect and promote human rights since the Second World War.

The argument is made that international harmonization of labour standards cannot be supported from a world-welfare point of view as there is little to suggest that market failures are uniform across countries and should be countered by similar measures (e.g. labour standards). Nevertheless, accusations of alleged unfair competition with regard to labour standards have come up time and again in trade relations. In Article 7 Chapter II of the stillborn 1948 Havana Charter of the International Trade Organization, members recognized that unfair labour conditions, particularly in the production for export, could create differences in international trade. Each member was to take whatever action was deemed appropriate and feasible to eliminate such conditions. A later iteration, the **General Agreement on Trade and Tariffs (GATT)**, was conceived with a more narrow mandate and did not address the issue of labour standards except in Article XX(e), which provides for prohibition of goods made with prison labour.

Multinational companies can influence employment standards in **developing countries** partly as direct employers, and also through their subcontracting activities. Levi Strauss were the first players to adopt voluntary guidelines in 1991, and since then codes of conduct have become widespread. The codes generally stipulate standards to be met on matters like worker safety, social insurance provision and compliance with national laws in areas such as over time. Indeed, many transnational corporations (TNCs) have whole departments dealing with social responsibility and the implementation of these codes (see also **Corporate social responsibility**). There are instances of companies using these codes of conduct to improve conditions along their supply chains, demanding compliance with minimum standards. However, their effect has been limited as these codes are voluntary in nature, and have, at best, been weakly enforced. There is no consensus on what rights should be protected by company codes. Most have standards on health and safety, child labour and broad contractual provisions. But some fail to include even the core labour standards set out by the ILO. Monitoring and enforcement arrangements and auditing are weak.

When it comes to subcontractors, some of the market conditions created by TNCs, including intense price pressures on suppliers, together with stringent delivery schedules, make it difficult to raise standards. There is also the issue of 'code fatigue' as factories supplying to a number of retailers are required to face an equally large number of auditing exercises and reporting requirements. Further, a number of developing countries, in order to attract foreign direct investment, have dismantled employment protection programmes. Thus, these codes have failed to address the erosion in workers' rights, or prevent the emergence of inequalities based on gender.

Liberalization

Liberalization or deregulation refers to the removal of regulatory mechanisms in favour of market forces and the retreat of the government from markets in general. It is based on the idea that market forces and not governmental policies ought to determine economic policies, and goes back to 18th century liberalism and thinkers such as Adam Smith, David Ricardo and Richard Cobden. Today, it forms part and parcel of the economic **neoliberalism** and privatization package.

Deregulation signified a reversal of the economic management strategies involving tight regulations that were hallmarks of economic policies in the industrialized world in the post-1945 period. The Keynesian policies in place then had been motivated by fears that unregulated competition could have serious political, social and economic consequences, threatening the very fabric of the state. Support for regulation came not only from governmental agencies and organized labour, but also from the corporate sector itself. Companies within a regulated market found themselves in a somewhat favourable position as regulations represented entry restrictions for potential competitors from abroad. Entry restrictions ranged from licences and state monopolies to a restriction on the number of competitors allowed in any particular sector. Examples of typical heavily regulated industries included, for instance, the transport and communications sector.

From the 1970s, however, pressure grew on governments to remove regulations and restrictive legislation. States were no longer to intervene and hinder market forces either by heavy regulation or by restricted market access through tariff and non-tariff barriers (see **Protectionism**). A retreat of official market regulations, especially with regard to cross-border flows of capital, goods, finance and services, was advocated. Government agencies were to restrict themselves to harmonizing different international standards and implementing the neoliberal agenda in order further to promote globalization.

The reason for deregulation is often couched in terms of the need to become globally competitive or retain the competitive edge. The USA in particular has been at the forefront of deregulation, not only within its own borders, but also in undermining international regulatory bodies like, for instance, the International Telecommunitions Union and INTELSAT. Most G8 countries and international organizations such as the **International Monetary Fund (IMF)**, the **World Bank**, the **World Trade Organization (WTO)** or the Organisation for Economic Co-operation and Development (OECD) have linked globalization with deregulation and the liberalization of market activities. This coalition provides a strong political basis for neoliberalism and makes its policies seem almost 'common sense' rather than an ideology and an orthodoxy in respect to globalization.

Liberalization, together with deregulation, has had far-reaching impacts on wages, prices, exchange rates, welfare, health care and the social insurance sector. The mantra of 'global competitiveness' and the measures taken to secure it have often meant states attenuating or terminating many redistributive wage and price policies, with cutbacks and compromises on spending on state-provided education, health, housing, and social security benefits. As a consequence, inequalities within societies have only been exacerbated, whether in the Global North or the Global South.

Deregulation has led to rapid market changes, together with the emergence of new mega corporations, as well as a new global class of purveyors of cultural commodities, entertainments and information technology, and a new class of professionals, including lawyers, management consultants and financial advisors. The deregulation of the financial markets, for instance, has led to a shift in the centre of gravity of the financial industry away from large transnational banks towards global cities. Indeed, some of the technologies of globalization have been made possible due to deregulation. Global electronic networks, for instance, have been facilitated by the privatization of public telecommunication services, the liberalization of electronic markets, and the deregulation of tariff structures, which, in turn, have led both to the creation of global communications giants and increasing convergence between sectors.

M

Mainstreaming fair trade

The development of fair trade certification marks has helped bring the concept of fair trade in from the margins, with both the market entry of more traditional players like Costa Coffee, Starbucks, Sainsbury's and Sara Lee, and the emergence of supermarket own-label fair trade products (Tesco UK, the Co-op). Supermarkets began to offer fair trade as a way to differentiate themselves from their competitors, especially discount retailers. And while mainstream coffee and chocolate brands may have been slow to adopt fair trade practices, a quick way for supermarkets to increase its fair trade offer has been through the development of own-label fair trade products.

The 1990s saw a change of focus on the part of **ATOs** to reposition their offering towards what would sell with more mainstream consumers (see, for instance, the **Day Chocolate Company**). However, with the entry of more mainstream players, ATOs fear that the movement would be diluted. They also fear that mainstreaming would mean losing the 'soul' of fair trade. Second-movers that engage with fair trade purely because they see a market opportunity cannot, it is argued, necessarily be trusted to keep their fair trade products on board if consumer interest begins to flag.

ATOs have developed rapidly in the past 20 years, moving from supplying niche market products driven by what producers could make to offering high quality mainstream products that have taken market share from more traditional players. Their success has encouraged competitor brands to re-examine their supply chains and address worker and farmer poverty, both by launching fair trade products and through their own company initiatives. The entry of mainstream players will require ATOs to rethink their business strategies as they compete for market share with companies that have scale economies and competitive advantages in distribution as well as brand awareness.

Make Poverty History

This is a campaign made up of various national Make Poverty History campaigns, all of which come under the broad aegis of the international Global Call to Action Against Poverty campaign. It was a call to action to the G8 nations to put into effect their pledge to halve world poverty by 2015, a promise made at their 2001 meeting. In the UK it soon became the biggest ever anti-poverty movement. With the UK hosting the G8 gathering of powerful world leaders in July 2005 as well as holding the presidency of the European Union for the second half of that year, the campaign gained momentum as it saw an opportunity to influence decisions at the highest levels internationally.

The campaign is a coalition of aid and development agencies which work together to raise awareness of global poverty and achieve policy change by the government. Though the different campaigns focus on different issues according to the circumstances within their country, they generally focus on issues relating to the millennium development goals and include concern for aid, trade and justice.

Max Havelaar

This is the name of a label created by a Dutch development aid organization, **Solidaridad**, in response to the request by one of the co-operatives they were working with, **UCIRI** (Mexico), for access to mainstream markets rather than the small sales achieved through the alternative trade world shops. The idea was for goods bought, traded and sold on fair trade terms to be visually distinguishable on any supermarket shelf by the product certification label. The name, Max Havelaar, came from a fictional Dutch literary character who exposed the exploitation of coffee farmers in Javanese colonies for the Dutch coffee market. The movement attained shelf space in supermarkets through mobilizing grassroots campaigns and support to create demand for fair trade coffee in supermarkets.

Soon after the labelling system came into being in 1989 in the Netherlands, a group of Max Havelaar labelling initiatives began to emerge in other European countries, including Belgium, Luxembourg and Switzerland. A democratic mixed board consisting of producers, the certification organizations and consumers oversaw the Max Havelaar organizational initiatives. The Max Havelaar label can still be found alongside the FLO product mark in countries where these labelling initiatives preceded the establishment of FLO and the international Fairtrade mark. See www.maxhavelaar.ch/en/homepage.

MFN (most favoured nation) status

This is essentially a method of establishing equality of trading opportunity among states by making originally bilateral agreements multilateral. It establishes the sovereign equality of states with respect to trading policy, and provides a treaty basis for competitive international transactions.

Under the **WTO** agreements, countries cannot normally discriminate between their trading partners, and this principle is known as most favoured nation (MFN) treatment. It is incorporated into all the three main areas of trade covered by the WTO. It is the first article of the General Agreement on Tariffs and Trade (GATT), which governs trade in goods. MFN is also a priority in the General Agreement on Trade in Services (GATS) (Article 2) and the Agreement on Trade-Related Aspects of Intellectual Property Rights (TRIPS) (Article 4). In each agreement, however, the principle is handled slightly differently.

Some exceptions are allowed. For example, countries can set up a free trade agreement that applies only to goods traded within the group, discriminating against goods from outside. Or they can give developing countries special access to their markets. Or a country can raise barriers against products that are considered to be traded unfairly from specific countries. But the agreements only permit these exceptions under strict conditions. In general, MFN means that every time a country lowers a trade barrier or opens up a market, it has to do so for the same goods or services from all its trading partners—whether rich or poor, weak or strong.

Middlemen *see* **Coyotes.**

Multifibre Arrangement (MFA)

This was an international trade agreement under which two countries could negotiate quota restrictions on textile and apparel imports from each other. Up to the end of the Uruguay Round, textile and clothing quotas could be negotiated bilaterally and governed by the rules of the Multifibre Arrangement (MFA). The global quota system in textiles and apparel emerged from the short- and long-term arrangements regarding international trade in cotton textiles, initially negotiated under the auspices of the General Agreement on Tariffs and Trade (GATT) in 1962. Those agreements were extended to materials other than cotton in 1974, and became known as the Multifibre Arrangement. It provided for the application of selective quantitative restrictions when surges in imports of particular products caused, or threatened to cause, serious damage to the industry of the importing country. The Multifibre Arrangement was a major departure from the basic GATT rules and particularly the principle of non-discrimination. On 1 January 1995 it was replaced by the WTO Agreement on Textiles and Clothing (ATC), which set out a transitional process for the ultimate removal of these quotas by 2004.

Textiles and clothing require relatively low amounts of capital and access to a large low-skilled, low-paid workforce, and therefore is the industry a number of developing countries turn to as they diversify away from primary production. And yet it is an industry that has seen many restrictions placed on it. Furthermore, exports from developing countries seemed to serve better the interests of importing clothing manufacturers in developed countries.

After the termination of the MFA, exports of clothing initially surged substantially to the European Union market, and to the USA. The largest percentage and absolute surges came from the People's Republic of China. Since the end of the ATC, there has been a growing and spreading set of trade restrictions targeted primarily at China, the largest shipper of textiles and apparel, through a series of agreements that are termed China containment.

Multinational companies/corporations (MNCs)

A multinational company (also multinational corporation, multinational enterprise or transnational enterprise) can be defined as a company that controls production facilities in more than one country. The existence of multinational enterprises, therefore, requires **foreign direct investment (FDI)**.

Foreign direct investment began to accelerate decisively after the Second World War. The promotion of foreign direct investment became part of the US foreign policy during the Cold War. Not surprisingly perhaps, most multinational companies were of American origin during those years. In the 1960s US multinational companies were joined by European and Japanese enterprises. And joining them in the 1980s were the so-called newly industrialized countries (NICs). Indeed, the number of companies operating simultaneously in several countries further multiplied six-fold between the late 1960s and the mid-1990s. Along with global organization through direct investment, companies have also formed thousands of trans-border strategic alliances, particularly since the 1980s. Today, foreign direct investment activities are not only located in the manufacturing sector but increasingly in the provision of services, with significant expansions in recent years in retail trade, finance, communications and information technology.

The role of MNCs is complex, with some seeing MNCs as agents of their home national governments, while others see them as beholden to no government. They are powerful players in the global arena. The **anti-globalization movement**, for instance, has argued against the large concentration of wealth in these corporations—the largest 100 global companies are said to control up to half of the world's total FDI, and the 15 largest have reached annual sales whose value exceeds the gross domestic product (GDP) of over 120 countries.

MNCs invest in a country for the perceived advantages of doing business there. These advantages might be the presence of natural resources, cheap labour, geographical location, skill levels, political and financial stability and favourable regulatory environments. As such, very often recipients of FDI are industrialized countries, the largest concentration being in the G7 countries. However, there has been an increasing outflow of manufacturing operations from western economies, as companies transferred production to Eastern Europe or Asia in order to take advantage of both lower labour standards and costs, and less stringent environmental restrictions.

Foreign direct investment has played a critical role in many of the most successful development stories, including Singapore, Malaysia and now the People's Republic of China (though Korea and Japan managed very well without much FDI). But while the activities of MNCs might have positive contributions for host countries, their role has never been unambiguously good. Amongst the showcased benefits for the host are an additional stream of tax revenue, the integration of the host country into the global economy as well as the transfer of technologies, new management styles and the introduction of new and more efficient work practices. However, not all these benefits are always realized. Conflicts over the distribution of the new wealth generated, for instance, are common. Governments may break the agreed terms on taxation and regulations. Technology transfer may be limited if the control over the production process remains firmly in the hand of the parent company. MNCs often try to avoid taxation altogether through transfer pricing. Further, MNCs want the freedom to assemble goods anywhere from parts made anywhere, whereas governments want to maximize the amount of wealth created on their own territories. Thus, states have been the sites of a struggle between territorial and supraterritorial capital.

Monetary policies could also lead to conflict. For instance, when a state's currency is devalued, imports become expensive, and a foreign MNC selling a product assembled from imported parts may be devastated. As such, MNCs prefer to make long-term investments in countries where the currencies are relatively stable.

MNCs are more likely to channel investment to states that restrict imports, as MNCs can avoid the import restrictions by producing goods in the host country. Furthermore, it is argued that the entry of MNCs works to the detriment of poor countries, as neoliberal policies foster the takeover of prime agricultural land, which is then used for the production of export crops, leaving locals to starve.

A strong line of critique against MNCs states that they are free to engage in investment and employment practices which contribute to poverty and insecurity in developing countries unencumbered by anything other than weak voluntary guidelines. In response to such criticism, more recently, MNCs have begun to participate in more broadly conceived development projects in the host state as a means of investing in goodwill (see **Corporate social responsibility**).

N

National Initiatives (NIs)

The National Initiatives (NIs) are based in the 21 countries which sell Fairtrade Labelled products—Austria, Australia and New Zealand, Belgium, Canada, Denmark, Finland, France, Germany, Ireland, Italy, Japan, Luxemburg, Mexico, the Netherlands, Norway, Spain, Sweden, Switzerland, the UK and the USA—and work for the promotion of Fairtrade in the countries where they are based. They encourage consumers to buy more Fairtrade products and lead public and political campaigns on the need for fairness in trade. (See also **FLO** and **Certification**.)

Neoliberalism

Neoliberalism is an updated version of (classical) liberalism. It is the prevailing economic orthodoxy that takes the logic of laissez-faire **capitalism** to the international level, transcending the nation state, and argues in favour of unrestricted capitalism, **free trade** and consumer-based individual ethics. It pushes for a bundle of interconnected policies, including financial and trade liberalization, flexible and deregulated labour markets, privatization of the economy, including public utilities, and low levels of public debt, often imposed on countries in transition or those in a **debt crisis**.

Neoliberalism became the dominant economic ideology in the late 1970s following the breakdown of the **Bretton Woods** exchange rate mechanism and the abandonment of the post-war Keynesian compromise. The policies of Ronald Reagan in the USA and Margaret Thatcher in the UK were characterized by a rolling back of the state, with large-scale privatization of government assets, economic deregulation, lower corporate taxes and anti-welfarism. With the demise of Communism as a credible challenge, neoliberalism has now become the 'common sense' doctrine, leading to Francis Fukuyama's pronouncements about the 'end of history'. In fact, most major political parties in the G8 countries today advocate a culture of self-help, individual responsibility and entrepreneurialism. It is also the doctrine of economic development favoured and actively fostered by international financial institutions such as the **International Monetary Fund (IMF)**. However, in all democratic states, the political supremacy of the free market is as yet incomplete and precarious and so far it has not been able to survive periods of protracted economic setback.

Nestlé

This is one of the four **MNCs** controlling a large proportion of the global coffee market, together with Sara Lee, Procter and Gamble and Kraft Foods. Nestlé has been blamed for tokenism in its fair trade efforts. It launched 'Partners' Blend' (launched in the UK in 2004), a Fairtrade-certified coffee, but this constitutes less than one-tenth of 1% of Nestlé's total volume, and involves only about 200 of the 3m. producer groups around the world dependent on Nestlé for a living. The granting of FLO certification to Nestlé created quite a stir as this was seen as another instance of a large MNC duping the public into believing it had changed its practices when only a miniscule proportion of its coffee was fairly traded, and its business practices with respect to the larger proportion of its produce had undergone no change whatsoever.

Network of European World Shops (NEWS)

This is a network of 15 national **worldshop** associations, comprising roughly 2,400 shops across 13 countries. The network was established in 1994 to facilitate networking and co-operation among members by providing information, to organize a biannual conference, and to develop and co-ordinate Europe-wide campaigns.

Non-governmental organizations (NGOs)

In a globalizing world, states are seen to be increasingly sharing their powers with, among others, a number of citizens' groups, known as non-governmental organizations (NGOs). NGOs consist of a group of people who conduct regular formal or informal meetings and engage in collective activities to achieve specified goals or policy objectives. NGOs are at the forefront of campaigning and lobbying national and international governance institutions to raise awareness and to achieve their policy goals. Indeed, the technologies of globalization have been well adopted and used by NGOs. The internet, for instance, has opened up new possibilities and opportunities for NGOs to engage in effective worldwide campaigns against what they see as threats, abuses or non-responsible conduct on the part of businesses or states. NGOs have become a significant part of the international landscape, forming part of an emerging global civil society that is more cosmopolitan in general orientation and less attached to individual nation states.

All NGOs share three main features: they are not for profit; they are committed to non-violent modes of action; and they are independent of national governments. The Red Cross, Greenpeace and Oxfam are prominent examples of NGOs and illustrate the range of issue areas NGOs are involved in. NGOs with a very significant international dimension are called international non-governmental organizations (INGOs).

NGOs and INGOs work in very diverse areas, and as their numbers and the range of their activities increase, so does their influence. They have created extensive national and international advocacy networks and have become part of the evolving system of global governance. Indeed, some see them as filling the 'democratic deficit' in a situation where, as finance and production become more global, there is no political machinery to deal with citizens' concerns. Many NGOs and INGOs work very closely with international governmental organizations (IGOs) such as the UN. NGO and INGO policy networks are particularly strong in human rights, the environment and development. In humanitarian relief efforts, for example, NGOs and INGOs often provide a well-developed organizational infrastructure and expertise while IGOs such as the UN and governmental agencies provide the necessary finances. In war situations, the neutrality of NGOs places them in a good position for conflict mediation and for the distribution of humanitarian aid.

There is no consensus on how many NGOs are currently operating in the world. What is clear, however, is that NGOs deliver more official development assistance than the entire UN system. Government agencies in general regard NGOs as useful partners for the distribution of foreign aid. NGOs are often quicker than governments to respond to new demands and opportunities. In many countries, NGOs are delivering services in urban and rural community development, education and health care, that faltering governments can no longer manage. And cross-border NGO networks offer citizens' groups unprecedented channels of influence.

So important and established have NGOs and INGOs become that they have received formal recognition by the UN and other international actors. Indeed, many UN conferences on global issues have two centres: one dominated by representatives of nation states; and a second attended by civil society groups (NGOs and INGOs).

However, for all their strengths, each NGO works for a particular outcome, and tends to be blinkered, judging every public act by how it affects their particular interest. Also, they often have limited capacity for large-scale endeavours, and have to find financial support to sustain themselves, which may compromise their objectives. And since they cannot survive without their grassroots base, they can compromise the truth to play to the gallery to gain membership and support.

Non-tariff barriers *see* **Protectionism**

North American Free Trade Agreement (NAFTA)

NAFTA is a free trade agreement between the USA, Canada and Mexico. It was negotiated between 1991 and 1993, replacing an earlier agreement between Canada and the USA by extending the free movement of capital, trade and financial services to the south to include Mexico. Its main purpose is the abolishment of barriers to trade and services, including the progressive elimination of customs in many areas of trade.

Compared to the European Union (EU), NAFTA lacks extensive institutionalization. It is characterized by intergovernmental modes of decision-making, so that the administration of agreements remains firmly in the hands of the governments of the three participating states and their representatives. These national representatives meet in the Free Trade Commission, specialized committees and working groups. Unlike the EU, NAFTA has no provisions for regional co-operation in areas other than trade. It is a purely economically oriented form of regionalism. However, an agreement on labour co-operation was signed in 1993. The agreement focuses on information exchange but does not provide for NAFTA-wide labour standards.

An important impetus for NAFTA was the end of the Cold War. Freed from the constraints of the superpower conflict, dynamics associated with the globalization process became the focus of attention. In the early 1990s there were widespread fears about the formation of a powerful and assertive European trading bloc, a 'Fortress Europe'. NAFTA was at least partly motivated by concerns about the form the EU was about to take.

Together with the EU, ASEAN and Mercosur, NAFTA is one of the main regional trading blocs. It is also significant in that it bridges the Global South and the Global North, uniting the developed and the developing world. This has implications for the internal structure of NAFTA; its economic diversity could potentially become a problem for internal cohesion. Indeed, the 1997 financial crisis in Mexico put a large strain on NAFTA though NAFTA weathered that test rather well, seeking actively for collaborative solutions.

O

Oxfam International

Oxfam International is a confederation of 12 independent aid and development **non-governmental organizations (NGOs)**. Its mission is to work with local partners on a global scale to reduce poverty. Oxfam International has a small secretariat based in Oxford and advocacy offices in Washington, DC, New York, Brussels and Geneva.

Oxfam (the Oxford Committee for Famine Relief) Great Britain was founded in 1942 to distribute food for famine relief in Europe. Over the years, Oxfam has developed a host of strategies against the causes responsible for famine. Subsequently, Oxfam's activities include the provision of medicine and medical support, foodstuffs and tools, the sale of fair trade produce and crafts from **developing countries**, and adequate training to enable people to achieve a certain degree of self-sufficiency. Its main focus is on poverty relief and development, humanitarian relief and national and international campaigning.

More recently, its issue areas have expanded substantially and now include international trade, education, debt and aid, livelihoods, health and HIV/AIDS, gender equality, conflict and natural disaster relief, democracy and human rights, and climate change. Fundraising activities, donations and the management of Oxfam charity shops help finance this international NGO. See www.oxfam.org.

Oxfam Fair Trade (OFT)

Oxfam Fair Trade (OFT) is one of the largest UK Fair Trade Organizations. Its mission has been to target disadvantaged producers and, through a fair trade relationship, help them build their capacities to access both export and domestic markets. Oxfam's Fair Trade programme started in the 1950s as an informal, voluntary activity to help poor people work their way out of poverty. The first Oxfam shop opened in 1948 but it was not until the late 1950s that the idea of selling crafts (initially from Chinese refugees in Hong Kong) was taken seriously. In 1964 the Oxfam Council of Management registered a company, Oxfam Activities Ltd, with a subsidiary, Oxfam Trading. Since then Oxfam fair trade activities have expanded considerably.

Oxfam Fair Trade monitors the impact of its intervention, and the performance, both its own and those of partner organizations. There is also a strong advocacy strain, with efforts to build consumer support for fairer terms of trade, including reforming current trade rules, and promoting ethical and social responsibility in the corporate sector. See www.oxfam.org.uk/what_we_do/fairtrade.

Oxfam Trade Campaign

This is Oxfam's campaign to change the rules governing trade in order to unleash the potential of trade to reduce poverty, to make trade 'fair'. Amongst its policy goals are: improving market access for poor countries and ending the cycle of subsidized agricultural over-production and export dumping by rich countries; ending the use of conditions attached to IMF-World Bank programmes which force poor countries to open their markets regardless of the impact on poor people; creating a new international commodities institution to promote diversification and end over-supply, in order to raise prices to levels consistent with a reasonable standard of living for producers, and changing corporate practices so that companies pay fair prices; establishing new intellectual property rules to ensure that poor countries are able to afford new technologies and basic medicines, and that farmers are able to save, exchange and sell seeds; prohibiting rules that force governments to liberalize or privatize basic services that are vital for poverty reduction; enhancing the quality of private sector investment and employment standards; democratizing the WTO to give poorer countries a stronger voice; and changing national policies on health, education and governance so that poor people can develop their capabilities, realize their potential and participate in markets on more equitable terms. See www.maketradefair.com.

P

Plantations

Fairtrade started by working with small farmers. More recently, traditional plantations have been allowed to qualify for certification if they meet minimum standards of pay and conditions. The introduction of certification for hired labour (as opposed to small farmers) has not been unproblematic, and questions are still raised as to the benefits of fair trade certification for workers on plantations, and for the small farmers who now have to compete with plantation owners—large multinationals or companies—which also have fair trade certification. Questions are also raised about fairness in the context of the inherently unequal land tenure system that plantations represent.

Tea, bananas, grapes and flowers are among the many products grown on commercial farms. Workers can participate in Fairtrade if they are organized (normally into trade unions) and if the company/owner that they work for is prepared to promote workers' development and share with them the additional revenues generated by Fairtrade. Plantations working with hired labour have to comply with the requirements of the standards to pay decent wages, ensure health and safety standards, and provide adequate housing and other social provision where relevant. Plantations seeking certification must also guarantee workers the right to join a trade union (though participation in unions is not a requirement).

Poverty

Ethical and human arguments central to a critique of trade have often said that it has made the rich richer and the poor poorer, and that it has dramatically increased **inequality** between and within nations. Even if it is argued that the poor have benefited from trade and globalization, the question remains as to whether it is a fair division of benefits, leading ultimately to the question of distribution and distributive justice, together with the question of whether the poor or disadvantaged get a fair opportunity and a fair share. These have also been the key concerns of the global justice movement, which calls for a serious reassessment of the adequacy of national and global institutional arrangements that characterize the contemporary world and shape globalized economic and social relations.

The **International Monetary Fund (IMF)** and the **World Bank** have been criticized for their standard pro-growth macroeconomic policies that they sell as the most effective route to poverty reduction. Market mechanisms are pointed to as the best means of achieving growth. Thus, these global institutions have, it is argued, shifted the discussion away from concerns with equity, to focus only on growth.

The United Nations Development Program has devised the Human Poverty Index to measure the proportion of the population that benefits from **development**. The HPI-1 measures the proportion of the population living in absolute poverty, and is calculated for **developing countries**, while the HPI-2 is used for Organisation for Economic Co-operation and Development (OECD) countries and includes a relative measure of income to reflect experiences of poverty amongst those who might be affluent in global terms, but who might not share the overall well being of the country where they live.

The year 2015 has now been set as the target to achieve the millennium development goals towards halving world poverty. The goals include eliminating hunger, achieving universal primary education, promoting gender equality and empowering women, reducing child poverty, improving material wealth, combating HIV/AIDS, ensuring environmental sustainability and developing a global partnership for development.

Primary commodities

Many of the world's poorest nations remain heavily dependent on the export of primary commodities. According to an Oxfam report, more than 50 **developing countries** depend on three or fewer such commodities for more than half of their export earnings. The export of these commodities has been seeing four adverse trends, particularly for countries with a larger share of such products in their export basket. These include: slow market growth in the sector; adverse price trends, including huge fluctuations in prices and deteriorating terms of trade; low value-added, as most of these products get their value-added through processing and marketing, both of which are not done by poorer exporting countries; and market competition, particularly from hugely subsidized products from wealthier countries (see also **Protectionism**). For instance, coffee prices have fallen by 70% since 1997, resulting in as much as US $8,000m. lost in foreign-exchange earnings for primary producers. Developing countries have a one-third share of world agricultural exports, and this has not changed since 1970.

Protectionism

Protectionism is designed to restrict transboundary exchange of goods and services (see **International trade**). Protectionism comes in the form of tariffs and non-tariff barriers. Tariffs are a duty applied to products or services from abroad. They are comparable to a form of import tax as they increase the price of the foreign product in the country imposing the tariff. Quotas, subsidies, administrative regulations and voluntary export controls are all examples of non-tariff barriers. Quotas are quantitative restrictions designed to limit either the quantity of imported goods or their value. Subsidies refer to certain allowances, cash grants, tax reductions or government contracts designed to foster specific domestic industries to increase their competitiveness. Administrative regulations cover a wide field, including all barriers to trade posed by health and safety standards, labour laws, bureaucracy, special marketing requirements, etc. In the case of voluntary export controls, a country voluntarily agrees to limit its exports to another state.

Protectionism is by definition contrary to liberal **free trade** ideals. Two arguments are made in favour of protectionism: the infant industry argument and the national security argument. The infant industry argument proposes the temporary protection of fledgling domestic industries from foreign competition. Such sheltered conditions are provided until these industries have become competitive and can benefit from **international trade** and **comparative advantage**. The national security argument makes the point that states ought to be self-sufficient in certain sectors for security reasons. An example is the protection of the production of military and security relevant technologies in the USA.

Traditionally, tariffs have been the most widely used form of protectionism. However, since the establishment of the **General Agreement on Tariffs and Trade (GATT)**, non-tariff barriers have become increasingly popular. Thus, while globalization has fostered international trade, there has been a backlash in the form of protectionist measures, taken by individual states or coming in the form of concerted actions of trading blocs or common markets.

Trade restrictions placed by rich countries are said to cost **developing countries** around US $100,000m. a year, which is twice as much as they receive in aid. They are particularly damaging for the poor, as barriers are targeted at goods they produce, such as labour-intensive agricultural and manufactured goods. According to an Oxfam report, subsidies to domestic farmers in the North account for more than $1,000m. a day. A huge surplus is usually generated, and this is dumped on world markets, devastating smallholder agriculture in poorer countries and destroying local markets. Furthermore, low and unstable prices for commodities are also preventing trade from working for the poor. And more recently, concern for the environment or labour rights, and efforts to set standards in these areas have been seen by Southern countries as new forms of protectionism imposed by the North.

R

Rainforest Alliance (RA)

Founded in 1989, the Rainforest Alliance is an international, not-for-profit organization that audits and certifies the production of commodity crops according to a strict set of environmental, social and economic criteria. It aims to link better use of land with better business practice and more informed consumer behaviour. The increasingly ubiquitous tree frog seal of approval guarantees that accredited products meet the body's strict set of criteria for sustainability. These include: conservation of wildlife, ecosystems, soil and water resources; integrated waste and pest management; fair treatment and good conditions for workers; and community relations.

The Rainforest Alliance is based in New York City. It involves businesses (from large multinational corporations to small, community-based co-operatives) and consumers worldwide in their efforts to bring responsibly produced goods and services to a global marketplace. This non-profit organization works in more than 60 countries around the world, collaborating with farmers, workers, business leaders, NGOs, governments, scientists and local communities, to develop and implement standards that are socially and environmentally responsible, as well as economically viable.

The Alliance started work in forestry, and was a founder member of the Forest Stewardship Council and the Sustainable Agriculture Network (both 1993) and the Sustainable Tourism Stewardship Council (2001). Today, it accredits timber, agricultural products (coffee, tea, cocoa, and fruit) and tourism. See www.rainforest-alliance.org.

Rice

Rice is the staple food for almost half of the world's population. Two billion also depend on growing and processing rice for their living, most of them smallholders in poor countries. Around 90% of the world's rice is grown by smallholder farmers in **developing countries**, typically on plots of less than one hectare. They depend on it for food and to pay for their families' health care, housing and schooling. Just five countries—Thailand, Viet Nam, the USA, India, and the People's Republic of China—account for 80% of exports, all supplying the long-grain market.

Rice is a staple crop that well captures the inequalities and asymmetries in global trade. In the USA, rice is produced on large farms employing few people, and at a cost higher than elsewhere in the world. This contrasts with a country like Sri Lanka, 140 times smaller, but where there are almost 50 times as many rice farmers. The USA heavily subsidizes its farmers and dumps their surplus rice on developing country markets, driving local farmers out of business. At the same time, developing countries have long been under pressure to open up their markets for rice and other basic foods, from the international financial institutions (IFIs) and from major agro-exporters. FLO took the first steps towards the introduction of **Fairtrade standards** for rice production in 2000. The aim was to open up new markets for the benefit of small farmers. Since the introduction of the standards, farmers who sell rice on Fairtrade terms receive a price that covers their costs of sustainable production. They also get a **Fairtrade premium** to invest in social, economic and environmental projects in their communities.

S

Shade coffee

This is coffee grown in the shade, protected from the sun by a canopy of taller shade trees. Traditional shade coffee plantations often contain much of the diversity of the original forest area, with an extraordinary diversity of plant species, insect species and soil organisms, even in that small plot. It is since the 1990s that there has been growing interest on the role of shade coffee as a refuge for biodiversity, particularly birds.

Shade coffee had been the norm in the past, but was replaced from about the 1970s by hybrid varieties and production methods that allowed coffee to be grown in the sun, with the added advantage of increased productivity per hectare. The new varieties were pushed by money from the US Agency for International Development (USAID) and other agencies. Colombia saw the most uptake of the new varieties and methods of growing. Mexico, on the other hand, with their land tenure structure supporting small peasants and indigenous farmers, saw least uptake of the new seed varieties.

In the 1990s the Smithsonian Migratory Bird Center (SMBC), which popularized the concept of 'bird-friendly' coffee, pioneered the certification of shade coffee (distinct from organic certification) as a means of providing farmers an economic incentive to protect their plots. The protection offered by organizations like SMBC might have come too late as highly diversified shade-coffee systems across South America are being cleared to give way to other land uses since returns from the system are deemed too low.

Social Accountability International (SAI)

This is a US-based non-profit organization set up to develop and implement voluntary and verifiable social accountability frameworks with a particular focus on workplace standards. In 1996 the SAI developed the Social Accountability 8000 (SA8000) standard in tandem with a range of stakeholders. SA8000 is modelled on **International Standards Organization (ISO)** frameworks and is based on International Labour Standards (ILS). It promotes management action to improve workplace conditions. The code was established by the Council on Economic Priorities Accreditation Agency and was designed to be an independently audited assessment of a company's ethical and social behaviour. The code addresses nine areas of employment practice, including forced labour, child labour, health and safety and working hours. The code is not enforceable by national law and is yet to be widely accepted by business.

Solidaridad

This is a Dutch development aid organization, which had been working with South American co-operatives, like **UCIRI**, to sell their products at **world-shops**. In 1988 UCIRI demanded access, on equitable terms, to the mainstream European market rather than being confined to sales at the alternative trade world shops. Solidaridad initially considered starting their own alternative brand to compete alongside commercially produced coffees, but eventually opted for the **Max Havelaar** label, which could be placed on coffee sold under any brand so long as the producers had received a 'fair' return.

Following the establishment of the Max Havelaar system in the Netherlands, Solidaridad has helped producer organizations to set up commercial fair trade companies, including **AgroFair** (1996) in the banana (and later fresh fruits) sector, and **Kuyichi** (2000) in the cotton/textile industry.

Starbucks

A coffee company based out of the USA which emerged and positioned itself as an 'alternative' to mass-produced, mass-merchandized coffee, and is seen as reflecting a turn from 'mass production' of the Fordist era to the 'mass customization' of the post-Fordist era. The success of Starbucks has been put down to its emphasis on the intangible Starbucks 'experience', including the ambience and the services. In recent years, Starbucks joined the Fairtrade bandwagon by sourcing a small percentage of its coffee from the Fairtrade market, thereby increasing its popularity across Europe, the USA and Canada. In 2000 Starbucks also changed all its own-brand chocolate to Fairtrade-certified, co-branding it with Divine.

In recent years, Starbucks has been at the centre of disputes in relation to fair trade. In 2005 the Ethiopian Government, with the backing of Light Years, an FTO, registered an application with the US Intellectual Property Office for trade mark ownership of the names of three of its prime coffee-growing regions—Sidamo, Harrar and Yrgacheffe. Starbucks uses these names for the high-quality beans they produce, but does not legally own these 'brands'. Starbucks then markets it under the 'Black Apron Exclusives' line, adding a premium of around US $26 to standard coffee pack prices, though the producers themselves are reported to receive less than $1 (net) in return. The Ethiopian Government calculated that if it owned the trade marks for these three regions they would receive roughly $8m. per year. However, Starbucks lobbied the Intellectual Property Office to reject Ethiopia's application as Starbucks would have to incur royalty fees if the trade mark was granted. Starbucks argued that Ethiopia should opt for geographic certification.

However, while such certification would guarantee that the product came from the region, it would not give the owner of the certification exclusive rights over the names in brand marketing, so that companies like Starbucks could continue using the names without having to pay licence fees to the owners. A protracted legal battle followed. Following out-of-court negotiations between the two parties, Ethiopia's 'ownership' of the trade names has been recognized by the global coffee roaster, in exchange for the Government's concession of a royalty-free licence for Starbucks' future use of the names. Starbucks' social responsibility credentials were revealed to be questionable in the face of their stocking only a little Fairtrade coffee while showing no willingness to empower producers in structural terms through company co-ownership, or advance Ethiopia's developmental agenda to secure greater value from the international coffee trade.

Structural adjustment

Structural adjustment is a term related to the conditionalities attached to **International Monetary Fund (IMF)** and **World Bank** assistance, recommending domestic and international economic policy changes for **developing countries**. In return for IMF loans the recipient countries agree to undertake so-called structural adjustment programmes entailing the liberalization of their economies to **international trade** and foreign investment (see **Multinational companies**), the reduction of state subsidies, privatization of state-owned enterprises, deregulation of economic activity, including the removal of price and capital controls, stringent budget constraints and export orientation.

There is a longstanding debate as to whether structural adjustment programmes initiated necessary reforms in developing countries or whether they reflected the interests of the creditors, leading to the wholesale **exploitation** of much of the **Third World.** Criticism focuses on the consequences of structural adjustment programmes including reduced local purchasing power due to lowered wages as national currencies are devalued, the elimination of tariffs, quotas or other controls on imports, thereby slowly displacing domestic producers through foreign competition, cuts in government spending on education, healthcare, the environment, and withdrawal of price subsidies on basic necessities such as food grains. The IMF uses such measures to increase foreign exchange earnings to facilitate debt repayment. It seeks to ensure that the money lent to a country is not spent for politically popular but unproductive purposes, like subsidizing food. It tries to ensure that inflation does not eat away all progress, and that the economy is stable enough to attract investment. In addition, it demands steps to curtail corruption.

However, the conditionalities, directly and indirectly, most severely impact on the poorest and most vulnerable sections of the population, thereby not only putting the brakes on any poverty reduction that might have been achieved, but also exacerbating inequalities within society. Imposing structural adjustment policies also raises questions concerning interference in the sovereignty in countries receiving help from the IMF.

Structural adjustment programmes have attracted severe criticism. Indeed, the 1980s, which saw the **debt crisis** and the implementation of a number of structural adjustment programmes around the world, is referred to as the 'lost decade'. The United Nations Development Report 1997 states that structural adjustment programmes, in many instances, tried 'to balance the economy at the cost of unbalancing people's lives'. During the 1990s the IMF and World Bank began to shift focus away from structural adjustment towards the new goals of poverty reduction and **sustainable development**.

Supply chains

The puzzle facing global supply chains attempting to trade fairly has been how to source products that are both competitively priced and ethically sound. As in conventional markets, there are a number of different supply chains within Fairtrade. For example, a large well-organized secondary level co-operative, such as Coocafé in Costa Rica, organizes the transport, processing and exportation of coffee produced by its nine member co-ops. A UK buyer purchases coffee directly from the co-op on behalf of its partner coffee company. The buyer contracts out the roasting, packing, etc., before the finished product is delivered to the coffee company's warehouse. Distribution is arranged through a variety of retail outlets including major supermarket chains. And the coffee company's main role is marketing and new product development.

A smaller co-op would pay for the processing and export services. A registered Fairtrade exporter would then sell the coffee to registered importers in Europe, which in turn sell on Fairtrade terms to small, independent licensed roasters which market the product to outlets such as the catering trade or health food shops. The importer also fulfils orders for the finished product from small coffee marketing companies. As it is not commercially viable for a small coffee company or retail outlet to directly import small shipments of coffee, this process allows these companies to participate in Fairtrade.

What the Fairtrade mark guarantees as an independent product certification label is that the disadvantaged farmers in the developing world at the very bottom of the supply chain get a better deal. It recognizes that they are at the sharp end of exploitation and injustice in international trade, and works to ensure that these farmers receive a fair and stable Fairtrade price and Fairtrade premium, receiving pre-financing where requested and benefiting from long-term, direct trading relationships.

Sustainable development

The term 'sustainable development' was first adopted by the Agenda 21 programme of the UN. According to the 1987 Brundtland Report, sustainable development is a process of 'developing' that meets the needs of the present without compromising the ability of future generations to meet their own needs. The term reflects the knowledge that the earth's resources are finite, and that the current patterns of growth are not sustainable. It is intertwined with the need to effect economic growth in the long term, meeting the basic needs of all, and extending to all the opportunity to fulfil their aspirations for a better life. However, sustainable development can only be pursued if population size and growth are in harmony with the changing productive potential of the ecosystem. It is not suggesting a fixed state of harmony, but a process of change in which the exploitation of resources, the direction of investments, the orientation of technological development, and institutional change are made consistent with future as well as present needs.

Some people now object to the term 'sustainable development' as an umbrella term since it implies continued development, and insist that it should be reserved only for development activities. 'Sustainability' itself is nowadays used as an umbrella term for all human activity, and sustainable societies are supposed to be rooted in 10 core principles: democracy; subsidiarity (power at the local level); ecological sustainability; common heritage; human rights; jobs/livelihood/employment; food security and food safety; equity; diversity; and the precautionary principle (whereby the proponents of a product or practice bear the burden of proving it is safe before it is used/implemented).

In the international arena, the environmental and economic regimes, however, seem to play out in contradiction to each other. While the environmental regime is concerned with the protection of the natural heritage for this and future generations, the economic regime is concerned with equal rights to exploit it. Environmental agreements are based on respect for natural limits; economic agreements on the right to carry through economic expansion successfully. The two also address very different systems of responsibility and accountability, with the environmental regime addressing sovereign states, while economic transactions involve transnationally active corporations that are not accountable to states.

Sustainable Fair Trade Management System (SFTMS)

The **World Fair Trade Organization (WFTO)** is developing the Sustainable Fair Trade Management System (SFTMS), which would be a globally recognized, light and efficient certification system, designed to transform any business into a sustainable fair trading business.

The SFTMS was originally designed for marginalized artisan co-operatives, groups and businesses to certify them as Fairtrade. Currently, these organizations are not catered for by the Fairtrade mark due to the complexity and variation of their products and processes. FLO's Fairtrade certification system was designed for commodity products, and it is technically difficult to adapt to other products. Also, in most countries in Asia, Latin America and

Africa, producers cannot sell Fairtrade-labelled products in their local markets because there are currently no national labelling initiatives licensed to issue the Fairtrade label.

The SFTMS changes all of that and it does so within the capabilities of a small producer and at relatively low cost. Unlike the Fairtrade label which is applied and paid for on a product-by-product basis, the SFTMS will apply to an entire business and all of its products and services. Based on management thinking, the system is also designed to empower small producers by providing a tool for continuous improvement.

The SFTMS Standard is currently in its third draft. Its second version acted as a verification tool that validated organizations against the 10 Fair Trade Principles of the WFTO. The evaluation comprised internal and external audit verification of the entire supply chain, following which a company could use the label 'Certified Fair Trade', an interim designation mark, on its label.

T

Tariffs *see* **Protectionism**

Ten Thousand Villages

This is a US-based organization to which the beginnings of fair trade are traced. In 1946 Ten Thousand Villages, started by the Mennonite Central Committee, started trading directly with producers of needlework from Puerto Rico. Ten Thousand Villages today work with over 130 artisan groups spanning over 38 countries in Asia, Africa, Latin America and the Middle East. Their products include home décor, jewellery, gifts and other handicrafts. As one of the first **Alternative Trading Organizations** (ATOs), they have built long-term relationships with their artisans across the world. It is also a founding member of the **World Fair Trade Organization (WFTO)**. See www. tenthousandvillages.com.

Third World

This term, a remnant of the Cold War, was used to refer to countries that did not belong either to the liberal West (First World) or to the Soviet bloc (Second World), with the Third World consisting of developing or non-aligned countries (see **Developing countries** and **Development**). This tripartite distinction lost its meaning with the collapse of the Berlin Wall and the events that followed in 1989, eliminating the 'Second World'. Meanwhile, many countries of the so-called Third World, such as those in South-East Asia, were entering a phase of rapid economic growth. Thus, a high degree of convergence of societies, economies and political systems was seen as emerging, leading Francis Fukuyama to suggest that the world was witnessing the 'end of history'.

Today, the term is broadly used to denote poorer regions of the world, especially former colonies. In the post-Cold War world it is, however, more common to refer to poorer regions in terms of one of the many binaries such as North-South, developing-developed, rich-poor, or on a continuum such as industrialized-industrializing-non-industrialized. Indeed, with global **capitalism** and economic activity increasingly becoming localized in regions below the level of the nation, and with management often at a supranational level, 'developed' and 'developing' sectors or the North and South need no longer be contiguous with national boundaries. Indeed, these terms are used more as metaphorical references with 'North' denoting the pathways of transnational capital, and 'South' representing the marginalized populations of the world. Thus, parts of the earlier Third World are on the pathways of transnational capital and belong to developed sectors of the economy, while parts of the First World that have been marginalized in the new global economy may contain pockets that show levels of poverty and deprivation commonly associated with the Third World.

Trade mark

For consumers, this sign indicates the trade source from which the good or service has derived or to which it is connected in some way. The sign could take the form of a letter, word, name, signature, numeral, device, brand, heading, label, ticket, aspect of packaging, shape, colour, sound or scent. Trade marks enable consumers to distinguish the 'origin' of a good or service from others in the market. Trade marks are also thought to reduce consumers' search costs by enabling quick selection between numerous available products, whose differences would take time to understand or whose features or quality cannot necessarily be tested prior to purchase.

Which brand a consumer actually decides to purchase derives primarily from trust in, or personal expectation of, the quality of a brand; the consumer has either seen an advertisement, had a recommendation from someone they know, or knows from prior experience of purchasing the brand. This is 'goodwill': a perceived intangible asset that consumers will buy based on the reputation of that brand. The importance of goodwill in consumer decision-making cannot be overstated. Consumers frequently choose brands with well known or established reputations over unknown brands. For this reason, economists view businesses as having an incentive to produce consistently high-quality goods and services to protect against lower-quality imitations. Trade marks therefore serve a 'quality' or 'guarantee' role for consumers. In turn, investments in brand reputation create an ex ante argument for protecting trade marks: a strong brand reputation enables companies to anticipate profits. Established trade marks thus acquire significant investment and **advertising** value.

While trade marks do not owe their existence to some act of invention, discovery or novelty (unlike patents or copyrights), they none the less function much like other forms of intellectual property rights by obstructing market competition. The legal power conferred on trade mark owners has not always been as extensive as it is today. In the USA, where the leaders of the global IP industry are based, two particular changes have redefined and enlarged the scope and capacity of trade mark owners to control markets. The first change expanded the definable subject matter of trade mark protection to include features not affixed to the product, such as advertising slogans, trade dress and trade names. Product packaging, designs and features have also become matters of proprietorial control. Second, the bundle of rights conferred on trade mark owners has been extended to protect the mark as a desirable property in its own right rather than as a source of identification of indiscernible product information (see also **TRIPS**).

Trade system

International actors engaging in **international trade** have created a trade system regulating the cross-border movements of goods, capital and services. The contemporary trade system endorses a neoliberal vision (see **Neoliberalism**) pushing for the progressive removal of tariff and non-tariff barriers to trade. The current system has its origins in the aftermath of the Second World War and Bretton Woods, which established the **General Agreement on Tariff and Trade (GATT)** which has brought major reductions in customs, duties, quotas and other measures that previously inhibited international trade. Following the **Uruguay Round** of multilateral trade talks, GATT gave way to the **World Trade Organization (WTO)**. The WTO represents the main institution of the international trade system, with greater competences to enforce existing trade agreements and to negotiate new measures for **liberalization** than GATT had. In addition to the WTO, various regional arrangements also exist to reduce the restriction to trade between their regional members.

The trade system has been undergoing revolutionary changes, as exports, for instance, have been growing much faster than global gross domestic product (GDP). Trade now accounts for a greater share of world income than ever before, with **developing countries** registering particularly rapid increases in the ratio of their exports to GDP. The composition of exports from developing countries has also been changing, with an increasing share in manufactured goods, and indeed, for some countries like the People's Republic of China, India and Mexico, even in high-technology exports. As such, changes in trade regimes can have a significant impact on increasing income and reducing poverty. It must be noted, however, that approximately two-thirds of all trade takes place between large **multinational companies (MNCs)**. And despite the overall growth in trade, the current international trade system is hugely polarized (see **Anti-globalization movement**).

Trade-not-Aid

Participation in trade has figured prominently in many of the most successful cases of poverty reduction. Indeed, it is argued that if **developing countries** increased their share of world exports by just 5%, they would generate US $350,000m., which is seven times what they receive by way of aid. Export growth is also considered a more efficient engine for poverty reduction than aid as it can concentrate income directly in the hands of the poor, creating new opportunities for employment and investment, thus increasing overall economic capacity. Recently, a book by Zambian economist Dambisa Moyo has argued that western assistance has given rise to a dependency culture in developing countries. Aid is seen as a handout that stifles innovation. Aid is not to be completely discounted though, at least in the short run, as it can support crucial investments in education, infrastructure and health. But official aid is often used to push developing countries towards further trade liberalization.

The idea that trade may prove more beneficial than aid in the long run is only now beginning to come into its own. For instance, after years of spending billions on aid projects in Africa, donors are now beginning to put money on the continent's entrepreneurs. And this is significant in a climate where the world financial crisis has increased protectionist tendencies among rich countries, worsening Africa's access to markets. Africa's average growth is projected to fall to 1.5%. The continent boasts 20% of the world's population but has only a 2% share of its trade. Meanwhile, organizations like **Oxfam** and **Christian Aid** have been saying that unless the trading relationship between North and South is significantly improved, all the benefits of official aid and debt relief may be worth little. But the reality is that rich countries continue to flood African markets with artificially cheap (hugely subsidized) food and products, while African producers, which get minimal help from their cash-strapped governments, find it ever harder to export.

Trade Justice Movement

The Trade Justice Movement is a coalition of organizations concerned with trade justice, including trade unions, aid agencies, environment and human rights campaigns, Fair Trade Organizations, faith and consumer groups. The movement is supported by more than 60 member organizations with millions of individual members, all calling for trade justice, rather than free trade, with rules weighted in favour of poor people and the environment. See www.tradejusticemovement.org.uk.

Traidcraft

Established in 1979 as a Christian response to poverty, Traidcraft, a trading company and a development charity, seeks to fight poverty through trade by promoting approaches to trade that would help poor people in developing countries. It is one of the UK's leading Fair Trade Organizations, and runs development programmes in some of the poorest countries in the world, whilst also campaigning in the UK and internationally to bring about trade justice. Traidcraft was instrumental in setting up the Fairtrade Foundation, which awards the Fairtrade Mark to products that meet internationally recognized standards.

Traidcraft consists of three main organizations bound together by a Deed of Mutual Covenant, which enshrines Traidcraft's Foundation Principles and sets out the basis for mutual co-operation. The Traidcraft Foundation is the founder member of the charity, Traidcraft Exchange, and holds a guardian share in the trading company. The trading company and charity share the same senior management team and support services.

Traidcraft's trading arm works with more than 100 producer groups in over 30 developing countries, producing about 450 different fair trade foods, crafts and textiles. They have a customer base of about 120,000 and a turnover approaching £20m. The charity, Traidcraft Exchange, was established in 1986, and works to enable poor producers in Africa and Asia to grow their businesses, find markets, and engage effectively in trade. See www.traidcraft.co.uk.

Transfair Germany

In 1992 a fair trade labelling organization in Germany pushed for a 'Transfair' certification mark to be recognized among the Max Havelaar community. It did not want to adopt the Max Havelaar organizational title which carried the 'historical baggage' unique to the Netherlands socio-political background. The Max Havelaar and Transfair labels can even today be found alongside the FLO product mark in countries where labelling initiatives preceded the establishment of FLO and the international Fairtrade mark.

Transfair USA

Transfair USA in some ways symbolizes the priorities of a number of Anglo-Saxon labelling initiatives, compared to European ones. They see certification as an end in itself, rather than as a tool for advocacy or a means to an end. Transfair USA created some negative publicity for itself in the world of fair trade by certifying **Chiquita**, the banana company, as European Fair Trade Organizations and ATOs saw this as jeopardizing the very principles of producer empowerment that certification stood for. Detractors saw this as another instance of a larger, mainstream organization using the label as a branding exercise and getting a new and more positive image on the back of certifying a small proportion of their product line (see also **FLO**).

Transnational corporations ***see*** **Multinational companies (MNCs).**

TRIPS (Trade-Related Intellectual Property Rights)

The **World Trade Organization (WTO)** Agreement on Trade-Related Intellectual Property Rights sets down minimum standards for most forms of intellectual property regulation within all member countries of the WTO. It is blamed as being anti-poor for having introduced controversial changes to the laws of intellectual property relating to **international trade**. For instance, the TRIPS definition of a trade mark extends ownership rights to anything perceptible to human beings that could serve as a signalling device (words, designs, sounds, scents, tastes …). With this broad array of elements over which to claim exclusive ownership, dominant firms now have unprecedented scope to block competition. TRIPS also removed the precondition that registration for trade mark protection be conditional upon the mark being in use as this was seen to be interfering with modern marketing strategies, thus creating a legal precedent for creating market monopolies in future market segments.

TRIPS rules on licensing also recognized and reinforced at a global level the concept of the trade mark as a protectable property in its own right, a 'stand-alone' commodity, amplifying the anti-competitive effects of trade marks to a global level as protection of the trade mark as property renders direct competition more expensive and more difficult, increasing the market power, prices and rents associated with popular brands. In discussions around TRIPS at the **Uruguay Round**, a highly moralistic tone was adopted in order to present US/EC demands as a measure to prevent criminal activity like piracy, theft or counterfeiting, though critics argue that the fine print was about ensuring rentier incomes for MNCs through global monopoly rights.

For all these reasons, TRIPS has been seen to be working against the poorer countries of the world. While the WTO is trying to ensure stringent protection for patents, it increases the costs of technology transfer. **Developing countries** would have to pay approximately US $40,000m. a year in the form of licence payments to companies based in the North, with the USA capturing around half of the total. The application of TRIPS to medicines, for example, could double the costs of medicines in poorer countries. Direct patenting of genetic material would entail that smallholder farmers would lose their right to save, sell or exchange seeds. Those opposed to TRIPS argue that developing countries should be allowed to maintain shorter and more flexible systems of intellectual property protection.

Twin and Twin Trading

This Alternative Trading Organization (ATO) was founded by the Greater London Council in 1985 and has been an incubator for commercial fair trade brands and businesses that today are leading fair trade brands in the UK market, including Cafédirect (1991) and Divine Chocolate Ltd (1997). In its early days it was part of a number of new European trading groups associated with secular activist movements on the political Left. Twin Trading was created to generate markets for produce from socialist countries whose access to markets in rich countries in the West was partially or entirely blocked. The company brought in goods from Mozambique, Cuba, North Viet Nam and later Nicaragua.

The aim of Twin and Twin Trading is to develop new forms of economic relations between the South and the North based on the principles of mutual advantage and independence of partners, and countering exploitative relations. Its emphasis on trading with co-operatives was particularly significant and was influential in shaping the subsequent Fairtrade labelling standards, which too focused on collective and co-operative forms of ownership in producer organizations.

Twin provides market distribution for other fair trade brand companies and traders, such as AgroFair, based outside the UK market. Twin Trading collaborated with Oxfam, Traidcraft and Equal Exchange to set up Cafédirect, and also operates as a trading arm for Cafédirect. It also later collaborated with The Body Shop and Christian Aid to support Kuapa Kokoo to set up the Day Chocolate Company, the first producer-owned Fairtrade brand. See www.twin.org.uk.

U

UCIRI

The Union of Indigenous Communities in the Isthmus Region (UCIRI) consists of small coffee producers of several communities of the lower and middle high slopes of the Sierra Juárez mountain range belonging to 20 municipalities of the state of Oaxaca. This group attained legal status in 1983 and began its operations as a co-operative by collecting the coffee produced by all its members in a central location. In 1983–84 the first coffee warehouse was constructed in Lachiviza. In the following year a dry processing plant was also installed, and the co-operative began marketing operations by 1985. Meanwhile, a group of Dutch and German agronomists and representatives of the fair trade market, invited by some grassroots church activists, visited UCIRI, and became interested in supporting their struggle. During this visit they discussed the economic potential and ecological benefits of organic coffee. This resulted in UCIRI's decision to shift to organic production and to sell to the German and Dutch markets by establishing a relationship with two ATOs: Gepa and Max Havelaar. In 1986 UCIRI got its export licence, and the same year the organic coffee production programme was initiated with the first inspection and certification through the German certifying agency NATURLAND (accredited by IFOAM, the European Union and the USA). In 1988 UCIRI and a Dutch organization, **Solidaridad** (Solidarity), together created the first fair-trade seal, Max Havelaar.

Today, UCIRI sells to over 10 organizations from seven countries. UCIRI opened a new roasting facility in 2001, and by 2002 was selling 100 tons of roast and ground coffee, and 150 tons of soluble coffee within Mexico under its own name. It is held up as a prime example of a community-based democratically organized initiative. See www.uciri.org/english/english.htm.

UN Conference on Trade and Development (UNCTAD)

This UN organization was established in 1964, and seeks to promote the development-friendly integration of **developing countries** into the world economy. UNCTAD has progressively evolved into an institution whose work aims to help shape current policy debates and thinking on development, with a particular focus on ensuring that domestic policies and international action are mutually supportive in bringing about sustainable development. It was the second UNCTAD Conference in 1968 that argued that trade not aid should provide the basis for Third World development. Certified fair trade has acquired a high legitimacy in UN organizations like UNCTAD. See www.unctad.org.

Uruguay Round

This was the last round of negotiations under GATT, which began in Uruguay in 1986 and lasted until 1994. The **WTO** was created in the Uruguay Round. Unlike earlier GATT rounds, the Uruguay Round is seen as being about restructuring the international economic system, rolling back the state, and opening up the Third World for the transnationalization of their economies. Officially, this was presented as bringing under multilateral rules and disciplines sectors of trade and important areas of economic activity that were outside international discipline, such as agriculture, textiles and clothing, and services, and to liberalize the trade in these US sectors and enable trade-offs among these.

Uruguay is considered a decisive moment in the history of globalization, since the agreement there secured the agenda of industrialized states and segments of international capital pushing to expand GATT's authority to do away with non-economic 'barriers to trade' and create the WTO. Indeed, it has been demonstrated that the WTO's governing structure benefits those industrialized economies (especially the USA, Europe and Japan) that already wielded disproportionate power in the global economy.

Utz Kapeh

This label was founded by Europe's **Ahold** supermarket chain in 1997 to signify 'certified responsible' coffee sourcing for its own-label coffee products. It grew out of the recognition that direct sourcing in coffee created to comply with Eurep-GAP food safety requirements could also serve to address consumer concerns about coffee farmers. Utz Kapeh-certified farms must meet minimum wage and working condition requirements, as well as environmental standards.

The Netherlands-based foundation sets no minimum price for growers, nor does it impose a set development-project premium as does fair-trade-certified coffee. Instead, it lays down strict production standards for growers. As there is no minimum price requirement, it is relatively cheap for companies to adopt and several European coffee roasters have implemented the code. Further, producer empowerment is not a stated goal of this certification model. The Utz Kapeh range of 'ethically' traded products are seen by some as a competitive threat to the Fairtrade movement.

More recently, Utz Kapeh has made tentative forays into US markets working through Ahold-owned supermarkets there. On the whole, however, Utz Kapeh has less consumer recognition than Fairtrade labels. See www.utzcertified.org.

W

World Bank

The World Bank is one of the world's largest sources of **development** assistance. It is another name for the International Bank for Reconstruction and Development (IBRD) and its four associated agencies. It is an international governmental organization (IGO) and came into existence as part of the **Bretton Woods** agreements in 1945 with the mission to facilitate the rebuilding of European economies shattered by the war.

With the recovery of Europe, the World Bank began focusing its activities on **developing countries**. Its underlying strategy has been to foster the creation of an economic infrastructure, which would 'kick-start' development. It provides long-term loans, grants and offers technical assistance to developing countries. Its financial help and technical expertise is used in many different areas ranging from infrastructure projects (such as roads, hydroelectrical dams) to reform of the health and education sector, as well as economic development in general.

Membership of the World Bank is restricted to the members of the **International Monetary Fund (IMF)**. Financial contributions provide a substantial part of the funds of the World Bank, and like the IMF, the World Bank has a system of weighted voting, thus giving power to states making the largest financial contributions. In addition, funds are also raised in private capital markets.

The World Bank has repeatedly been the subject of criticism for being a tool of the USA and the West (see **Anti-globalization movement**). In addition, it has often been critiqued for its underlying neoliberal philosophy (see **Neoliberalism**), focusing on free market solutions despite sufficient evidence that structural adjustment policies such as privatization, free trade policies and budget discipline are often harmful to development.

Over time, and with an increasing body of evidence against some of these approaches, the World Bank has been changing its stance. For instance, it now accepts that some controls over short-term speculative flows are necessary to protect national economies. In recent years, it has extended its agenda and moved from a concentration on economic growth to poverty reduction strategies. Partly in response to its critics, the Bank has also begun to invest heavily in sustainable development projects. It now emphasises growth that is stable, sustainable and equitable, whilst also seeking to ensure wider participation in its projects. See www.worldbank.org.

World Development Movement

This is a UK-based anti-poverty campaigning organization working for economic justice, which includes the right of poor communities to determine their own path out of poverty, and end harmful policies which put profit before people and the environment. In order to make their case, they lobby decision-makers, organize public campaigns and produce evidence through research to win change for the world's poorest people. They investigate, expose and challenge government policies and corporate actions that harm vulnerable communities and trap people in poverty. The organization does not fund or run projects but works with Southern activists to research and promote solutions to poverty. See www.wdm.org.uk.

World Fair Trade Organization (WFTO)

This was formerly known as the International Fair Trade Association. It was created in 1989 and is a global association of 324 organizations in over 60 countries. Membership is limited to organizations that demonstrate a 100% commitment to fair trade and apply its 10 Principles of Fair Trade. These are: creating opportunities for economically disadvantaged producers; transparency and accountability; trading practices; payment of a fair price; child labour and forced labour; non discrimination, gender equity and freedom of association; working conditions; capacity building; promotion of fair trade; and environment. WFTO members who are monitored against these principles are listed in the FT100 index of world-leading fair trade brands, businesses and organizations. It is the only global network whose members represent the fair trade chain from production to sale. In 2004 the WFTO introduced the fair-trade mark (FTO) which identifies registered Fair Trade Organizations worldwide (as opposed to products as in the case of FLO International or Fairtrade) and guarantees that standards are being implemented in line with its 10 principles or standards. See www.wfto.com.

Worldshops

These are specialized retail outlets offering and promoting fair trade products that also typically organize various educational fair trade activities and play an active role in trade justice and other North-South political campaigns. They are non-profit organizations run usually by local volunteer networks. Although the movement emerged in Europe (and a vast majority of worldshops are still based there), worldshops can also be found today in North America, Australia and New Zealand. Worldshops were the route fair trade products took into the North, with these shops selling fairly traded goods, largely handicrafts. The first growth in fair trade sales came through increased listings in **Alternative Trading Organizations** (ATOs) such as Oxfam and worldshops. Even today, handicrafts are distributed through a network of 2,870 worldshops run as not-for-profits by NGOs.

World Trade Organization (WTO)

The WTO was established in 1995 to replace the provisional General Agreement on Tariffs and Trade (GATT). GATT, one of the three institutions set up by the **Bretton Woods system** to govern the international political economy in the post-1945 world (the other two being the **International Monetary Fund (IMF)** and the **World Bank**), included a series of treaties and administered a series of international negotiations to facilitate free trade at the international level. The WTO was the outcome of the last GATT round of trade negotiations, more popularly known as the Uruguay Round of Multilateral Trade Negotiations (MTNs), launched in September 1986 at Punta del Este in Uruguay and concluded in 1994 in Marrakesh, Morocco. After lengthy negotiations, the loosely structured GATT was transformed into the WTO, which has the status of an international governmental organization.

The WTO is described as the widest-ranging multilateral trade agreement ever negotiated. It includes a multilateral agreement on trade in goods, the general agreement on trade in services (GATS), agreement on trade-related aspects of intellectual property rights (TRIPS), understanding on rules and procedures governing the settlement of disputes (DSU), a trade policy review mechanism (TPRM) and plurilateral trade agreements. The WTO covers 28 agreements in total in its ambit.

The WTO set the stage for a process of perpetual negotiation (unlike GATT 1947 where multilateral negotiations had to be agreed to specifically and launched periodically). It provides an institutional set-up for the trade system. It forces all signatories to accept every one of the multilateral trade agreements. They cannot withdraw from any of them without withdrawing from all of them.

The main functions of the WTO are: to administer WTO trade agreements, to provide a forum for trade negotiations, to handle trade disputes, to monitor national trade agreements, to offer technical assistance and training for **developing countries** and to facilitate effective co-operation with other international organizations.

The WTO and its predecessor, the GATT, have often been criticized for facilitating the spread of neoliberal globalization (see **Neoliberalism**). First, the WTO agenda setting appears to be partial towards the interests of the rich developed countries and large **multinational companies (MNCs)**, resulting in imbalanced and biased rules of trade. It is argued that its rules on intellectual property, investments and services protect the interests of rich countries and powerful multinational companies, while imposing huge costs on developing countries. One example often mentioned by critics is the failure of the WTO to remove non-tariff barriers and subsidies from the heavily protected agricultural sectors in Western Europe, the USA and Japan. Second, environmental protection, labour standards, health and safety standards, **human rights** issues and national interests are all deemed secondary to its chief concern, which is free trade. And finally, there is the issue of participation. The development of the global political economy has over the last 50 years enhanced the role of international organizations such as the WTO, entrusting them with ever increasing powers in shaping international norms and expectations. However, only states can be WTO members, and the WTO agenda is driven by governments. This raises the problem of transparency, wider participation in international decision-making processes and democratic governance at the international level. Public dissatisfaction with the decision-making procedures, for instance, was part of the driving force behind the massive protests at the ministerial conference in Seattle in 1999 (see **Anti-globalization movement**). See www.wto.org.

STATISTICS

Table 1 Sales of Fairtrade Certified Products in the UK

	1998	*1999*	*2000*	*2001*	*2002*	*2003*	*2004*	*2005*	*2006*	*2007*	*2008*	*2009*
Coffee	13.7	15.0	15.5	18.6	23.1	34.3	49.3	65.8	93.0	117.0	137.3	157.0
Tea	2.0	4.5	5.1	5.9	7.2	9.5	12.9	16.6	25.1	30.0	64.8	68.1
Cocoa products*	1.0	2.3	3.6	6.0	7.0	10.9	16.5	21.9	29.7	25.5	26.8	44.2
Honey products*	n/a	n/a	0.9	3.2	4.9	6.1	3.4	3.5	3.4	2.7	5.2	4.6
Bananas	n/a	n/a	7.8	14.6	17.3	24.3	30.6	47.7	65.6	150.0	184.6	209.2
Flowers	n/a	n/a	n/a	n/a	n/a	n/a	4.3	5.7	14.0	24.0	33.4	30.0
Wine	n/a	n/a	n/a	n/a	n/a	n/a	1.5	3.3	5.3	8.2	10.0	16.4
Cotton	n/a	n/a	n/a	n/a	n/a	n/a	n/a	0.2	4.5	34.8	77.9	50.1
Other	n/a	n/a	n/a	2.2	3.5	7.2	22.3	30.3	45.7	100.8	172.6	219.4
TOTAL	16.7	21.8	32.9	50.5	63.0	92.3	140.8	195.0	286.3	493.0**	712.6	799.0

Source: *The Fairtrade Foundation (http://www.fairtrade.org.uk/what_is_fairtrade/facts_and_figures.aspx)*
* The figures against these products represent the cocoa part of all products containing cocoa and the honey part of all products containing honey.
** Following review, some of the 2007 figures have been amended but the total remains the same.

Table 2 Estimated Retail Value of Fairtrade Certified Products by Country (in euros)

Country	*2006*	*2007*	*Increase (%)*
Australia/New Zealand	6,800,000	10,800,000	59%
Austria	41,700,000	52,800,000	27%
Belgium	28,000,000	35,000,000	25%
Canada	53,800,000	79,600,000	48%
Denmark	23,200,000	39,600,000	71%
Finland	22,500,000	34,600,000	54%
France	166,000,000	210,000,000	27%
Germany	110,000,000	141,700,000	29%
Ireland	11,600,000	23,300,000	101%
Italy	34,500,000	39,000,000	13%
Japan	4,100,000	6,200,000	51%
Luxembourg	2,800,000	3,200,000	14%
Netherlands	41,000,000	47,500,000	16%
Norway	8,600,000	18,100,000	110%
Spain	1,900,000	3,900,000	105%
Sweden	16,000,000	42,500,000	166%
Switzerland	142,300,000	158,100,000	11%
UK	409,500,000	704,300,000	72%
USA	499,000,000	730,800,000	46%
TOTAL	1,623,300,000	2,381,000,000	47%

Source: The Fairtrade Foundation (http://www.fairtrade.org.uk/what_is_fairtrade/facts_and_figures.aspx)

Table 3 Europe's World Shops and their Turnover

Country	*Worldshop Association*	*Number of Worldshops*	*Sales of Worldshops (in million euros)*
Austria	ARGE Weltläden	89	10.6
Belgium	Oxfam Wereldwinkels	207	7.9
Denmark	Fair Trade Denmark	14	0.6
Finland	Maailmankapupojen liitto	19	1.0
France	Fédération Artisans du Monde	145	10.0
Germany	Weltladen-Dachverband	486	22.0
Luxembourg	Arbechtsgrupp Weltbutteker	7	0.7
Netherlands	Landelijke Vereniging van Wereldwinkels (DAWS)	391	27.7
Sweden	Världsbutikerna för Rättvis Handel	43	0.9
UK	British Association for Fair Trade Shops (BAFTS)	117	13.2

Source: Krier/DAWS 2008

Table 4 Estimated Fairtrade Retail Sales Value by country (in million euros)

Country	*2007 (in m.euros)*	*2008 (in m.euros)*	*2009 (in m.euros)*	*% growth 2007–09*
Austria	52.8	65.2	72.0	29.4
Belgium	35	45.7	56.4	46.8
Denmark	39.6	51.2	54.4	28.9
Finland	34.6	54.4	86.8	96*
France	210.0	255.5	287.7	30.4
Germany	141.7	212.7	267.4	59.1*
Ireland	23.3	94.4**	118.5	100.8*
Italy	39.0	41.2	43.3	10.4
Luxembourg	3.2	4.2	5.3	50
Netherlands	47.5	60.9	85.8	62.9
Norway	18.1	30.9	34.6	53.4
Spain	3.9	5.4	8.0	75.9*
Sweden	42.5	72.8	82.6	55.1
Switzerland	158.1	168.7	180.1	13
UK	704.3	880.6	897.3	21.9
Sub-Total Europe	1,553.6	2,043.8	2,280.2	35.6
USA	730.8	757.7	851.4	16.5
Canada	79.6	123.7	201.9	153.6*
Japan	6.2	9.5	11.2	80.6
Australia and New Zealand	10.8	18.5	28.7	165.7
Sub-Total Non-Europe	827.4	909.4	1,093.2	32.1
TOTAL	2,381	2,953.2	3,373.4	41.6

Source: FLO Annual Reports 2007, 2008–09 and 2009–10
* Growth rate is not representative due to a change in calculation methodologies.
** 30.1 in 2008–09 Annual Report: this reflects the change in calculation methodologies which was done retroactively for 2008.

Table 5 Fairtrade Premium Use 2009

	Africa	*Asia*	*Latin America and the Caribbean*
Total Fairtrade Premium (in million Euros)	12.6	5.6	33.8
Community	22%	25%	24%
Education	16%	12%	4%
Environment	0.2%	0%	1%
Health	6%	18%	3%
Business and Production	46%	20%	36%
Women's Programmes	3%	4%	2%
Other	3%	14%	18%
Not Yet Spent	4%	7%	12%

Source: FLO Annual Report 2009–10

Table 6 Countries where Fairtrade Certified Producer Organizations can be found

Latin America	*Africa and the Middle East*	*Asia*
Argentina	Benin	China
Belize	Burkina Faso	India
Bolivia	Cameroon	Indonesia
Brazil	Comoros	Kyrgyzstan
Chile	Congo (Democratic Republic of)	Laos
Colombia	Côte d'Ivoire	Pakistan
Costa Rica	Egypt	Papua New Guinea
Cuba	Ethiopia	Philippines
Dominican Republic	Ghana	Sri Lanka
Ecuador	Kenya	Thailand
El Salvador	Madagascar	Timor-Leste
Guatemala	Malawi	Vietnam
Haiti	Mali	
Honduras	Mauritius	
Jamaica	Morocco	
Mexico	Mozambique	
Nicaragua	Palestinian Autonomous Areas	
Paraguay	Rwanda	
Peru	Senegal	
Windward Islands (Dominica, Grenada, Martinique, St Lucia and St Vincent and the Grenadines)	Sierra Leone	
	South Africa	
	Swaziland	
	Tanzania	
	Togo	
	Tunisia	
	Uganda	
	Zambia	
	Zimbabwe	

Source: FLO Annual Report 2008–09

Table 7 Number of Producer Organizations by Geographical Region in around 2008

Geographical Scope	*No. of Producer Organizations (2007 figures in brackets)*	*Percentage*	*Most Important Products*
Caribbean	16 (19)	3.2%	Bananas (Fresh fruit/Vegetables)
Central America	126 (97)	25.4%	Coffee
South America	188 (157)	37.8%	Coffee
Northern Africa	4 (3)	0.8%	Dried fruit
Eastern Africa	51 (58)	10.3%	Coffee
Western Africa	36 (32)	7.2%	Fresh Fruit/Vegetables
Middle Africa	3 (3)	0.6%	Coffee
Southern Africa	2 (3)	0.4%	Tea
Western Asia	1 (0)	0.2%	Nuts and Oilseeds (Olive Oil)
Central Asia	1 (0)	0.2%	Seed cotton
Eastern Asia	4 (4)	0.8%	Tea
South-Eastern Asia	33 (24)	5.8%	Coffee and Rice
Melanesia	3 (3)	0.6%	Coffee
Total	497 (418)	100%	

Geographical Scope	*No. of Hired Labour Organizations (2007 figures in brackets)*	*Percentage*	*Most Important Products*
Caribbean	15 (5)	3.7%	Banana
Central America	2 (0)	1.1%	
South America	46 (32)	23.7%	Banana and Flowers/Plants
Northern Africa	6 (4)	3.0%	Fresh Fruit/Vegetables
Eastern Africa	42 (36)	26.7%	Flowers and Plants
Western Africa	8 (5)	3.7%	Fresh Fruit/Vegetables
Southern Africa	37 (31)	23%	Fresh Fruit/Vegetables
Southern Asia	29 (22)	16.3%	Tea
Total	185 (135)	100%	

Source: Fairtrade Labelling Organizations International, *The Benefits of Fairtrade*, Second Edition, Bonn: Germany, August 2010.
Note: The information is based on FLO audits between 2007 and 2010, and most of the data refers to an approximate period of 12 months around 2008; it has not been possible to present data for an exact calendar year.

Table 8 Number of Individual Members by Geographical Region

Geographical Scope	*No. of Individual Members 2008*	*Growth (2007-08)*	*Most Important Products in the Region**
Caribbean	23,000	143%	Cocoa
Central America	100,000	64%	Coffee
South America	97,000	13%	Coffee
Northern Africa	470	31%	Dried Fruit
Eastern Africa	394,000	12%	Coffee (Tea)
Western Africa	87,000	1%	Cocoa (Seed Cotton)
Middle Africa	34,000	300%	Seed Cotton
Southern Africa	170	-48%	Tea
Western Asia	530	NA	Seed Cotton
Central Asia	770	NA	Nuts and Oilseeds – Olive Oil
Eastern Asia	6,100	0%	Tea
South-Eastern Asia	44,000	10%	Coffee
Southern Asia	58,000	57%	Seed Cotton
Melanesia	1,400	-64%	Coffee
Total	845,000	22%	Coffee
Geographical Scope	*No. of Hired Labour Organization Workers (2008)*	*Growth 2007-08*	*Most Important Products*
Caribbean	2,300	238%	Banana
Central America	460	NA	NA
South America	6,200	44%	Flowers and Plants
Northern Africa	8,200	6%	Fresh Fruit/ Vegetables
Eastern Africa	49,000	15%	Tea (Flowers and Plants)
Western Africa	2,700	80%	Fresh Fruit/ Vegetables
Southern Africa	13,000	17%	Fresh Fruit/ Vegetables
Southern Asia	46,000	54%	Tea
Total	127,000	31%	Tea

* Most important product in terms of number of individual members

Source: Fairtrade Labelling Organizations International, *The Benefits of Fairtrade*, Second Edition, Bonn: Germany, August 2010.

Note: The information is based on FLO audits between 2007 and 2010, and most of the data refers to an approximate period of 12 months around 2008; it has not been possible to present data for an exact calendar year.

Table 9 Male and Female Members and Workers by Product

Certified Product	*Number of Women, Small Producer Organizations (2008)*	*Number of Men, Small Producer Organizations (2008)*
Banana	210	80
Cane Sugar	19	81
Cocoa	14	86
Coffee	20	80
Dried Fruit	34	66
Fonio	14	86
Fresh Fruit/Vegetables	15	85
Fruit Juices	18	83
Herbs and Spices	19	81
Honey	12	88
Nuts and Oilseeds	28	72
Quinoa	31	69
Rice	16	84
Seed Cotton	13	87
Tea	27	73
Wine Grapes	16	84
Total	20	81
Certified Product	*Number of Women, Hired Labour Organizations (2008)*	*Number of Men, Hired Labour Organizations (2008)*
Banana	12	88
Flowers and Plants	50	50
Fresh Fruit/Vegetables	35	65
Fresh Juices	22	78
Sportsballs	36	64
Tea	44	56
Wine grapes	28	72
TOTAL	35	65

Source: Fairtrade Labelling Organizations International, *The Benefits of Fairtrade*, Second Edition, Bonn: Germany, August 2010.

Note: The information is based on FLO audits between 2007 and 2010, and most of the data refers to an approximate period of 12 months around 2008; it has not been possible to present data for an exact calendar year.

Table 10 Fairtrade Premium by Geographic Region

Region	*Small Producer Organizations Fairtrade Premium 2008 (in euros)*	*Percentage 2008*	*Hired Labour Organizations Fairtrade Premium 2008 (in euros)*	*Percentage 2008*
Caribbean	5,054,000	16.7	1,103,000	9.2
Central America	7,985,000	26.3	221,000	1.9
South America	10,013,000	33	3,478,000	29.1
Northern Africa	31,000	0.1	343,000	2.9
Eastern Africa	3,279,000	10.8	4,482,000	37.5
Western Africa	1,156,000	3.8	298,000	2.5
Middle Africa	150,000	0.5		
Southern Africa	22,000	0.1	715,000	6.0
Central Asia	3,700	0.0		
Western Asia	48,000	0.2		
South-Eastern Asia	330,000	1.1		
Southern Asia	1,079,000	3.6	1,303,000	10.9
Melanesia	70,000	0.2		
TOTAL	30,350,000	100	11,944,000	100

Source: Fairtrade Labelling Organizations International, *The Benefits of Fairtrade*, Second Edition, Bonn: Germany, August 2010.

Notes: The information is based on FLO audits between 2007 and 2010, and most of the data refers to an approximate period of 12 months around 2008; it has not been possible to present data for an exact calendar year.

The Fairtrade premium on seed cotton and cocoa appeared remarkably low. Considering Fairtrade sales volumes for these two items, it is likely that the actual premium income was 50–100 percent higher for cotton, and at least 50 percent higher for cocoa. Also, as the M&E study included only 92 percent of all certified producer organizations, the actual Fairtrade premium income is probably about 9 percent higher than the total figure presented here.

Table 11 Fairtrade Premium Spending

	Fairtrade Premium Spend 2008: Small Producer Organizations	*Percentages 2008*	*Fairtrade Premium Spend 2008: Hired Labour Organizations*	*Percentages 2008*
Community	6.0 million	23.7	4.4 million	41.5
Education	1.8 million	7.1	1.8 million	17
Environment	189,000	0.8	57,000	0.5
Health	1.3 million	5	491,000	4.6
Women's Programmes	574,000	2.3	73,000	0.7
Investment in Business (Career Development for Hired Labour)	3.9 million	15.6	1.4 million	14
Investment in Production and Processing	5.3 million	21.1	NA	NA
Other Premium Use	3.2 million	12.4	1.1	10.1
Not Project Specific	579,000	2.3	132,000	1.2
Premium Not Spent	2.5 million	9.8	1.1 million	10.4
Total Premium Spent	25.2 million	100	10.6 million	100

Source: Fairtrade Labelling Organizations International, *The Benefits of Fairtrade*, Second Edition, Bonn: Germany, August 2010.
Note: 62 small producers and 12 hired labour organizations who received Fairtrade premium did not record how they had spent their premium revenues. The information is based on FLO audits between 2007 and 2010, and most of the data refers to an approximate period of 12 months around 2008; it has not been possible to present data for an exact calendar year.

EUROPA WORLD

www.europaworld.com

Librarians, to register for your 30-day **FREE** trial visit: **http://tinyurl.com/ewfreetrial**

EUROPA WORLD AND THE EUROPA REGIONAL SURVEYS OF THE WORLD ONLINE

An interactive online library for all the countries and territories of each of the world regions

Europa World enables you to subscribe to *The Europa World Year Book* online together with as many of the nine *Europa Regional Surveys of the World* online as you choose, in one simple annual subscription. The *Europa Regional Surveys of the World* complement and expand upon the information in *The Europa World Year Book* with in-depth, expert analysis at regional, sub-regional and country level.

Key Features:

- Impartial coverage of issues of regional importance from acknowledged experts
- A vast range of up-to-date economic, political and statistical data
- Book and periodical bibliographies – direct you to further research
- Extensive directory of research institutes specializing in the region
- Ability to search by content type across regions
- Thousands of click-through web links to external sites.

A CHOICE Outstanding Resource

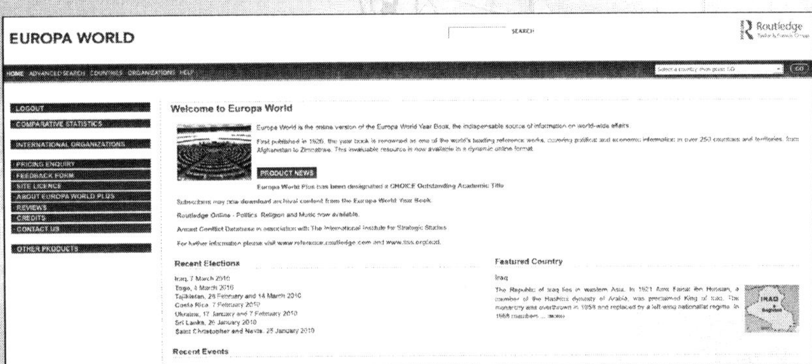

30-DAY FREE TRIALS AVAILABLE 30-DAY FREE TRIALS AVAILABLE 30-DAY FREE TRIALS

Alternatively, to register for your free 30-day trial or for more information please contact your sales representative:

UK and Rest of World customers:
Tel: +44 (0)20 701 76062
Fax: +44 (0)20 701 76699
Email: **online.sales@tandf.co.uk**

US, Canadian and South American customers:
Tel: 1-888-318-2367
Fax: 212-244-1563
Email: **e-reference@taylorandfrancis.com**

Taylor & Francis
Taylor & Francis Group